Marcus's STORY

Finding Strength and Hope
When the Worst Happens

Benedicte T. Nielsen

© 2020 Benedicte T. Nielsen

Marcus's Story: Finding Strength and Hope When the Worst Happens
First edition, April 2020

HopeCopePress
Katy, Texas
benedictenielsen.com

Editing: Shayla Raquel, shaylaraquel.com
Cover Design: Lilly Hallquist, lillyhanna.com
Interior Formatting: Melinda Martin, melindamartin.me

Marcus's Story: Finding Strength and Hope When the Worst Happens is under copyright protection. No part of this book may be used or reproduced in any manner whatsoever without written permission except in the case of brief quotations embodied in critical articles and reviews. Printed in the United States of America. All rights reserved.

ISBN: 978-1-7344005-0-2 (paperback), 978-1-7344005-1-9 (epub)

*When we meet real tragedy in life,
we can react in two ways—either by losing hope
and falling into self-destructive habits,
or by using the challenge to find our inner strength.*

—*Dalai Lama*

*In loving memory of Marcus,
whose cancer journey inspired me to share his story.*

*"It's not how much we give
but how much love we put into giving."*

—*Mother Teresa*

Contents

Foreword 1

Chapter One: The Phone Call 3

Chapter Two: Living in Denmark 5

Chapter Three: Our American Dream 13

Chapter Four: Warning Signs 15

Chapter Five: A Parent's Worst Nightmare 23

Chapter Six: First Line Treatment 37

Chapter Seven: At Home after Treatment 49

Chapter Eight: One Step Forward, Two Steps Back 61

Chapter Nine: Declining Health 71

Chapter Ten: Back to the Hospital 77

Chapter Eleven: "This Is All So Wrong" 85

Chapter Twelve: Final Decline 97

Chapter Thirteen: Signs of Hope 111

Chapter Fourteen: HealthBridge 121

Chapter Fifteen: Irreversible Brain Damage 129

Chapter Sixteen: Choosing to Celebrate 133

Chapter Seventeen: Downturn 139

Chapter Eighteen: Christmas 143

Chapter Nineteen: A New Year 149

Chapter Twenty: Taking Charge 165

Chapter Twenty-One: Getting Ready to Be Home 175

Chapter Twenty-Two: Home at Last 183

Chapter Twenty-Three: The Relapse 201

Chapter Twenty-Four: A New Approach—A New Hospital 205

Chapter Twenty-Five: New Hope 217

Chapter Twenty-Six: Gearing Up for the Bone Marrow Transplant 231

Chapter Twenty-Seven: Bad News Comes in Waves 243

Chapter Twenty-Eight: The Big Decision 253

Chapter Twenty-Nine: Wishes Do Come True 257

Chapter Thirty: Letting Go 261

Epilogue: I'm Free 265

Appendices 271

Acknowledgments 277

About the Author 279

Foreword

I recall the first time I met Marcus with a clarity as if the scene were captured in a photograph. He lay on the gurney, brought in by his adoring mother and the team of attendants required to safely transport him between his home and the hospital. Various pieces of machinery that kept Marcus alive traveled all along his weak body. As a former pediatric intensive care unit physician, I recognized the rhythmic cadence of his mechanical ventilator. At his feet was the multihued digital monitor that detailed his heart rate, respiratory rate, blood pressure, and oxygen levels. Large backpacks lay underneath the gurney that housed medications and extra equipment should something unexpected happen to Marcus or the machines that sustained him while en route.

It is worth mentioning at this point that everything described above was for a routine clinic visit, not an emergency visit or an admission to the hospital. For Marcus, his mother, and his family, this was part of his life. Each detail was a strand of string that, when wound together, composed part of the tapestry of their daily lives. Having worked in some of the largest children's hospitals in the world, this was a familiar scene to me, and yet there was something . . . something different about Marcus, something different about his mother that I could not fully make sense of. There were more strands to see, more strings to unravel that would help fill out the tapestry of this remarkable boy and his family.

I spent many hours getting to know Marcus and his family during clinic visits and hospitalizations, but it was not until I had the enormous privilege of visiting him in his home did the tapestry reveal itself even more. His room was decorated with posters of his hero, the Argentinian soccer legend Lionel Messi. I felt the soft comfort of the blanket that covered Marcus in his bed. I saw the backyard where I could imagine in my mind's eye Marcus playing soccer with his brother, fashioning himself into Messi and scoring the game-winning goal of the World Cup as only children can magically do. I saw his brother's (Lucas) room where they undoubtedly spent countless hours playing. I saw the kitchen table where I envisioned the family eating dinner. The American poet Maya Angelou describes home as "the safe place where we can go as we are and not be questioned." I was visiting Marcus on his terms, not mine at the hospital, and I got to see Marcus as he was.

At the most fundamental level, the book that lies in your hands is a love story. As is true for most love stories, there are difficult times and unpleasant truths that remain unresolved in both our hearts and our minds. But there are also challenges faced and conquered, great odds overcome. The details of his life as lovingly told by his mother made Marcus more alive for me than ever before, and the tapestry of Marcus Nielsen came into full view. It is a story of great courage and of great loss, but also of great hope, as his mother provides sagacious advice from her own experiences that can help guide all parents of seriously ill children while they navigate the often murky waters of the health-care system.

—Dr. Kevin Madden, Assistant Professor,
Department of Palliative, Rehabilitation & Integrative Medicine
at MD Anderson Cancer Center

CHAPTER ONE

The Phone Call

"The labs and the ultrasound show evidence that Marcus has cancer," Dr. Brack said with a serious voice.

Immediately, dizziness overwhelmed me, as if I were about to throw up. I remained calm and talked to her. Then I cried but tried hard not to.

"Are you sure?" I asked her. "How can you be sure?" I repeated.

She explained the results of the testing they had run on Marcus and that she had suspected Marcus had cancer after examining him. She said she was going to meet us at Texas Children's Hospital. We should not go anywhere; we should simply wait for her in the exam area.

CHAPTER TWO

Living in Denmark

Life is all about journeys, the good ones and the not-so-good ones. My childhood was in the first category. Like everyone else, we had family issues, but overall, the country I grew up in offered some valuable building stones for my adult life. I would come to depend on all of them and more.

In her book, *A Piece of Danish Happiness,* American-Indian author Sharmi Albrectsen discusses why the Danes lead the world in the happiness rankings. She proposes that a life philosophy based on our special set of unwritten social norms called Jante Law is the reason for all the happiness in Denmark.

The emphasis in Denmark is on the collective good rather than individual gain. Albrectsen points out that Danes have a unique mechanism for managing expectations and staying focused on what is real: community, family, leisure time, environment, and free choices are trademarks of Danish society and their corresponding happiness.

My parents married in 1965, and the year after, my oldest brother Alexander was born. Four years after, my brother Christopher was born. At that time, they lived in Rungsted in Denmark, the city where the writer Karen Blixen was born.

On October 21, 1972, I was born at Gentofte Hospital north of Copenhagen. After I was born, we moved to a bigger house in Espergærde farther up the coast, a ten-minute drive from Helsingør (Elsinore in English). Helsingør is known for its castle, Kronborg, where William Shakespeare's play *Hamlet* is set. Even though Denmark is small, the country has a rich history and beautiful old monuments.

Chapter Two

My parents bought a huge family home in a quiet area of town close to a forest and the beach. I stayed at home with my brother Christopher all through my early childhood. Alexander, the oldest, started school when I was born. My mother did not want us to go to day care, preschool, or kindergarten because she wanted us to stay home with her even though she was busy working from home. By education, my mother was a cook and a very creative one. She was a self-employed consultant and ran her own business from home. She wrote recipes for Danish magazines, wrote cookbooks, and taught cooking classes. Before she was married, she traveled to Middle Eastern countries arranging food demonstrations with Danish dairy products and Danish agricultural products. Along with other cooks, my mother worked abroad for Danish agricultural organizations to promote the export of Danish products such as butter, cheese, yogurt, chicken, and eggs. When she was in her twenties and early thirties, she was adventurous and eager to see the world. She told me stories about her exciting career abroad.

My father got his training in business with an emphasis on export relations. During his active career, he worked as the export manager for Danish companies such as LAMA that fabricated mattresses and Chr. Hansen, a global Danish bioscience company that develops natural solutions for the food, nutritional, pharmaceutical, and agricultural industries. Due to his work, he traveled extensively not only within Europe but also to South America and Australia. When my father was gone on business trips, I felt as if he were gone for years. In reality, it was no longer than two to three weeks at a time.

On top of his training, he was a multiform artist: linguistic professional, musician, painter, and creative chef. He was humorous, charming, and fun. He was fluent in Danish, English, German, French, Spanish, Italian, and Portuguese. He could play the contrabass, the sax, the trombone, and the drums.

My father was a true animal lover. He shared this passion with my brothers and me by buying pets for us. He built a small basin in our backyard for his goldfish. Outdoors, he also had three land turtles and beautiful white fantail pigeons. He built an open cage for them where they could eat and stay at night; otherwise, they were free to fly around outside. They were tame and returned to their cage for food and shelter. Caring for and nurturing pets as a child helped me develop responsibility early on. My mother and father trained me to take care of them, and I did all the work, which I did not mind. I loved animals and tending to them.

My childhood base was our house, my pets, my family, and my friends who lived down the street. It was very simple.

From first grade to ninth grade, I went to Tibberup School in my hometown of Espergærde. I liked school and had many good friends. I went to jazz ballet and received private lessons in piano. I also started playing handball, which is a popular sport in Europe. I was good at sports because I was fairly athletic and competitive, probably a trait I had picked up from my two older brothers. I also went to summer language schools in England, Austria, and Germany. Those were challenging and exciting.

In school, I received good grades and decided to obtain my high school diploma from Espergærde High School. My specialization was in modern languages, as my passion was foreign languages. In the meantime, my parents had divorced. My mother got the family house and my father moved into a beautiful apartment with a sea view close to Elsinore.

Overall, my childhood reflected all the reasons Danes are happy. The Danish lifestyle is relaxed with an emphasis on family life. The work-family balance is crucial for Danes' happiness, and a meaningful leisure time is part of that balance. I knew my parents valued their close friends and, for that same reason, taught my brothers and me the importance of building strong, lasting friendships.

Despite a sometimes harsh climate, spending time in the outdoors matters a lot to Danes. Danes often refer to the phrase, "There is no such thing as bad weather, only unsuitable clothing." I walked or biked to school during all the different seasons. That was how it was.

I graduated high school with strong grades. After graduation, I decided to spend one year abroad. My main goal was to improve a foreign language on two levels: speaking and writing. In their youth, both my parents had been adventurous. I think they agreed "to travel is to live," as expressed by the famous Danish writer Hans Christian Andersen. Their wonderful accounts from trips abroad inspired me to explore the world myself. As a young surgical nurse, my father's sister Sorella had traveled the world working for WHO in developing countries in Africa, Asia, and South America. She entertained me many times about her experiences in these exotic cultures. She was fluent in the same languages as my father but was especially fond of the French language.

I ended up choosing France because I had discovered that there was a bilateral student-exchange program between Denmark and France, enabling me to do a French high school exam in one year. I would not have to pay any student fees, which meant I needed to pay only for a place to stay and for my living costs. I applied for the program and was accepted to a high school called Lycée du Grésivaudan in the astonishing mountainous area of Grenoble, France.

In the summer of 1992, I returned to Denmark with a French high school exam with honors in my hands, ready to start a new chapter in my life.

The good news about education in Denmark is that it's all free. The term *free* means that taxpayer money funds the Danish education system. Not only do students get free education, but they also get free stipends from the Danish government to support boarding and other living expenses. Well aware of the benefits of being a student in Denmark, I chose to apply for law school in Copenhagen.

In Denmark, the law degree consists of a Bachelor of Law and a Master of Law. Both degrees are offered at university level and take five years to complete. I have always been interested in social sciences and how countries are governed. I also strongly believed that a law degree would open many doors for me, as many Danish lawyers are occupied in the public sector, either working for government agencies or municipalities. I was not keen on becoming a practicing lawyer working eighty hours a week. I had no intentions of going into the legal business for the money. Money is a means, not an end. I knew that early on.

For me, the importance was my vision that I wanted to do something meaningful that had to do with people. I hoped to be able to go on business trips to other countries. Also having nice colleagues was a priority. I did not want be part of a competitive work environment where everything revolved around clients and making money.

When I studied law, I got a part-time job working as a receptionist and housekeeper in a small hotel in Copenhagen. It was supposed to be a summer job, but I kept it during my second year of college because I liked it so much. It was a practical job, while law school was theoretical. I liked both aspects and I earned some extra money to supplement my government student stipend. Life was busy and good, but then I encountered a new man.

I had moved to a dorm in Lyngby, close to Copenhagen, and in November 1995, I attended a friend's graduation party. That night, I met my would-be husband, Jacob. He sat next to me at dinner. He was tall, handsome, funny, charming, and smart. He had short hair and big blue eyes and was a reservist in the Danish Army. He had just finished his master's degree in engineering and was looking for a job. We talked and danced all night. Immediately, there was chemistry and mutual interest. I think we were destined for each other because Jacob considered not showing up for the party because he had been gone on a military training camp. Once he had returned to his dorm after many days of hard training, he was exhausted. Nevertheless, he decided to attend the graduation party, and that night we met for the first time.

Later on, we started dating and moved in together into a small two-room apartment in Copenhagen. Copenhagen, the capital of Denmark, dates back more than one thousand years and, like Denmark, has a rich history. Being young, in love, and without children, we did not need a lot of space. Jacob got a job in a small-size engineering consulting company in Copenhagen, and in the summer of 1998, I graduated with my master's in law. During my last years of study, I exchanged my job at the hotel for a part-time position as a paid legal intern in the Danish Immigration Service.

Sadly, in 1996, my father had fallen ill. He had suffered from high blood pressure for years. He got a blood clot in his leg and had to be on strong declotting medicine after the incident. As with all medications, there were unwanted side effects, and one of them was strokes. Early 1996, he had a stroke and was rushed to the hospital. He survived but had to undergo rehabilitation for months. The stroke affected half of his body, including his ability to talk and eat. He had to retrain many functions. He was able to walk with the assistance of a walker and function in his own apartment with medical assistants helping him a few times a week. It was the first time I experienced firsthand how devastating brain damages were. His younger sister Sorella was a tremendous help. Since my parents were divorced, there was no

Chapter Two

wife to help my father; thus, he was dependent on other family members to step in.

He did well for several months, but then he had another stroke. This time, it hit him badly. Afterward, he was bedridden and in a wheelchair. He needed help with everything but could still talk a bit and, with difficulty, eat and drink on his own. He had to move into a nursing home where he died from pneumonia at age seventy, less than one year after moving in.

Two and a half years later, the day before Christmas Eve, my mother died from a stroke in her lungs. She was a lifelong smoker with a congenital heart condition, so her health had been deteriorating, but she refused to seek medical help for her health issues.

By age twenty-eight, I had lost both my parents.

I graduated from law school at the same time my father died. Some months after, I got an attractive position as an immigration lawyer in the Danish Ministry of Interior. I worked there for almost ten years and enjoyed many challenging assignments. My work involved serving as a lawyer for the politically elected Minister of Interior and making decisions in cases regarding applications for visas and residence permits. I rotated to different positions in the department and got the opportunity to work with European Union policy and travel to places such as Stockholm, Helsinki, Brussels, Yerevan, Belgrade, and Sarajevo. I was interested in politics and law and had a successful legal career working for the Danish government.

In June 2005, I married Jacob, and on May 27, 2006, Marcus was born. He was a healthy baby who quickly developed ahead of expectations. He crawled before turning four months, walked at nine months, and was speaking fluently at age two. He reminded me of my late father in both personality and skill set.

When we had Marcus, Jacob and I lived in a small town house on the outskirts of Copenhagen. We needed more space and bought a family house in Hillerød, thirty minutes north of Copenhagen. Conditions for paid maternity leave in Denmark were favorable, and I spent about ten months at home with Marcus. Then Marcus was ready for nursery, and I returned to my job in the Ministry of Interior. Jacob continued to work for a small Danish engineering company, which in the meantime was acquired by

Schlumberger, the world's largest oil field services company working in more than eighty-five countries and employing approximately 113,000 people.

To broaden my work experience, I was eager to work in a local municipality. I got a job in the mayor's office at Fredensborg Municipality, a fifteen-minute drive from our home. I managed to negotiate a part-time contract so I could spend more time with Marcus in the afternoon. On August 24, 2008, Lucas was born, and I started another paid maternity leave with him.

With Schlumberger on board, Jacob had to travel more frequently to destinations in Europe, Asia, and North and South America. He was usually gone for two to three weeks, flying often to Houston, Texas, the headquarters of the company's oil and gas activities.

With both of my parents gone, I felt left alone with Marcus and Lucas while Jacob was gone on business trips. Luckily, my mother's younger sister and my mother's cousin, who lived down the street, stepped up to help babysit the boys in my time of need. Jacob's mom and two of his aunts also came to help me with the boys.

At the end of 2008, Jacob started talking about the possibility of relocating to the US. Schlumberger had offered him a position in Houston, and he was eager to move over there with our family. For him, it was an easy decision, but for me, it was harder. I had to give up working and leave my friends and family behind. I felt we had a good family life in Denmark, and both of us had good jobs. After many considerations, we decided to try it. We rented out our house but packed everything else in a container destined for a new adventure in America.

CHAPTER THREE

Our American Dream

In August 2009, we arrived in Houston and moved into a two-story rental house. Marcus and Lucas started in preschool and nursery to learn English, as we spoke only Danish at home. Jacob liked his new job, and we all settled in, although it took some time to get adjusted to the heat and the American lifestyle. I missed my job; despite having my Danish background in law, I could not work as an immigration lawyer. I needed an LLM or JD from the US. Instead, I volunteered as a legal intern at the ACLU of Houston. Eventually, I decided to enroll in a paralegal certificate program, and at the beginning of 2012, I graduated with a GPA of A-plus. Immediately after, I started a position as an immigration paralegal at Liu & Associates, PLLC in Houston.

We ended up enjoying the easy lifestyle in Houston, and the boys did well too. We visited Denmark every summer. Marcus started kindergarten at a private American school called the Village School, and Lucas joined that school the year after. My husband started running in a running club in nearby Katy and made many new friends. The boys attended the Danish Saturday school called Vikingeskolen where I volunteered as a Danish teacher and board member. We were active in the Danish Club of Houston and had a great network. Years passed. My husband and I were blessed with two healthy sons.

CHAPTER FOUR

Warning Signs

It was January 2014. Marcus walked down the stairs to our living room complaining his neck was hurting. I thought he might have slept in a weird position and that he was sore for that reason. He told me some liquid came out of his ear on his pillow when he woke up. It sounded like he had an ear infection, and I told him we had to see his pediatrician, Dr. Brack. I got an appointment that same day. After examining Marcus, Dr. Brack concluded he had an ear infection in his left ear. In fact, Marcus had a ruptured eardrum and she had to prescribe antibiotics. The lymph nodes on his neck were swollen, a common sign of infection. I wondered why Marcus had not complained about having ear pain. Then again, he was seven years old and a tough boy.

That same evening, Marcus started his treatment for an ear infection. His medicine was sticky and sweet. I mixed it with water and Ribena, the black currant fruit drink he loved so much. His younger brother Lucas was a bit jealous, as he did not get any medicine. Marcus quickly improved. However, about a week after he started taking the antibiotics, he developed a red rash all over his body. I thought it was probably an allergic reaction because of the antibiotics. Marcus had always been a healthy and strong boy and had never taken antibiotics before. I took Marcus back to see Dr. Brack, who quickly identified the rash as an allergic reaction to amoxicillin. The good news was that his ear infection had cleared. Marcus could stop taking his antibiotics and did not need further treatment. As for his rash, I could give him some allergy medicine and apply an ointment until the rash disappeared. Marcus was good to go. It could have been much worse, and what a relief to leave the doctor's office knowing Marcus was completely cured from his ear infection.

It took a few days before Marcus's rash improved. It clearly bothered him. On Saturdays, we used to attend the Danish school in Houston. Lucas enjoyed going to this school where the children spoke Danish and were a part of the Danish society in Houston. Marcus had reached a point where he felt the school was boring. The Saturday following the allergic reaction, Marcus was not feeling enthusiastic about joining his class so I let him sit outside in the common areas. I told the other parents about Marcus's allergic reaction. After seeing the blotchy rash all over his body, some of the parents felt sorry for him. Others thought he used the rash as an excuse to skip Danish class that day. I loved Marcus so much and I knew he was not playing tricks. I told him he would soon be well again. I was proud of him for being honest about how he felt. Not every child would behave that way. Marcus did not waste any time. He had brought some homework from his American school he could work on while the Danish classes were in session.

Some weeks passed, and Marcus was back to his baseline. I did notice that he still had some swollen but painless lymph nodes on the side of his neck. When touching them, they felt soft. Upon examination, my husband could feel them too. I consulted the school nurse, who informed me that no particular infections were circulating among the children. Marcus played and had the same energy level as always. He had no fevers and overall did well in school. At that time, I was not worried about the swollen lymph nodes. I knew they were not supposed to be there, but I imagined they would eventually disappear.

At the beginning of April, Marcus and I revisited his pediatrician. The lymph nodes on Marcus's side of his neck had not disappeared, which was a cause of concern. In fact, he had more of them. Dr. Brack was not in the clinic that day, so another pediatrician, Dr. Brack's sister, Dr. Torn, saw Marcus instead. She was as sweet, lovely, and caring as Dr. Brack. Dr. Torn examined Marcus and noticed swollen lymph nodes on other parts of his body too. She told me that she wanted to run labs on Marcus. *Labs?* I thought. *Why?*

She believed Marcus had contracted infectious mononucleosis, also known as mono. She ordered Marcus and me to go straight to Texas Children's Hospital West Campus in Katy. She wanted labs and a chest X-ray done. This was unexpected. Could this not wait until the next day? I called Jacob at work and asked him to pick up Lucas from his after-school program.

Once at the hospital, when the nurse was about to draw his labs, at the sight of the needle, Marcus grabbed onto me. Unable to speak, he panicked, crying loudly. I patted Marcus on his back and told him he would be okay. I was not successful in calming him down. Luckily, the nurse was able to call two child life specialists to come talk to him and help him settle down. One of the child life specialists brought an iPad, and Marcus picked a movie he could watch while the nurse drew his labs. I was grateful for those child life specialists. They knew exactly how to distract Marcus and make him more comfortable. They talked to him with such gentle, sweet voices. After the drama was over in the lab room, we proceeded to get chest X-rays taken. As we got home, Lucas was already in bed. Marcus and I had a late dinner, and after this exhausting day, Marcus went straight to bed.

Around 9 P.M., Marcus's pediatrician called me. *Why is she calling me at night?* She immediately told me the good news that Marcus's labs came back normal and that he did not have mono. His chest X-ray also looked normal. I mentioned that I wanted to take Marcus and Lucas on an Easter trip to New Orleans and asked her if that would be okay. We had talked about making a trip to Hawaii to celebrate Marcus's eighth birthday during the Memorial Day holiday. Would this be safe? The doctor confirmed it was safe to continue life as normal. Letting out a huge breath, I ran upstairs and told my husband the good news. Then I went to Marcus's bedroom, and he was fast asleep—adorable.

We felt comfortable knowing that the doctors had conducted a complete checkup of Marcus so we could start planning our summer vacation to Denmark. I was eager to go back to Denmark. I missed my home country, my family, my friends, the fresh air and cool weather, the food and everything Danish. It was such a joy to have something to look forward to in the upcoming months.

During the Easter break in April 2014, the boys and I flew to New Orleans to spend a few days exploring Cajun food and a different culture influenced by the French.

I liked traveling alone with the boys. I used to call them my tiger cubs.

Chapter Four

It was the first time I took them on a trip without Jacob. He was busy with work and had to stay home.

My philosophy was never to postpone the good things in life—just the bad ones. Something inside me told me I had to make the trip with the boys to New Orleans. We were gone for four days. We stayed at a nice high-rise hotel not too far away from the Mississippi River, which we could see from our hotel room.

The boys loved watching the container ships sailing on the river, making sharp turns when the river twisted. It was like being on an adventure with them. The boys were sure the container ships would tilt over when they made those sharp turns. From our hotel window, they watched and watched, unable to stay still as they waited for the big drama when the container ship made the turn and tipped over into the river.

"I don't think the container ship will tip over into the river," I told them.

"Why not?" Marcus asked as he dropped his head.

"Yes, it will. Look, Mummy!" Lucas exclaimed while pointing out the window to the container ship.

"Listen, the captain has been sailing on the Mississippi River many times, and he knows how to navigate with cargo on board—even on very little space," I said.

Patiently, they kept staring at the turning container ship and screamed with excitement when it looked like it was about to tilt over. When they realized it did not happen, they decided to celebrate that the container ship made the turn safely.

"I was right," I bragged. "What a good thing it did not tilt over." I shared a smile.

During our time in New Orleans, we visited the Mardi Gras Museum, saw the Easter parade in the old part of town, and visited the WWII museum. One of the top attractions was the jazz cruise we took on the Mississippi River aboard the steamer *Nachez*. It turned out Marcus enjoyed listening to jazz. For Marcus, being on board this steamer was a unique experience.

During our trip, we visited Manning's famous restaurant in town, the restaurant belonging to the famous football family. Already at that age, Marcus had a passion for football. He was thrilled to eat at Manning's Restaurant and to take pictures of the football decorations displayed in the restaurant. Marcus tried grits and liked it. He had fish dishes too. We met a local waiter who had decided to stay in New Orleans during Hurricane Katrina. Marcus was interested in learning more about this natural disaster.

"How were you able to survive during the hurricane?" Marcus asked, sitting at the edge of his chair.

"Well, I refused to leave my house when first aid responders came by during the evacuation of the flooded city," the waiter explained. "I moved to the attic of my house and survived for several days with the food and water I had stored in the attic."

"Were you not nervous about staying there alone?" Marcus asked the waiter with a curious voice.

I think Marcus was impressed the person had the courage to stay. Marcus understood the dangers involved in refusing to follow the governmental evacuation order.

"Regardless of the danger, I was convinced it was the right decision for me to stay put in my house. You see, I survived and was able to help rebuild New Orleans after the devastating damages Katrina left behind," the waiter concluded while Marcus and Lucas listened carefully with eyes wide and rounded.

Back in Houston, it was time to make more family plans. Feeling highly energized, our family registered to do the Family Fun Run in the Danish capital of Texas called Danevang. My husband ran the 5K with Marcus while Lucas and I did the one-mile fun run. Marcus finished in less than thirty minutes, an amazing time for a seven-year-old. In fact, Marcus beat Anna Holliday, the current Danish consul in Houston, who used to be an elite runner.

Once again, a sense of calm hit me. Nothing serious could be wrong with Marcus. Marcus was an excellent athlete. He did swim classes and was an astonishing soccer player and an avid footballer. However, he still had swollen lymph nodes. I talked to other moms at the Fun Run, and we all agreed that Marcus looked too healthy and strong to be sick. After seeing Marcus running so energetically that day, we had no doubt he was in good health.

It was May. For my Mother's Day gift in 2014, Marcus had decorated a white foam cup and made it into a vase. The vase had lovely details on it such as flowers and hearts. He also made a paper flower, which was sitting in the vase. He had used different colors and had written "Happy Mother's Day" on it. The boys had also made the most adorable cards for me; Lucas even made one written in Spanish, even though he had just started to learn Spanish and lacked experience in that language. Every time I looked at his flower arrangement, it filled my heart with love and I thought about Marcus. Not only did it fill me with love, but it filled me with happiness because I felt loved. Loved by Marcus, loved by Lucas.

Marcus's birthday was on May 27. Right after school finished at the end of May, we flew out to Oahu, Hawaii. We had rented a nice apartment in the tropical paradise of the Aulani Disney Resort. Lucas and Marcus played, swam, and enjoyed every moment on this flourishing Hawaiian island.

Marcus's eighth birthday fell on Memorial Day. Marcus had a passion for army history. In school, he enjoyed learning about US history, and at home, we had studied World War II history. It was Marcus's wish to visit Pearl Harbor on his birthday. We saw the iconic USS Arizona Memorial, the USS Bowfin Submarine Museum & Park, and USS *Missouri BB-63* ("Mighty Mo" or "Big Mo"). People remember the USS *Missouri* best as the site of the surrender of the empire of Japan, which ended World War II. We stood on the deck of USS *Missouri* while a guide lectured us on all the details of the Japanese surrender. The guns on board the USS *Missouri* were fascinating to watch and explore. The boys pretended to play with the guns on board the battleship. They ran from one gun to the other, fantasizing about being soldiers shooting the enemy. The weather was sunny and windy. Just beautiful but warm. That night, Marcus had lobster and other seafood for dinner. He had a genuine interest in cooking, and he loved exploring new food. It was a special night for a very special boy.

One of our last nights was movie night. They showed a Disney movie outdoors on a big lush lawn in front of our apartment building. My husband remained in the apartment with Lucas, as he was already in bed. Marcus, on the other hand, was determined to join the movie night. I went down to watch the movie with Marcus. We sat on the green lawn close to the huge movie screen. It was dark, and we looked at the stars in the sky. It was a beautiful night. Halfway through the movie, I noticed Marcus felt cold. Unable to focus on the movie, I asked him if he was cold, and he answered yes. I hurried back to our apartment and got some blankets to cover him. He was tired but wanted to watch the movie, so I let him stay. He rested his head on my lap, and I tried my best to warm him. I felt a strong connection to Marcus that night. It was alarming that Marcus felt cold, as he had always been a warm boy. Not long after clouds covered the sky, it got windy and it started to rain. Marcus and I decided to leave the movie night and rush back to the apartment.

On another occasion, Marcus showed an unusual behavior. He and I had planned to go snorkeling in the private lagoon in the Aulani resort. The water was cold but pleasant. Marcus was wearing his snorkeling gear—complete with fins, mask, and breathing tube. The lagoon had amazing fish, and I thought we would spend a decent amount of time in the lagoon. Jacob and Lucas were watching us through a window, and Marcus and I waved to them. Suddenly I lost track of Marcus in the water. I could not find him anywhere. I quickly swam to the wall and saw Marcus standing on the deck and removing all his snorkeling equipment. He said he got cold and wanted to get out. He seemed upset. He only spent a few minutes in the water. This behavior was so unlike Marcus. It was as if something bothered him. He would usually be the last person to get out of the water.

I treasure the memories of the trip to Hawaii, and I'm grateful that we made this trip as a family. It made us all strong. All the strength we got from this trip was something we would need very soon.

Once back in Houston, the boys began summer camp at the Village School. They were excited and eager to be with their friends. I was busy at work in the law firm and had to finish as much work as possible before heading to Denmark on vacation. I had scheduled Marcus's eighth-year physical exam with his wonderful doctor, Dr. Brack, during the first week of camp. Sitting at work, I considered canceling and rescheduling Marcus's doctor's appointment until after our vacation to Denmark when we had more time. Marcus didn't want to miss his camp, and I had loads of work to do at the office. On the other hand, something inside me told me not to cancel it. After the trip to Hawaii, I was worried something was wrong with Marcus.

At their baptism, I carried both my sons. I promised to take care of them and protect them as long as I lived. Up until that point, I had fulfilled that promise and I intended to keep doing so. Work and camp had to wait.

CHAPTER FIVE

A Parent's Worst Nightmare

Early June on a Wednesday, I left work to pick up Marcus from camp. Marcus was in full swing playing with his friends. He was in a good mood—simply happy. I told the staff at camp that Marcus had a quick doctor's appointment, after which we would come back and pick up Lucas.

Dr. Brack entered the exam room, and I filled her in about the trip to Hawaii and our upcoming vacation to Denmark. The three of us were in great spirits, and she was thrilled to hear about Marcus's birthday vacation to Hawaii. Dr. Brack later told me that when she saw Marcus in her clinic that day, he looked like a million bucks. He was tanned, muscular, and healthy-looking. He had the biggest smile on his face and the softest blond straight hair one could imagine. He was adorable, so innocent. Simply the perfect boy one could envision. Marcus did not raise any complaints to Dr. Brack. As expected, she quickly started examining Marcus.

She started with his neck, then she asked Marcus to lie down on his back so she could examine his abdomen. She moved on to examine his armpits, then his mid abdomen again, and moved farther down to his groin section. Midway, she stopped talking. I waited. *Why isn't she saying anything?* I thought. She focused her full attention on my son, and her face looked serious. Her eyebrows drawing together, she finished her exam. My pulse quickened. I had never seen her look like this before. Finally, she stopped her exam.

"Marcus's spleen is enlarged," Dr. Brack explained. "Compared to the last physical exam of Marcus in April, Marcus now has an increased number of swollen lymph nodes in his neck, armpits, and groin."

Chapter Five

I listened attentively. I had to take Marcus immediately to Texas Children's Hospital in Katy for labs and an ultrasound of his spleen. I asked her if it could wait until the day after. She was clear: it could *not* wait. I called Jacob to let him know what Dr. Brack had told me. I asked him to go pick up Lucas from his summer camp, as I anticipated the visit to Texas Children's Hospital would take several hours. I had to focus entirely on Marcus.

Once Marcus and I got to the hospital, we went straight to the lab to have his labs drawn. As he sat down on the chair in the lab, his face reddening, making an effort not to cry, he grabbed onto me as I moved closer. Marcus tolerated it better this time compared to the first time. After the nurse had successfully drawn the labs, we went up to the ultrasound exam room where a technician was waiting for us. She was polite and talked to Marcus about the ultrasound procedure she was about to perform on his spleen. Marcus lay down on the bed, and the technician squeezed a cold gel onto his stomach. Seeing the gel on his tummy reminded me of the times when I was pregnant and had to get an ultrasound done to see how the baby developed. For me, it used to be exciting to watch the screen with the baby while the technician explained what she saw on the monitor. This time with Marcus, my mind raced through random possibilities of what was going on with him. At the beginning, I could not tell if what I saw on the monitor was normal or abnormal since the nurse did not say anything. She said the radiologist was going to do the reading.

"Where is Marcus's spleen on the screen?" I asked the technician.

She pointed it out. Looking at the ultrasound images, I saw something dark with a lot of weird white stuff in the middle. I looked down. Maybe it was just an infection in his spleen.

We waited ten minutes, then other ten minutes, then another ten minutes. The technician had left the room and talked to the staff in the offices behind us. When she came back, I let her know I was about to leave with Marcus and that it was fine for me to get the results from the scan the day after. She stressed that we had to remain in the room.

"Why do Marcus and I have to stay when he's already done?" I questioned her.

"Because the doctors have to talk," the technician explained.

What doctors? What is going on? A sudden dizziness hit me. I started to believe something was seriously wrong with Marcus. The technician said nothing, and it seemed as if she was avoiding us.

I felt like we waited for hours, but it was probably just about one hour or so of waiting time before the technician returned and told me the doctor wanted to talk to me on the phone. She directed me to a phone in the waiting area adjacent to the exam room and told me to pick up the phone. I sat down on a chair while Marcus was still waiting in the exam room.

When I answered the phone, I realized it was Dr. Brack. I was happy to hear her voice, but my joy did not last long. What she told me changed everything.

I didn't know where to look. I refused to believe that Marcus had cancer. Maybe the doctors made a mistake and Marcus was okay after all. Marcus sat close by and didn't look sick to me. I put on a happy face and decided to call Jacob right away.

I explained to him that Dr. Brack was on her way to meet us. The only fact I could tell him was that Marcus had cancer. That was all I knew at that point in time. I sensed Jacob's voice lose its power, but he remained calm. I promised to call him back later after the meeting with Dr. Brack.

Dr. Brack arrived, and we sat down to talk. Marcus did not hear our conversation, as I let him rest in the exam room. Dr. Brack walked me through what was going to happen: We should drive home and get some sleep. In the morning, we were to bring Marcus to the Texas Children's Hospital (TCH) Main Campus in the Houston Medical Center. She had already called a colleague of hers who worked as an oncologist fellow at TCH. Her colleague had arranged for us to report to the ER at 9 A.M., and further studies would be done on Marcus.

Dr. Brack assured me that the doctors at TCH were the very best in the country. I asked her what type of cancer Marcus had, and she said it could be lymphoma, a cancer of the lymphatic system, or leukemia, a blood cancer. The doctors needed to run detailed tests on Marcus to determine the exact type of cancer he had. She explained that it would be best not to let Marcus eat anything in the morning so he was ready to get any procedures completed.

After our meeting, Dr. Brack walked us down to my car parked in the hospital parking lot. It struck me that when I walked through the door

Chapter Five

entering TCH with Marcus, the world looked different from when we walked out again. I wanted to roll back time to before I heard the words that Marcus had cancer, but I could not. Unfortunately, Dr. Brack was very clear about this horrible diagnosis. I had hoped she was not so certain. I kept hoping the doctors were mistaken and they would find out Marcus had caught a random disease that was easily treatable and not life-threatening. Her honesty was overwhelming yet appropriate and professional. What an amazing doctor and how fortunate for us that she was Marcus's doctor in that particular moment.

Driving home in darkness at first, there was complete silence in the car. Marcus and I were both exhausted after spending hours at the hospital. We needed time to digest. We allowed those moments of silence to just *be*. Silence is a precious gift. In that space between our words, it's where we find ourselves. When the mind is quiet, when there are no thoughts and no words to be said, we can hear our own hearts talking to us.

"Do I have cancer?" Marcus broke the silence.

This was not a good time to open up a discussion about cancer. On the other hand, how many times have I read that you should not lie to a child? Many times.

"The doctors believe you have cancer, Marcus, and that's why we will go to the hospital tomorrow so the doctors can help you," I replied.

Marcus knew a lot about cancer and was aware the disease was potentially deadly. I explained to him that today the doctors could treat it and that he would be all right.

I could not fall asleep that night. I had a terrible headache even two tablets of Aleve could not remove. I wanted to sleep and not wake up to face more ordeals. I had one wish, and it was to erase that day completely from my life.

Sometimes in life, we get upset about the wrong things. We go to bed in the evening thinking we don't want to get up early in the morning, go to work, go to school, or go to whatever appointments are scheduled that day and meet with people we dislike. Why is it that we hate the idea of waking up to a normal day with normal day-to-day activities? Why do we not appreciate normalcy? Normalcy could, in fact, be a good thing—meaning life is safe to wake up to with no disease present, no drama, and no bad surprises awaiting you.

That night, I fell asleep very late. The following morning, Jacob and I had to tell Lucas that Marcus was sick and had to go to the hospital. Lucas was five years old, close to six. Lucas was too young to understand what that meant, as Lucas had never visited a hospital before. We took Lucas to his soccer camp at the Village School and briefly explained to the staff that Marcus had cancer and we had to take him to TCH. They were shocked to hear the news. They promised to take good care of Lucas.

It was Thursday morning, and the ER was busy. A young nurse greeted us, after which we waited in the exam room for a while. Jacob started playing chess with Marcus, a game Marcus's friends had taught him in school. The nurse came back and described what was going to happen next. She hooked Marcus up to multiple monitors. She also inserted an IV in Marcus's hand. The doctors had found out what type of cancer Marcus had and would come and talk to us.

Shortly after, an oncology fellow arrived. It was Dr. Brack's colleague, a young and sweet female doctor. The oncology fellow clarified that the doctors had received the final pathology analysis from the lab. The pathology report showed that Marcus had leukemia, a type called Childhood Acute Lymphoblastic Leukemia (ALL), a cancer in the bone marrow. ALL is the most common type of cancer in children and is curable in most cases. When I heard the word *curable* coming out of the doctor's mouth, I felt assured that Marcus was going to survive.

The oncology floor is the busiest floor at TCH. The hospital has inpatient pediatric patients not just from Houston and other parts of the US, but also from other countries. Rich families from the Arabic countries seek cancer treatment for their children at TCH. They choose to fly their child back and forth to treatments at TCH rather than getting treatment in their own country. This was a strong indication to me that TCH was the best hospital in the whole world and that Marcus would be safe with specialized doctors in all departments of the hospital.

I was not used to seeing so many sick children in one single place. When we got off on the ninth floor and walked down the hallway, we saw parents, nurses, and doctors all over. Some doctors were busy typing on the computers in front of the rooms in the designated nurses' and doctors' stations. The horrible smell of medicine was everywhere. Walking down to Marcus's room was heartbreaking, passing all the children with no hair. It was easy to distinguish cancer patients from their siblings. Some patients looked like they had been internees in a WWII concentration camp and had just been freed by Red Cross workers. These children's eyes were so empty and innocent. They looked skinny and unhealthy; some were wearing hats to hide their baldness. There was no doubt they had experienced suffering a child should never experience. Not just physical pain but emotional pain too. Some patients were too young to realize they could die from cancer. Others were mature enough to understand the impact of their disease.

I did not believe that Marcus would end up looking like these poor children. Being so strong and otherwise healthy, Marcus would do astonishingly. Only other kids would end up like this. Not our Marcus. To me, Marcus was special and unique. There was no way cancer could beat him.

Marcus got a nicely equipped room with his own TV, restroom, and bath. Next to Marcus's bed was a pullout sofa for one caregiver to stay overnight. The room had a spacious closet where Marcus could put his backpack and hang his clothes. He had brought several of his favorite stuffed animals and a Spider-Man fleece blanket to make his bed cozy.

"I'm going to put Wolf here next to my pillow. Wolf is going to protect me," Marcus exclaimed, placing his stuffed animal Wolf close to his pillow. "I'll spread out my blanket here." He organized it neatly on top of the hospital duvet.

A young nurse came in and handed Marcus a kid's menu card. At TCH, inpatient children get to pick their own menu from a huge selection of dishes, drinks, and side dishes. To be honest, this kind of service was quite impressive.

I said to Marcus, "This is just like living in a hotel with your own waiter outside. You have your own room, your own TV, and you can decide what you want to watch. Marcus, I bet Lucas will get jealous when he sees this."

After having carefully studied the menu, Marcus made his selections and stated, "Tonight, I would like to have cheese pizza and fruit for dessert and water."

The young nurse came back and said, "I'll give you a tour of the floor so you know where to find what you need. And I'm going to show you the game room and playroom."

Marcus was thrilled to hear about the game room and to learn where it was located on the floor. So far, he was happy and forgot just for a moment that he was in a hospital. At that time, we heard a baby crying, almost screaming, loudly next door in the corner room. That scared me. What was a small baby doing on the oncology floor? In my world, a tiny baby could not get cancer. It was unbelievable that an innocent baby could get such a terrible disease. It struck me that behind these hospital walls was a world I had not known ever existed, and it was not pretty. The smell of medicine, the busy doctors, the sick children, and the sound of crying children made me feel uncomfortable. I could not wait to get out of there.

Yet I could not show this to Marcus. He needed a strong, confident mom, not a shocked, speechless mom. By instinct, I used a technique of reminding myself that all these children were here to get a cure to their cancer, enabling them to return to their normal lives, play with their friends, and go to school and learn new things. I was used to hearing the laughter of children in Marcus and Lucas's school. I missed the sound of laughter on this floor. It was not a place for laughter. In Denmark, we often joke that a patient has to be very healthy to survive a hospital stay. Now I understood why.

The game room was a success and offered a race-car game and other electronic games Marcus would love to play with. My husband and I promised Marcus that he could come back later that day and play. At this time of the day, Marcus still had not eaten anything. To maintain Marcus's fluid balance, he got hydration through the IV in his hand. The plastic fluid bag was hanging on a rollable IV pole. The rate of the fluid dripping from the bag was modulated with an electric pump programmed by the nurse. At first, it was difficult for Marcus to roll the pole, as he had to steer and roll it at the same time with his left hand. He was rushing to get around, and it was a bit of a challenge for him to keep up his usual high speed since he was new in this "game."

The tour included a visit to the Ronald McDonald House, that "home-away-from-home" for families so they could stay close by their hospitalized family members. This was my first time entering a Ronald McDonald House, and it was not going to be my last time. Supporters help fund Ronald

Chapter Five

McDonald Houses. The majority of the programming funds come from individuals, organizations, and businesses; the hospitals are not involved in running the houses. I was pleased to learn that the Ronald McDonald House at TCH offered snacks, a kitchen to make tea, and a fridge for any personal perishable items we wanted to bring to the hospital. Everything was free of charge, even meals such as pizzas. All Ronald McDonald House staffers are volunteers. Most of them were students, moms of pediatric cancer survivors, and senior citizens—all of whom offered help and courage to the parents while keeping the Ronald McDonald House clean and stocked with supplies.

I immediately knew I would appreciate all the services they could offer. I had found a place where I could talk to other parents, a safe base where I could take a break from the hospital environment just outside the door. I never saw a nurse or a doctor inside the house. The Ronald McDonald House was strictly for patients, their siblings, and caregivers. I felt the nature of this space in the middle of the oncology floor to be one of hope and calmness. Just the smell of coffee and food that greeted me upon entry made me think I was entering a Starbucks, a place I always enjoyed visiting.

Although it was comforting to have a "safe place" away from the medical world, I would learn much later that it would also be beneficial to have someone who could act as a parent/caregiver specialist, much like the child specialists, who would provide much-needed communication between the medical people and the family.

At the end of the tour, we got a glimpse of the entrance nursing station where posters on the walls gave clear instructions about *not* entering the floor if sick or febrile or having symptoms of any type of disease. It became evident to me that access to this floor was limited. Everyone wanting to enter the floor had to pass the reception where nurses would assess him or her and ask questions about their current health situation.

This was the new reality for Marcus and us. It slowly became clearer to me that this floor was a floor for very sick children.

When we returned, the nurse guided Marcus and us to a different floor to do an ultrasound of Marcus's heart. The technician who performed the ultrasound did not say anything and focused entirely on his task. Not knowing if he was looking for something abnormal or if this was just a routine check prior to starting treatment, I was troubled.

Once back in Marcus's room after the ultrasound procedure, the nurse told me not to worry, as this was a necessary step prior to starting treatment. The doctors wanted to be sure that Marcus's heart was healthy. If his heart was unfit, this could influence Marcus's treatment plans. Luckily, it turned out that Marcus's heart was in good shape.

Next item on the agenda was for Marcus to get a bone marrow biopsy and a spinal tap. Before the doctors could proceed with this invasive procedure, Jacob and I had to meet with the oncology doctor. The doctor came prepared with enormous amounts of paperwork. The doctors had to assess the leukemia burden in Marcus's bone marrow and spinal fluid. Many different types of leukemia exist, and it mattered which form of leukemia Marcus had and how far it had progressed. Marcus was diagnosed with T-cell ALL, which starts out in the bone marrow and can move into the spinal fluid. In Marcus's case, they had to remove a small amount of bone and a small amount of fluid and cells from inside his hip bone (bone marrow). A spinal tap, also called a lumbar puncture, is a medical test in which fluid is collected from an area surrounding the spinal cord. In the lab, the pathologists study the sample for traces of bacteria and other infectious agents. They also test it for blood cell count, protein, and other blood components. I did not like the thought of the doctors penetrating Marcus's spinal fluid and bone, as this to me sounded like risky procedures. I had to come to terms with these procedures, as this was the only way to look into his bone marrow and spine. Marcus had to be sedated for this procedure, and this, too, made me anxious. Marcus had never been under anesthesia of any sort.

Jacob and I went over side effects and risks with the doctors, and I didn't like what I heard. The doctor used medical terms unfamiliar to me. With no background in medicine, I was in new territory. I disliked the medical world because it reminded me of disease, pain, and death.

We asked the doctors a number of questions to get some clarifications about how Marcus would feel after the procedure and if it would hurt afterward. He would have some pain in the incisions and in his back, and they would give him medicine for that. Still, I'd rather have them do the procedure on me, not Marcus, but we had no choice than to give permission to these procedures. Additionally, the doctor told us that Marcus was to get intrathecal chemotherapy.

Chapter Five

"What is intrathecal chemotherapy?" I asked the doctor.

"It's a type of chemotherapy that's administered into the fluid between the membranes that line the brain and spinal cord. We use intrathecal chemotherapy to treat cancer that has spread to the CSF or to prevent cancer from spreading to the CSF," the doctor answered.

"What do you mean by intrathecal and CSF?" I asked.

"Cerebrospinal fluid—or CSF—is a clear, colorless body fluid found in the brain and spine. Intrathecal means that the medicine is administered into the spinal canal," the doctor replied.

I felt like it could not get any worse now. Marcus had leukemia, and now the doctor talked about injecting chemotherapy into his spine.

It was as if things were happening too quickly to process.

"Is it really necessary to give Marcus all this?" I tried to object. I placed my hands over his head.

"Yes," the doctor replied. "It's because Marcus has T-cell ALL, and this type of leukemia has a tendency to spread to the CNS. In boys, there is also a risk of spreading to the testicles," the doctor explained.

This was horrible news. I stared at the doctor, my mouth agape.

"Could leukemia turn into testicular cancer, and what is CNS again?" I questioned, rubbing my temple as I tried to comprehend everything she said.

The doctor explained that Marcus did not have testicular cancer.

"About two percent or so of boys have testicular disease at diagnosis of T-cell ALL, but this relates to the spread of leukemia, not testicular cancer. As far as CNS goes, that stands for central nervous system."

The doctors needed our consent in writing so Marcus could proceed to get his bone marrow biopsy and spinal tap done and receive intrathecal chemotherapy. There was no way out, no alternative—just this way forward to save Marcus.

The doctor discussed which trials we could choose from for Marcus. Hospitals implement different clinical cancer trials and the parents choose which protocol to enroll their child in. Clinical trials are research studies. People live longer lives from successful cancer treatments that are the results of past clinical trials. Therefore, by enrolling Marcus in a clinical trial, Marcus adds to doctors' knowledge about cancer and helps improve cancer care for future pediatric patients. Jacob and I wanted the doctors to use the results from Marcus's treatment for their research. Marcus was also interested in contributing his results to science. The doctor had a trial in mind for Marcus, and Jacob signed the paperwork for that protocol. The truth is that regardless of the trial, the doctors would recommend Marcus get the same treatment.

The extent of information we received during the conference overwhelmed me. It was intense and detailed information, and there was no time to go home and consider what would be the best option for Marcus. As laid out by the doctor, the medical team had already picked the protocol that would suit Marcus best.

Watching my husband sign the consent paperwork felt like we let go of Marcus. Marcus had cancer, and because of that, we had no control over what was going to happen to him. We had to trust the medical team. After all, they were the experts and they dealt with this stuff every day. Marcus was just a new child in line to start chemotherapy treatment. The doctors expected that the chemotherapy treatment would work, but there was no guarantee. Sometimes it didn't work.

Just as I hoped the conference was over, the doctor informed us that Marcus needed a tiny operation to get a peripherally inserted central catheter (PICC or PICC line). I'd never heard of a PICC line before, and it was another shock to me that Marcus needed such a medical device placed in his arm to receive chemotherapy. It was as if I had to have a medical degree to understand all these new medical terms.

A PICC line is a form of intravenous access that can be used for a prolonged period such as for long chemotherapy regimens or extended antibiotic therapy. The doctor told us it was standard procedure for a child to get a PICC line. She elaborated on the benefits.

"A PICC line is more comfortable compared to the many needle sticks that would have been needed for giving medications and drawing blood. The goal is to spare Marcus's veins from these frequent needle sticks. A PICC line can also spare Marcus's veins and blood vessels from the irritating effects of IV medications."

The doctor told us that child life specialists worked on the oncology floor and a child life specialist would visit Marcus prior to the procedures. Child life specialists are pediatric health-care professionals who work with children and families in hospitals and other settings to help them cope with the challenges of hospitalization, illness, and disability. Their most important goal is to explain a child's diagnosis to him or her in a way that's appropriate for the child's age and level of understanding. Specialists also explain medical jargon to kids and prepare them for procedures. They use teaching dolls or utilize real or pretend medical equipment. Sometimes they use art and play to help children express their anxieties about their diagnosis or procedures that they may not be able to verbalize.

A young, friendly child life specialist named Alyssa came to talk to Marcus. She had a doll and some kids-size medical devices so she could demonstrate on the doll what a PICC line looked like and what its function was. After Alyssa had shown Marcus how the PICC line worked on the doll, Marcus got to play doctor and pretend to give the doll medicine through its PICC line. Marcus seemed confident handling the syringe and showing me how his PICC line was going to work. Marcus loved science so this allowed him to experiment with the doll and to adjust to the medical equipment that would soon become part of his daily life.

I quietly observed Marcus, a healthy little boy having fun playing with the doll in such a natural way. Looking at him for a moment, I forgot all about our current setting. Alyssa did such a wonderful job talking to Marcus. I wanted to hug her. A big smile on her face, long straight hair, and a calming presence—that's what she brought with her inside Marcus's hospital room. I cannot emphasize enough how important those child life specialists became to Marcus and our family. As a newcomer to the medical environment, Marcus needed the extra support the child life specialists could offer. And so did we. I was thankful for this gift.

Alyssa also carried a piece of cardboard and round color stamps to do an exercise with Marcus. "Marcus, you pick three colors," she instructed him peacefully, preparing him to focus on his next assignment.

"Okay," Marcus replied and picked red, purple, and yellow.

"You take these stamps and put red, purple, and yellow dots all over this paper," she explained. Marcus quickly marked the whole paper with beautiful dots.

"So these dots represent all your healthy blood cells in your blood, Marcus," she said. "Your blood contains three types of important cells. One type is called red blood cells, another is called white blood cells, and the last type is called platelets." She reached over to the stamps. "Now I'm going to add some orange stamps."

She quickly stamped random orange dots all over the cardboard.

"So these are the leukemia cells we do not like," she explained.

Then she took a blue stamp and made lines and small crosses over the orange dots. She paused and handed Marcus the blue stamp.

"The blue stamp is the medicine that will eliminate all the bad leukemia cells and make you healthy again. Marcus, now you take the blue stamp and take out all the leukemia cells," she said in an encouraging voice.

Marcus did not hesitate. He swiftly completed the task, and the result was a lovely piece of art he showed me immediately after.

"I promise I will come back to check on you later today, Marcus. Your mommy can call me if you need me or have any questions." She left to attend to other children on the floor.

CHAPTER SIX

First Line Treatment

Marcus came back from the PICC insertion and first intrathecal chemotherapy procedure in a wheelchair. He looked weak and pale. He was officially a cancer patient now. The anesthesia had started to wear off. All procedures went as planned. What a relief. Marcus tolerated the anesthesia well, and when he was alert enough, he could have something to drink and eat.

"Mommy, it hurts," Marcus uttered with a quiet voice.

"Where does it hurt, honey?" I asked.

Marcus pointed to his PICC line site on his left arm and to his back. I called the nurse because Marcus kept hurting. The nurse gave him an ice pack to cover the PICC line site and some pain medicine. Some time elapsed, and I could see Marcus was not comfortable even with the ice pack on and the pain medicine kicking in. I felt the drama start to build up. Marcus began crying as the pain became intolerable for him. He wanted to have the PICC line removed. I comforted him and let him know that soon the pain would go away. After some time, he calmed down and was able to relax.

I remember Alyssa mentioning there was a library on one of the floors above us. When Marcus was feeling better, we decided that he could pay the library a visit and borrow some books. Although slowly, Marcus was able to walk again in the afternoon. Once we arrived in the library, Marcus cheered up and shortly forgot about the pain in his arm and back. He was impatient and ready to explore the whole library.

Jacob suddenly called me and told me to rush down to Marcus's room because we had to sign more paperwork regarding Marcus's treatment. I asked the librarian if I could briefly leave Marcus in the library while I ran down to sign important paperwork, and the librarian promised me to look after Marcus. He was wearing a hospital bracelet with his name, date of birth, and medical number on it, and she promised to call me if Marcus needed me.

"Mommy, I'm fine here. You can leave," Marcus assured me. He was ready to go on board in all the books and DVDs he just found out he could borrow. This opportunity to borrow new books and DVDs was too exciting for him to miss.

It turned out the conference about the paperwork took longer than expected. The doctor talked and talked. I regretted letting Marcus stay in the library. Was he okay? Once again, we had to sign consent forms allowing Marcus to receive blood transfusions if necessary. Blood cells and blood components may be lower than normal for a variety of different reasons in cancer patients. The doctor explained that because Marcus had blood cancer, leukemia, the doctors expected that Marcus would likely need to receive transfusions of blood and blood products during his treatment.

Initially, I found the idea of giving Marcus another person's blood disgusting and rather invasive. It took me awhile to comprehend the scenario that the chemotherapy Marcus was about to get would weaken him to a degree that blood transfusion would be necessary to give. Half of my attention was directed toward Marcus, who was in the library, and the other half was focused on understanding the consequences if Marcus did not get blood transfusions. It was hard to remain on track during these detailed discussions. It was late in the afternoon. During the course of this initial day at the hospital, the doctors had already overloaded us with tons of information. This was not easy to comprehend, and I noticed that I felt filled up to the maximum capacity. When would this flow of information stop? I needed a break—now. Frustration started to build up. I wanted to say stop to the doctor. I wanted to leave the room and find Marcus to ensure he was okay. I missed him. Yet it was essential that Jacob and I understood the effects of the chemotherapy treatment Marcus was due to receive. I was stuck between a rock and a hard place.

The picture became clearer and clearer. Cancer is not treatable in one afternoon. The side effects of the disease and treatments are awful. Treatment is supposed to be lifesaving, but at the same time, it can also be life-threatening. At the hospital, they had to monitor Marcus closely in order to follow his response to treatment and to ensure possible side effects were taken care of.

What choice did we have but to sign the consent forms and allow Marcus to receive blood transfusions? We did not wish for Marcus to have repeated fevers and infections, difficulty breathing, mouth sores, bruising, and excessive bleeding—all of which could happen with low blood cell counts.

On the other hand, I was concerned about the risk of disease and transfusion reaction from donated blood—not to mention that Marcus may have a mild allergic reaction even if he received the correct blood type. We ended up signing the consent forms allowing Marcus to receive blood transfusions.

I rushed the doctor to finish the meeting so I could go get Marcus in the hospital library. When I returned to the library, I saw Marcus sitting in a wheelchair all alone with tears in his eyes. The librarian had left. I could tell he was aching. I got upset, as nobody was looking after him and nobody called me to inform me that Marcus was in pain. I shook my head in disbelief. I rolled Marcus down to his room where Jacob was waiting. We helped him back into his bed so he could rest his hurting back.

It became evident that the chemotherapy and that day's procedures had started to affect Marcus. He was not himself anymore. It's difficult for parents to witness when their child is not well or is sad. It feels like the parent is hurting too. Marcus was usually a charming and active boy. Sitting in the wheelchair, he was wearing his own clothes, which helped to maintain his normal look, but his charisma had vanished. It was as if the medicine had already changed him.

I was angry at the leukemia because it was causing Marcus to be in the hospital and feel miserable. I also felt pity for him. I felt guilty because Marcus had cancer. Was there something we did or did not do that caused the cancer? Repeatedly, the doctors explained to us that we were not responsible for causing Marcus's cancer. I also blamed myself for not noticing Marcus's symptoms quickly enough and for not having pushed Dr. Brack or the other pediatricians to find the cause of the persistent swollen lymph nodes. I started to get anxious and to question myself. Would Lucas also get leukemia? Is he at higher risk now due to Marcus's situation? Again, the doctors assured us that childhood leukemia does not run in families. In other words, leukemia is not hereditary. Still today, doctors do not understand leukemia well enough to pinpoint reasons or circumstances that can explain why otherwise healthy children develop leukemia. I tried to forget I had told Marcus that being in a hospital was like staying at a hotel. I had lied to him. It was not like a hotel at all.

Later in the afternoon, the nurse entered his room with Marcus's first round of IV chemotherapy. With ease, she administered it through Marcus's PICC line, which was held in place by a dressing. Marcus had two ports: a red and a blue one. That way, Marcus could get both his chemotherapy and fluids simultaneously. For the first time, we saw the benefits of the PICC line in action. Marcus remained unaffected by the nurse working at his bedside. It was comforting to witness how elegantly she handled Marcus's PICC line, hooked him up to his IV chemotherapy and fluids hanging on the pole, and managed programming the pump. It seemed like this was what she did all day long in the hospital. After all, it seemed that all the children on the floor had a PICC line, so it couldn't be that special. While Marcus was napping, Jacob and I made plans for the rest of the day. Even though exhausted after the previous meetings and intense information overload, we had to remain cool and mobilize some energy.

I decided to drive back home to get some extra clothes and things for myself so I could stay several days at the hospital with Marcus. If he tolerated the chemotherapy treatment well, the doctors could release him from the hospital after four to five days. This meant we had to make plans for Lucas while Marcus was in the hospital. Fortunately, Lucas was in summer camp at school the day Marcus was admitted to the hospital and the day after, which was a Friday. During the weekend, we could arrange playdates for Lucas at his friends' houses.

It was in the middle of the afternoon. The weather was beautiful and hot in Houston. Traffic was light, just what I needed. Driving home in my car, I experienced increased self-confidence and felt a sense of calmness inside because Marcus was in the hospital and his daddy was with him. With self-talk, I convinced myself the chemotherapy would do the job and cure Marcus completely. I was alone in the car and I got a break away from the stressful hospital atmosphere. I felt positive and hopeful. The staff at TCH was professional and knowledgeable and had Marcus's complete treatment plan lined up even before they had met Marcus. They were well prepared and confident, and I believe it helped me cope with the situation better than expected. There was no drama or rushing. From the beginning, Marcus's case was not unusual or difficult. He was just another child in line for treatment. The cure rate for children diagnosed with T-cell ALL was 90 percent. Marcus simply had to follow his protocol, and then he would recover and be back to our normal Marcus. He was going to be in the 90 percent group. I chose hope, not fear or sadness.

When I came back to Marcus's room, I noticed he felt better. The nap was good for him.

"Mommy? Daddy? I want to go to the game room," Marcus said.

"Sure, Marcus, you can do that," I said, getting ready to escort him to the game room.

I loved it. Marcus was happy and ready to play again. He was able to walk down the hallway pushing his pole with chemotherapy. The game room, which was opposite the Ronald McDonald House, was busy with other boys already playing.

He grabbed the steering wheel and put his right foot on the speeder while sitting in the seat of the race car. In front of him was a screen showing the race-car track. The second Marcus pushed the play button, he was in game mode. He held the steering wheel tightly and almost jumped out of the seat to push the gas pedal farther down. Marcus forgot all about his PICC line and chemotherapy dripping into his veins.

"I'll ask Daddy to take a photo of you while playing the game," I told Marcus.

He did not react to my comment. The game had his full attention. Although he was tired, it turned out that Marcus tolerated the chemotherapy very well. This afternoon was a little victory.

At dinnertime, a cafeteria staff member delivered a dinner tray to Marcus with cheese pizza and peaches in syrup as dessert. His pizza was a disaster—he refused to eat it. It could be that the chemotherapy made him nauseated or that he expected the pizza to taste like a margherita pizza at George's Pastaria on Dairy Ashford, a favorite pizza restaurant close by our home. I tasted Marcus's cheese pizza for myself. The crust was rubbery, tasteless, and very uninspiring. A big food lover, Marcus was obviously disappointed. I told him I would make a delicious dinner for him when we got home again.

"Mommy, I wish you could cook your homemade spaghetti carbonara for me when I get home," Marcus urged.

"Okay," I said. "I'll make it with bacon, onions, and mushrooms, right?"

He nodded, a smile forming on his lips.

"And then, I'll fry it lightly in butter on the pan. Then I can make a cheese egg mix with eggs, grated Parmesan cheese—oh, *lots* of Parmesan cheese!—and heavy whipping cream."

"Mommy," Marcus interjected, "but not too much salt and pepper!"

I rolled my eyes and laughed. "I won't put too much salt and pepper in, I promise."

Marcus couldn't sit still. He started pacing. "Then I can help you cook. You boil the spaghetti, and then I help you mix it all together." Suddenly his eyes bulged. "You *have* to put a lot of Parmesan cheese in the sauce, okay?"

Marcus loved cheese.

"I promise, I promise!" I said.

"This dish is so yummy," Marcus concluded as if he had ordered the food already.

This talk was mouthwatering, and I got hungry just talking about the food.

"Can we also make rice with creamy mushroom sauce?" Marcus asked.

"Sure, we can make anything you want," I replied.

We laughed. This opened up a whole conversation about all the food we wanted to cook together when Marcus got home. Not all boys Marcus's age were interested in food. My mother was the first person in Denmark to publish a cookbook made specifically for children. UNICEF published it, and she donated all proceeds to the UNICEF committee. My mother was a visionary, being the first person to come up with the idea of bringing children into the kitchen to cook easy recipes with their parents. My two older brothers and I were models in the cookbook, showing how to do the recipes as my mother instructed us.

Marcus and Lucas always enjoyed looking in the cookbook with childhood pictures of my brothers and me. The pictures included our beloved family dog Liva, a huge brownish Great Dane. Although Marcus never got a chance to meet my parents, it seems like he had inherited their appreciation for food and many of their skills, qualities, and interests. Marcus also appreciated traveling.

It was a pleasure to see how Marcus had grown into this little foodie. For his second-grade reflection, Marcus was asked to answer this question: What was your favorite thing about second grade? He answered it honestly and wrote, "It was that we get cookies in school every Friday and we go to the field." This described what he liked the most about school: food and sports.

The first night, Marcus and I had to get used to the hospital routines when nurses came in to check on Marcus and when medical assistants came in to take his blood pressure and measure his temperature. Throughout the night, they interrupted us. Marcus received IV fluids on top of the chemotherapy, which made him wake up a few times to use the restroom. He was not used to getting so much fluid and hated to get up several times during the night. I had to get up and help him go to the restroom. The fluids were hooked up to his PICC line arm, and he wanted to roll the pole in the dark. Not a good idea. I had to turn on the lights.

When the IV pump was done or when the line was obstructed, it beeped loudly. That noise was not to be missed. Marcus joked he wanted to be "beep-free" and that he could not wait to get home. The baby next door cried on and off during the night. I felt so bad for the baby and the mother that I wanted to go in and comfort him or her. We did get some sleep but not very much.

The following days at the hospital passed with no major drama. One of the days, Dr. Brack came to visit him. She brought gifts for Marcus; among others, there was a big red plastic Spider-Man ball. She went to the hospital cafeteria to get my husband and me some lunch. As always, she was so nice and wonderful. She was confident Marcus was safe at TCH. She told us that the test of Marcus's spinal fluid showed no sign of disease. This was good news. This meant the leukemia had not spread to his spinal fluid, which meant he needed less aggressive treatment in his spine and central nervous system.

The other tests revealed that Marcus had 75 percent leukemia blasts in his bone marrow. I had asked if this was normal, and the doctors told us

Chapter Six

this is what they typically see at time of diagnosis. In that respect, Marcus's clinical picture was normal. Normal sounded reassuring.

In June 2014, it was World Cup time in Brazil, uniting soccer lovers all over the world, including Marcus. He was ready to follow his favorite soccer players, Lionel Messi from Argentina and Neymar Jr., who played for Brazil. Ms. Scavo, his second-grade language arts teacher, visited Marcus at the hospital with his science teacher, Ms. Winston. Ms. Scavo gave him the official *2014 FIFA World Cup Magazine*. It contained the program of all the World Cup soccer games and nations represented in the tournament. The magazine included all soccer player profiles and foldout posters for the wall.

In second grade, Marcus had researched a topic of interest for a school project. An avid soccer fan, Marcus researched soccer player Messi, who played professionally for FC Barcelona in Spain. He produced a PowerPoint and presented the information he learned in front of the class. The night before his presentation was due, Marcus decided he wanted to wear Messi's Argentina strip (jersey and shorts) for the presentation. That was a great idea, but the problem was Marcus didn't have the jersey or shorts. Once Marcus came up with an idea, it was impossible to make him forget about it. There was no way out. He was determined to wear the strip to make the presentation perfect.

That night, I had to rush out to a store to get Messi's Argentina strip. Luckily, I found one in Marcus's size. What a mommy does for her child!

In Marcus's academic plan from the Village School, his language arts teacher, Ms. Scavo, made the following comment about the presentation: "Marcus shared his passion for soccer by doing research on Messi and presented the information learned through an amazing PowerPoint. I loved that Marcus dressed the part while presenting! He was well-informed and was very well-spoken. Everyone enjoyed learning from him."

He was an eager boy who enjoyed learning. I told my friends and family I never worried if Marcus would succeed in life. Watching him grow up and seeing his qualities and drive, I told them that Marcus could achieve anything in life. He was smart, charming, handsome, funny, and caring. He had so many talents and was hardworking and detail-oriented, like myself.

The first portion of Marcus's inpatient stay lasted five days. His induction program consisted of six different types of chemotherapies. Induction therapy is a term used to describe the first major treatment or therapy administered to a cancer patient.

One night at TCH, Marcus became so angry that he refused to swallow his prednisone tablets because the taste was disgusting. I was desperate because Marcus had to take his medicine. All Marcus's medicines were lifesaving because they all fought the leukemia at different levels; thus, I could not let him skip any of them. It was late in the evening, and child life specialists had left for the day. I was beyond tired, and Jacob had already gone home to take care of Lucas. I had to find a way to make Marcus understand he had to swallow the pill. I managed to find a night nurse who appeared for his shift refreshed and with a positive attitude. He sat down to talk to Marcus and showed him a trick.

"Marcus, I have an idea that works for other kids," the night nurse said. "You take a piece of Fruit Roll-Up, and then you cover the pill in it. When you swallow the pill, you won't taste the medicine. Pretty cool, right?"

Marcus suddenly looked interested after hearing about the Fruit Roll-Up—one of his favorite candies.

"What flavor do you like, Marcus?" the nurse asked him.

"I like strawberry," Marcus replied.

The nurse went to the kitchen and came back with a strawberry-flavored Fruit Roll-Up. He showed Marcus how to make a little ball with the pill and the Fruit Roll-Up completely covering the pill. Marcus forgot all about not wanting to swallow his pill. The nurse got him some milk, and in one go, Marcus easily swallowed his pills.

"Wow! Amazing job, Marcus. You did it!" I high-fived him.

I thanked the nurse for helping Marcus. In fact, he not only helped Marcus, but he also helped me. At TCH and any other children's hospital, the staff relies on the caregivers to help. After all, the parents are there all the time and they know their child.

I was learning how much I would be on the front line of caring for Marcus. From the moment your child is diagnosed with cancer, you have to step up to become a nurse and doctor on top of being a parent. A parent must be the child's advocate, and it takes knowledge, will, and energy to fill that role. From one second to the next, your role changes and nobody is going to ask you how you feel about it. The medical professionals expect you

Chapter Six

to be capable of doing this while you're still processing the news from the cancer diagnosis and trying to cope along with the rest of the family as they grieve.

The doctors told us that after induction, Marcus would continue to consolidation therapy for several months and, after this, over a year of maintenance treatment. The total duration of the treatment program was two to three years depending on how Marcus would respond to the treatment. Even after successful completion of the protocol, the doctors would have to follow Marcus through regular blood tests to rule out relapse. The reality was that sometimes, despite the best care and significant progress made in treatment, leukemia could come back. When this happens, the doctors call it a recurrence or relapse. Between 15 and 20 percent of children who are treated for the type of leukemia Marcus had will achieve an initial complete remission but will have the disease return.

It came as a shock to me that Marcus would need treatment for two to three years. The doctors expected he would have to miss school for about half a year, after which time he could return and still follow his maintenance program. He would be tired and have a low immune system; thus, he would probably miss class a lot.

Jacob and I had to deal with numerous questions. Could we travel to Denmark? Could we travel domestically? Could Marcus do sports? How would all these changes affect Lucas and our family life? Could Lucas have playdates in our house when Marcus received chemotherapy? Could we invite adult visitors into our house? The doctors did a great job explaining these new limitations. Hygiene became a top priority. When Lucas came home from school, he could not go see Marcus until he had washed his hands. We could not allow any sick visitors into our house, especially not any sick children due to Marcus's compromised immune system. Any little bug that would otherwise be harmless to healthy people could be fatal to Marcus. There was a constant fear that Marcus would get an infection that could easily kill him. All this meant that our lives were now full of precautions. It didn't terrify me, however, that we had to make all these changes in our home and in our private lives. They were manageable.

The doctors were happy with the way Marcus tolerated the chemotherapy, and we learned that there was a chance the doctors could discharge him

First Line Treatment

on Monday, June 9. That Monday was hectic but exciting. I felt like crying tears of joy knowing that Marcus could return home. I also didn't regard Marcus's situation as a serious one in the beginning. I later discovered I was wrong. The situation was definitely still serious. Marcus already had leukemia. The doctors didn't know if the treatment was going to work or not. We could see a very small light at the end of the tunnel with many obstacles along the way. As long as we could see the light, there was hope. Hope that Marcus would eventually survive this and grow up to become a man. Hope that we as a family would survive this. All I could do was store away the fear and focus on doing the best thing for Marcus at each step of his treatment.

It was Monday, June 9, and Jacob had relieved me at TCH. The doctors told us that Marcus could be discharged that day or the following day. I had driven home to prepare the home for Marcus. It was like getting Marcus home for the first time after I gave birth to him. It felt like Marcus got another chance to live. It was a gift to bring him back home again. Except this time, he was not a healthy newborn baby boy, but a young boy with a life-threatening disease. I rushed home and went straight to our supermarket, Kroger, to buy cleaning supplies so I could clean the whole house before he got home. I bought all Marcus's favorite foods: strawberries, grapes, tomatoes, cucumbers, carrots, RITZ crackers, and rice.

I bought many Clorox disinfectant wipes, the same type I had seen the staff use in the Ronald McDonald House. I took down the shower curtain in Marcus and Lucas's bathroom and washed it. I was scared it had bacteria that could get Marcus sick. I wiped all the handles on the doors where all germs collect. I cleaned and I cleaned even though my back was aching. I didn't care how much pain I had. It had to wait. The house had to be perfect for Marcus's return, and I had limited time left before I had to drive back to TCH. I changed his bedsheets so he had fresh and clean ones to sleep in when he got home. I arranged for Lucas to be picked up by our Danish friends living close by so Lucas could stay at their house and eat dinner and play. Jacob and I were 100 percent concentrated on getting Marcus home. Unexpectedly, Jacob called me to let me know that the doctors would discharge Marcus in the evening. This news was amazing and reassuring.

Before we could leave the hospital, we had to go to the nearest pharmacy to pick up all the medicine Marcus needed once he was home. To avoid infection, TCH also had to arrange for a home health nurse to come to our home once a week to change Marcus's PICC line dressing. The home health nurse was to give us instructions on how to flush Marcus's PICC line every day. If it wasn't flushed, it would clog and become useless.

I hurried back to TCH expecting the best. Once back with Jacob and Marcus, I realized it would take several hours before we could leave TCH with our son. First, we had to wait for the doctor to complete and submit the prescriptions. Then Jacob had to drive to CVS Pharmacy to collect the medicine. He did so and returned. It was dinnertime, and Marcus was getting tired. So were we. We had no time to eat dinner, but Marcus was able to eat.

Dr. Schafer, the leukemia oncologist on shift for the night, entered Marcus's room, and we sat down and went over all Marcus's medicines. Dr. Schafer made a tremendous effort to explain to us the importance of all the medicines. Jacob had collected a huge bag of medicine. I was confident we could soon leave. Dr. Schafer noted that one medicine was missing. A mistake had been made by the pharmacist. The doctor went back to the computer and resent the prescription to CVS Pharmacy, and Jacob went over one more time. He returned, and after rechecking the medicine, Dr. Schafer agreed that everything was in good order.

In Marcus's medicine bag, we had eight different medications. Prednisone was part of his home chemotherapy treatment. The other medicines were to treat side effects of the chemotherapy; he also had prophylactic medicines to prevent infections.

I had to administer all these medicines to Marcus according to a fixed schedule. I felt a huge responsibility to make sure he got the correct medicines at the correct times during the day.

The nurse had to finalize the discharge paperwork. I wanted to go home with Marcus, but it took forever. It was 10 P.M. before we left TCH. Marcus was in a wheelchair, and Jacob rolled him down to the underground garage. After loading our car, it was so full of bags that it looked like we were returning from a long vacation. We had received binders with materials about leukemia. In the meantime, at our friends' place, Lucas had fallen asleep on their couch after a long day of play. I missed Lucas too. I missed him a lot.

CHAPTER SEVEN

At Home after Treatment

While Marcus was admitted to TCH, Jacob had brought Lucas into TCH so he could visit Marcus. The boys used to play every day, and they missed each other. Lucas, being the younger of the two, completely relied on Marcus as a playmate.

Lucas had never been away from Marcus for so many days before. At home, it had been quiet with just Lucas around. The air in the house was usually full of laughter, screaming, and fighting between the boys. The house was only still and calm when both boys were asleep.

Marcus's first night at home was good.

"I love being beep-free," Marcus exclaimed the morning after he woke up. We both laughed. I had enjoyed sleeping in my own bed too without disruptions.

"Did you sleep well?" I asked him when I came up to his bed.

Then his speech was rushed, and he pushed his blanket to the side and dropped his chin to the chest.

"Mommy, my sheets are wet. I had an accident," Marcus cried.

"Don't worry, honey. It's just because you had extra fluids at the hospital before you got home," I said, offering him a small smile. "I'll change the sheets quickly."

Marcus had always struggled to stay dry overnight. He used to be proud that he could stay dry throughout the night, and now he felt everything was ruined. It was something that made him upset, and I knew it. When the initial morning drama was over, he changed into dry clothes and came downstairs to eat breakfast with Lucas. I soon realized that Marcus was jealous because Lucas could go to summer camp and have fun while Marcus had to stay home. Jacob took Lucas to camp while I opened Marcus's medicine bag and tried to organize his medicines.

At 9 a.m., we had an appointment with the home health nurse. He was to come to our house to change Marcus's PICC line dressing and teach us how to flush the PICC line with saline. Before he came, the staff at TCH had arranged for a box of medical supplies to be delivered to our house. The big box contained dressing kits, caps for Marcus's PICC line, adhesive remover wipes, saline syringes, and disposable gloves. A nice, young African-American nurse rang the bell.

"Come on in." I opened the door and shook his hand.

His name was Arthur. He was athletic-looking and seemed nice. My husband had returned from dropping off Lucas at camp, and he was now ready to get instructions on how to flush Marcus's PICC line and change the ports.

"Come on into the kitchen to meet Marcus," I said, gesturing into the kitchen.

Arthur smiled. "Hello, Marcus, how are you?"

"I am okay, I guess." Marcus attempted a weak smile, then kept his eyes down. Hesitantly, he asked, "What are you going to do?"

"I'm going to change your PICC line dressing and give you a nice fresh one. The one I use is much more comfortable than the one you got at the hospital. You're going to like it." He glanced around the room. "Where's the big box?" Arthur asked, referring to the one we received earlier in the morning with the medical supplies.

"Oh! Let me grab it for you." I got the box for him, and he opened it. He pulled up a place mat and folded it out.

"Is the dinner table clean?" Arthur asked.

"Yes," I replied. "I just cleaned it."

Arthur put the mat out on the dinner table. On the mat were different sections. Each section on the mat had a number referring to each step you needed to complete in the flushing process before moving on to the next step. The mat contained drawings of two sterilizing pads called alcohol wipes, two saline syringes, and two caps.

Marcus stared with big eyes at all the medical stuff on the mat and the dressing kit. He was anxious before the dressing change even happened.

Arthur changed Marcus's dressing in five minutes. He was careful, taking all possible precautions to keep all the medical supplies clean. He even wore a mask. Marcus didn't like the disinfection of the skin and PICC line area. He said his skin was burning when Arthur cleaned it. Arthur tried his best to keep Marcus comfortable, but Marcus had a tendency to get dramatic very quickly. I don't blame him because he wasn't used to having a PICC line in his arm.

Marcus had to tolerate nurses and doctors touching him and messing with his body. His body was no longer private in the sense it used to be. He had entered a very different world. He wanted to be with his friends and play, just like Lucas. He wanted to be a child. The discomfort was evident, and Marcus did not hide it.

When Marcus was at home, Jacob would be the one in charge of flushing the PICC line, as he was the more technical person between the two of us. Arthur instructed Jacob in simple hygiene procedures such as washing his hands before handling the medical supplies and disinfecting his hands. Then my husband had to clean each port with the alcohol wipe and let it dry. During drying, the disinfection happens. This is why it is so important to let it dry first. You have to count fifteen seconds before moving on to the flushing part. Only that way do you ensure all the germs are eliminated.

Jacob quickly picked up the technique used to flush Marcus's PICC line. Finally, he learned how to change the ports on the PICC line. As I expected, he mastered all the techniques immediately.

After all procedures were completed, Arthur and I made an appointment for the next time Marcus's PICC line dressing was due to be changed. Every time it needed to be changed, the nurse would come to our home and do it.

As part of his daily hygiene routines, Marcus needed to have a bath. His PICC line dressing was a problem because it could not get wet. If the dressing got wet, it had to be replaced with a new one and Arthur had to be called out again. For that reason, it was important to keep the dressing dry and away from germs. At the hospital, I learned a simple trick to protect his PICC line dressing from getting wet when showering. I could cover his dressing with kitchen cling plastic wrap so Marcus could avoid getting it wet.

Chapter Seven

I filled the bathtub with warm water. Marcus went up and started washing himself. He had to use a special disinfectant soap. I asked him to rest his right arm with the plastic wrap on the side of the bathtub so it didn't drop into the water. Marcus was adorable. He was so excited about getting into the bathtub that he started splashing the water.

"Marcus, you have to stop splashing the water, or your dressing will get wet," I told him. "The wrap is not completely safe. You still have to be careful."

"Okay, Mom. I'll try to remember," he replied but continued to splash a bit. "I just love my bath so much. That's all."

For his oral care, Marcus had to use a special mouthwash because the risk of mouth sores increase when having chemotherapy. At TCH, the mouthwash was prepared by the in-house pharmacy and the nurses would bring a bottle to the room. At home, I could mix it myself instead of buying it at our local CVS Pharmacy. After brushing his teeth, he had to take ten milliliters of the oncology mouthwash in a medicine cup, swirl it for ten seconds in his mouth, and spit it out. He did not like the taste of that mouthwash. Of course not—it was salty and not enjoyable—but he did it anyway.

I realized quickly that Marcus's home care was rather complicated. I explained to him that this was temporary. This first month was intense, but after the first month, the doctors would remove his PICC line and he could go swimming with Lucas again. Instead of the PICC line, they would insert a port under his skin close to his heart. The port wouldn't be annoying and would allow him to do all the activities he used to do.

As I preferred to organize things visually to keep track of each steps in Marcus's care, I decided to make a medicine sheet for each day of his induction treatment. That way, I could make notes about Marcus and document what medicines Marcus had taken.

I opened a Word document and created a table. In the first column, I added the medicine. Then followed a column for the date after which I made separate columns for AM, NOON, PM, and BEDTIME. Some medicines he had to take on specific days; others every day and multiple times a day. I printed out enough copies for the whole month of induction. I found an empty binder and put all of Marcus's leukemia paperwork in the binder organized by dividers. This was helpful because moving forward, I only needed to bring the binder with us for his appointments in the hospital. I knew all his leukemia paperwork was organized and easy to pull out from the binder. (Examples of these sheets and the notebook organization can be found in the appendix.)

The first few days at home were times of adjustments. I did my best to talk to him and explained that we would get through this together. I had notified my bosses in the law firm where I worked that Marcus had fallen ill and that I could not come to work for the next month or so. They understood that I had to stay home to take care of Marcus.

Marcus started thinking about important questions such as "Why does God do this to me?" and "Will I die?" One day at lunch, Marcus became furious. He was fed up with the medicine, the PICC line, and the isolation from his friends. It took him some days before he realized how his life had changed. Marcus was analytic and questioned me about all sorts of things. Tension built up inside him. He was driven by the belief that he had been done wrong.

"I hate God!" he yelled. "No child should go through what I experience. This is not fair."

Eyes reddening, he made no attempt to wipe loose tears away.

"Marcus, you cannot say you hate God. God is not evil."

"If God were nice, I would not have to be sick. God gave me leukemia," Marcus said with a pained expression.

I got up and fetched him something to drink.

"Listen, Marcus," I said. "I understand this is how you feel, but trust me: God is going to make you healthy again. God is helping you and the doctors. Look, the doctors already gave you medicine to get rid of the leukemia. You are going to be fine," I explained as I tried to change the subject.

For now, Marcus was satisfied with my answer, but I had promised him a lot. I promised he would get well again and that the suffering would end. I hoped it was true.

I also questioned why God did this to Marcus and our family. Why us? In addition, why did God give Marcus leukemia? Marcus was so strong and healthy—why should he have leukemia and why would God make him suffer for no logical reason? Those were tough questions, and there were no answers. I realized that in the cancer world and the medical world in general, the doctors do not always have an answer for you. They cannot give you promises about outcome. The human body is governed by biology. Biology is unpredictable, not completely understood, and therein lie the limitations.

On Thursday, June 12, Marcus had his first outpatient appointment at TCH Clinical Care Center (CCC) on Fannin Street. Jacob, Marcus, and I went in. The CCC was a huge building in the Texas Medical Center. It was across the street from the inpatient building. The two buildings were conveniently connected by a skywalk. When we entered the CCC in the morning, a hectic atmosphere greeted us. Doctors, nurses, and other medical personnel rushed to get to work on time. Patients were coming in for appointments. In the elevator going up to the oncology floor, I witnessed more sick children than I had seen in my whole lifetime. Some children had disabilities and were bound to a wheelchair or a stretcher. Other children were cancer children. I could tell right away by looking at them. I felt sorry for the parents who were there with disabled children because these children were born that way with no possibility for curative treatment. At least Marcus was otherwise healthy and scientists had invented a cure for him.

Fifty years ago, there was no cure for childhood leukemia, so those children would die within a few months after diagnosis. They would die from infections or the leukemia itself. Science had made so many advances in leukemia research, and during the last ten to twenty years, the cure rate for childhood leukemia has increased dramatically.

For every visit in the CCC, we had to wait a long time. The waiting area had one section with video games and another section with a TV showing cartoons. The area was friendly and inviting with bright colors. If one did not know, it could serve as a childcare facility, as no medical equipment was present. Only the cancer children made you think otherwise, but many of them were happy and so were their parents. I guess the happy families were the ones with children responding well to the treatment and already in remission. Maybe they were close to completing their protocols. Maybe this was their last appointment for a long time. Siblings were everywhere, running and playing. Parents struggled to keep control of them as they ran away. Some toddlers were hungry so the parents pulled out snacks and drinks for them. Sometimes the little ones were the cancer patients and the older ones were the healthy, lucky ones with hair on their heads seeking entertainment from their iPad or cell phone.

It was June, and school was already out in Houston. This was why so many siblings were present. Cancer in their family forced them to be in the CCC. Honestly, no child should have to be there, nor any parents. Yet again, it was better to stay at home and come in for outpatient visits in the CCC than having to stay in the hospital. Marcus and I made a pact. We agreed we would do anything to avoid getting back to the hospital. In other words, our primary goal was for Marcus to remain "beep-free."

One of the methods I used deliberately was to appreciate whatever positive I could see in a situation. It served as my survival strategy. Knowing that the situation could be worse (but wasn't) came as a comfort to me. Marcus could have had an inoperable tumor in his brain with only two more weeks to live, but he didn't have that. He could have been born with disabilities, but he wasn't. Marcus could have remained undiagnosed and could have died from pneumonia, but he didn't. We could have lived in a country with limited medical treatment options, but we were in Houston, a city world-famous for its high level of medical care. This way of putting our situation into perspective was helpful to me. I was thankful for the care Marcus received and the professionalism we witnessed at the hospital. I was confident. Not one second did I doubt Marcus was not in the best hands at TCH.

After calling Marcus in, the nurse took his temperature with a thermometer in his ear and then measured his blood pressure. After that, she proceeded to draw his labs. After the labs, the nurse guided Marcus to a bin to collect a prize. This was the best part. He was very interested in the goodies, and every time he came in, he looked forward to collecting his prize. One time, he picked a small water bottle for Lucas. He always thought about him. After a while, the lab results were ready and we got a printout. The nurse told us Marcus didn't need any blood transfusion that day. Back then, I still struggled to understand the lab results.

Reviewing the labs, I didn't pay attention to the amount of leukemia blasts in the lab results. I later found out that the first place to see if the chemotherapy worked was in the blood. If the treatment worked, the first indication would be that the leukemia blasts disappeared in the peripheral blood. The nurse was not a doctor; therefore, I didn't question her about the labs. She said everything was fine and we could go home with Marcus.

One side effect from the prednisone was increased hunger. The doctors told us that some children would feel extremely hungry and require additional meals and snacks every day. Marcus belonged to the group of children that became extremely hungry compared to what he would usually eat when he was healthy.

Marcus had a passion for food. This passion developed further because of his extreme hunger brought on by the prednisone. When he woke up in the morning, the first thing he would ask me was what we were going to have for dinner. After he got home from the hospital, he was able to eat seven huge meals a day. I had never experienced anything like this before. Occasionally, I would go to our local Subway shop and buy sandwiches for lunch. I could not bring Marcus with me to a public place like Subway. The doctors had advised us against bringing Marcus to public places and thereby increasing his risk for infections. It was safer for him to be at home. I would be gone for about ten minutes or so, and he could call me on my cell phone if he had questions while I was gone.

"I can eat a foot-long Subway sandwich," he said. "I would like . . ." He thought for a moment and then rattled off every single item he wanted: "Italian bread, ham, shredded cheddar cheese, then toasted, then add lettuce, cucumbers, tomatoes, and ranch dressing. Done."

I doubted he could finish a foot-long Subway sandwich. I certainly couldn't.

I was wrong. Marcus could finish it in one go.

I had to go grocery shopping very often to get fresh produce and snacks for Marcus. During June 2014, the World Cup in soccer was in full swing in Brazil. He was cheering for Argentina and Brazil. He believed the final would be a match between Germany and Argentina with his favorite soccer player Messi scoring the winning goal. I promised Marcus he could watch all the soccer matches during the World Cup.

One time, Marcus was at home watching a World Cup game while I rushed to Kroger for groceries. Before leaving the house, I told Marcus he could call me if he missed me. Then I left. Two minutes later, I had barely entered Kroger and my cell phone rang. Marcus just wanted to tell me that one of the teams had scored a goal. I let out a huge breath.

"Oh, that's nice," I said, reaching for a shopping cart. "It's going to be an awesome match. Very exciting, Marcus."

"I have to go back to the game, Mommy." He told me goodbye and hung up.

I went down to the vegetable and fruit section of Kroger, which is right after entering the store. Then my cell phone rang again.

"Hi, Mommy, it's me again," Marcus said. "The team has scored again. Now it's two to zero!" Marcus shouted with excitement.

Once again, I was relieved he was okay. There was no emergency.

"Listen, I'll be back in five minutes, okay?" I said, urging him not to call me again unless it was an emergency. I asked him to stay focused on the game and give me a report once I returned home.

How intense life was for Marcus! One goal in one game was enough to excite him, and it was definitely enough for him to want to share his passion with me.

When Marcus woke up in the morning asking about dinner, I suggested he decide what we should cook. I encouraged him to be my helper in the kitchen. I was scared if he got a cut in his finger while using a knife because this could lead to complications. He had an increased risk for bleeding, and he could easily get an infection in the wound. As always, I had to make sure what he did in the kitchen was safe.

Marcus's favorite dishes were rice with mushroom sauce, spaghetti dishes, and fried rice with chicken and vegetables. Marcus got so involved in cooking that he started to make his own recipes. He decided he wanted to open a seafood restaurant when he grew up after retiring from his professional soccer career. He wanted to open several locations such as one in Galveston, Texas, by the Gulf of Mexico, where he would have plenty of access to fresh seafood. When we found out Marcus was sick, Jacob bought Marcus an iPad. That way, he could Skype with his friends. With his new iPad, Marcus started taking photos of the rice dishes he made and emailed them to my oldest brother Alexander, who used to own a restaurant in Saint Petersburg, Russia. Marcus asked Alexander if he wanted to work as a consultant in his seafood restaurants. Alexander found the idea fascinating and agreed to function as a consultant.

"Which position are you going to have in your restaurant, Marcus?" I asked him.

"I'll be the boss and will hire chefs and servers and many helpers," he said with determination. "I want you and Daddy to come eat in my restaurant."

"I would love that, especially if the food is free." I laughed.

"Of course, everything is free for you in the restaurant," Marcus promised.

For a moment, I envisaged Marcus as a grown-up man welcoming guests into his restaurant with his usual charm. Marcus never doubted himself or his own skills. I absolutely loved that, despite facing cancer, he still laid out plans for the future and he believed in them.

One of the first days home after being discharged from the hospital, I gave Marcus a piece of white paper and some country stickers. Each sticker had a name of a country on it and a symbol originating from that country. Marcus had studied a number of different countries in school. He was also familiar with some countries because of his interest in soccer. When he identified a soccer club he liked, such as Barcelona, Manchester United, or Bayern Munich, he would research and find out in which country the soccer club had its base.

The curiosity for foreign cultures and people of other civilizations was equally developed through his interactions with peers. He had friends in school from many different cultures. At home and in school, he was raised with an open mind and respect for other cultures. Marcus easily completed the assignment I gave him. The title on the paper was "My Favorite Places." He listed the following countries: France, Brazil, Greece, Germany, China, Japan, Spain, and Italy. One day, he hoped to visit these places. I loved how he was able to list so many countries with such ease. He knew where he wanted to go in life.

He had many dreams. One day in the bathroom, after he had brushed his teeth, I told him he was such a handsome boy. He charmed all the girls in school and all the women he met on his way with his big smile and creative attitude.

"Marcus, do you know that when you grow up, you're going to make the girls crazy," I told him.

"Yes, I know, Mommy, and I cannot wait," he said with a big smile on his face. I could feel his charisma fill up the whole room, and we both laughed while he started dancing.

"You are too funny," I said and redirected him back to his evening routine before going to bed.

CHAPTER EIGHT

One Step Forward, Two Steps Back

Friday, June 13, Marcus was due at TCH CCC for his next bone marrow biopsy in his hip joint. Once again, he was going to have full anesthesia. This meant he could not eat or drink anything before the bone marrow procedure except for water. First, a nurse called him in for vitals (temperature and blood pressure measurement), then she drew his labs. After the lab results were ready, Marcus had to meet with Dr. Stephen Simko. He examined Marcus's tummy and checked his lymph nodes. Dr. Simko was in a good mood.

"Are Marcus's lymph nodes on his neck still swollen?" I asked Dr. Simko as I repeatedly ran my hands through my hair.

Dr. Simko rechecked Marcus's neck and his other lymph nodes. "What lymph nodes?" he said and looked at me with an upturned face.

"So does this mean they are back to their normal size?" I held still in expectation.

"Yes, he feels completely normal and his spleen is normal too. I'm very happy with the way he looks today," Dr. Simko replied, keeping strong eye contact with me. "The chemotherapy is doing its job, and this is what we expected to see."

He leaned back in his chair.

"I am so glad." I felt a warmth spread through my body.

"Marcus is ready for his bone marrow procedure and his next course of IV treatment after the procedure. I will call you on Tuesday, June seventeenth

Chapter Eight

with the results from the bone marrow biopsy," he said as he sent me off with a curt nod.

I liked when Marcus's doctors were in a good mood. Immediately, I sensed if any doctor became serious, stopped talking, hesitated, or showed any signs of concern during the examination of Marcus or while reviewing lab results on the computer. The doctors' body language revealed everything.

We had been struggling for half a year to find out why the swollen lymph nodes persisted, and now Dr. Simko told me they were gone. I was over the moon with happiness and relief.

After waiting for hours, a nurse called Marcus in for the pre-assessment with the anesthesia doctor. After that, more waiting time. After that, yet more waiting time. I couldn't give Marcus any food because he had to be fasting for the procedure.

After hours of waiting, it was Marcus's turn. I walked into the little procedure room with him and was able to stay there until the anesthesia kicked in, then I had to leave the procedure room. Even though he wasn't getting open-heart surgery, I was worried about him. I believed he had been through enough already, and then I realized this was only the beginning of a long, long journey with endless treatments and follow-up appointments. I had to rewire my brain to think differently. I convinced myself I could do this because I had to. Since I had no other choice than to sit and wait for the procedure to be completed, I had to put aside my negative feelings about being stuck here inside the hospital against my will. I had to remind myself that all these treatments were temporary, that the doctors would cure Marcus. In fact, Dr. Simko had just told me Marcus's condition had improved. Remember, no more swollen lymph nodes. I should be more than thrilled. I took a moment for myself and started fantasizing. *Maybe a year from now, we'll be in Denmark eating our favorite Danish homemade food with Marcus and Lucas's grandparents.* I started imagining us enjoying life; Marcus would be playing soccer with Lucas and his cousins on a sunny day, or Marcus would be going fishing with my brother Alexander in a little boat and they would bring home fresh fish for dinner. Then somebody called me.

"Mrs. Nielsen, Marcus is ready for you," the nurse called.

"That was quick. How is he doing?" I asked impatiently.

"Marcus tolerated the procedure well. He's in here." The nurse guided me to Marcus's recovery station. I rushed over to Marcus's bed to give him a big hug. It was the best hug ever.

Marcus was in the common post-procedure area. Little children were crying; others were still sleeping in their beds. Marcus was already awake and hungry, ready to move on.

"Can I get something to eat now?" he asked the nurse.

"In just a few minutes. I want you to drink something first and tell me how you feel." She offered him some juice.

Marcus took a sip of his juice. "I feel okay now. I'm hungry. Can I please eat my snacks?" he asked again.

I looked in my bag for Marcus's snacks. He loved small tomatoes, cucumber sticks, carrot sticks, and bell pepper sticks. I gave him the whole bag, and he ate all his vegetable snacks without interruption. It was afternoon, and it was the first food he had eaten that day. No wonder he was hungry.

Looking at Marcus's vegetable snacks, the nurse said, "I have never seen a child eat this after a procedure. You must eat very healthy food. That's impressive, Marcus!"

"I like to eat healthy," Marcus said with confidence. "I like many fresh vegetables, but my brother Lucas doesn't like fresh tomatoes." He brought his attention back to me. "Mommy, can I have my fruit snacks now?"

"Sure, Marcus, here you go." I gave him a Ziploc bag filled with fresh strawberries and grapes.

Marcus was the biggest vegetable eater in our house. He loved fruits too. Because of his compromised immune system during treatment, I had to be extra careful giving him fresh fruits and vegetables.

On fresh fruits and vegetables, spores can easily grow and those can cause food poisoning. The same applied to breads in humid climates like Houston. One of the first comments the oncologists had at TCH when we met with them was that it's okay to be afraid of germs when you have a child battling cancer. It's even normal to become paranoid and see germs all over. For this reason, I had placed sanitizers all over our house. We all used it even after washing our hands.

When the nurse in the waiting area deemed Marcus was ready to leave, she found a wheelchair for him so I could roll him back to the oncology floor at CCC. He was due for his IV chemotherapy treatment. This meant more waiting, more time in the CCC, more chemotherapy. Marcus was already exhausted from the prior treatment. I, too, was exhausted and wanted to go home. Was this not enough for one day? The answer to this question was no. It was important to keep throwing chemotherapy at the leukemia throughout this first month, the goal being to bring Marcus into remission as soon as possible.

Finally, the nurse brought Marcus's chemotherapy and enthusiastically said that she was going to start his treatment soon. During that day in CCC, I called my husband and updated him about the course of the day. He had already picked up Lucas from his summer camp, and they waited patiently for us to come home. We left CCC around 5 p.m.

Once home, I started cooking dinner. Everyone in the family was hungry so I had to put something together quickly. I realized that outpatient visits took a toll on Marcus and me.

The weekend went by, and Marcus was tired but otherwise doing fairly well. Jacob was in charge of flushing Marcus's PICC line, and I managed all of Marcus's medicines. We had already adjusted to the new routines.

The isolation from Marcus's friends was difficult to handle. Marcus missed being in school. He missed having fun. I couldn't take him to any public place unless it was an open space offering limited risks of infections. The doctor had told Marcus that he could run or walk as long as he had energy to do so.

One morning, Marcus said he wanted to go for a little run. It was before noon so it wouldn't be super hot in Houston yet. First, Marcus went out on the street to warm up. We met one of our friends named Chris living down the street. In the summer, Chris's son Luke used to play in the community pool with Lucas and Marcus. Chris was active, mowing the lawns for some of the neighbors. When he saw Marcus, he stopped for a moment, then moved closer to him.

"Hey, Marcus. How are you?" Chris asked with a genuine smile.

"I have leukemia," Marcus answered, showing no emotional discomfort.

Chris became speechless and shook his head in denial.

I took a moment to explain to Chris what was going on with Marcus.

"I am so sorry to hear that," Chris said, trying to console us.

"It's fine. I'm going to be okay, Chris," Marcus assured him, arms swinging as he started walking.

Marcus was getting ready to go for a short run. A few months before, Jacob had bought a pair of blue Nike running shoes for Marcus. Marcus decided to wear those for his morning run.

I had prepared some bottles with ice water for Marcus to bring on the run. I figured Marcus would get tired during the run and I didn't want him to feel like a failure if he had to walk home. I wanted to be sure that he could quickly come home if he felt exhausted.

"Marcus, I'm going to take my car and drive next to you while you run on the sidewalk," I explained to him.

"No, Mommy, you don't need to do that," he replied.

"Yes, I think it's a great idea. I can bring your water bottles and I can bring some snacks too if you get hungry."

Sure enough, Marcus was only able to run for about ten minutes. Then he had no more energy left. It became evident he was not our strong, healthy Marcus anymore. The disease and the treatment had started to affect his body in negative ways. I asked Marcus to stop a few times to get a sip of water. I didn't want to see him push himself too hard.

"Marcus, I'll stop here. I think you should jump into my car so we can drive home. It's hot. You already had a great run," I said, trying to encourage him.

Marcus gave up. "Mommy, I'm too exhausted. I can't run anymore."

I stopped so he could get into my car. We drove home. Marcus was sweaty and tired. I told him how proud I was of him for wanting to run even though he was sick.

On Tuesday, June 17, 2014, after his outpatient visit, I called Dr. Simko to get the results from the bone marrow biopsy. He was pleased to tell me that Marcus's leukemia blasts had dropped from 60 percent before he started treatment to 23 percent. Dr. Simko elaborated.

"This is a good result, but it means that Marcus is not an early responder," Dr. Simko explained.

"What do you mean by early 'responder'?" I asked.

"It means that the child goes into remission quickly after treatment

Chapter Eight

has started. This is what we want. We want an early response," Dr. Simko explained.

"But Marcus is not in remission yet. It's my understanding that you want Marcus to reach zero percent leukemia blasts. Right?" I asked him for clarification.

"Yes, that's true. Some children don't respond immediately. He still has more weeks to go. We'll see how his numbers look the next time we do a bone marrow biopsy. We want the blast percentage to keep going down. Just follow the treatment plan as you have done already."

I thanked Dr. Simko and called my husband right after. I told him the good news that Marcus's leukemia blasts had decreased, but that Marcus was not an early responder. I also wrote an email to the grandparents and shared the good news. Even though this result was not optimal, the treatment had some effect and the leukemia burden was decreasing.

With cancer, it's not wise to celebrate prematurely. A person's life depends on a number. I only wished that Marcus's number would go down and that the following week he would be in remission.

"Mommy, I have decided I want to eat healthier and eat less sugar," Marcus declared one day. "That way, I can help my body beat the leukemia."

"What a great idea!" I replied.

"I should eat more vegetables and more fruits. They have vitamins that can make me strong."

Marcus had suddenly matured and become responsible.

On Friday, June 20, Marcus was due for his next outpatient visit. My husband came with us. It was yet another long day. Marcus didn't need any blood transfusion and was ready for his chemotherapy infusion right after his bone marrow biopsy. The message from the doctor's team was for me to call the Tuesday after to get the bone marrow results.

During the weekend, Marcus was increasingly tired. He didn't want to play with Lucas the way he used to because he lacked energy. One time, he decided to go into our backyard to play soccer with Lucas. Marcus was a much faster and more skilled soccer player than Lucas, as Lucas was five years old and had not played soccer as long as Marcus had. Marcus was eight years old and stronger too. I watched the two of them playing on the dry grass. It was evident that Marcus struggled to keep up the pace and run around. I saw

Lucas attacking with the ball; he ran toward Marcus, made a quick move to the side, and passed Marcus with ease. I did not believe what I saw. Lucas outplayed Marcus on the soccer field!

"I can't play anymore, Lucas," Marcus shouted. "I'm sorry."

Marcus pressed one hand to his abdomen, withdrawing from the field as he realized he had to give up.

For Lucas, this was a triumph, a victory. To me, it proved how weak Marcus had become. It was so unlike Marcus to let Lucas dribble past him in soccer.

On Tuesday, June 24, 2014, I called Dr. Simko to get the results from the bone marrow biopsy. The first time I called, he said the results were still pending. He couldn't explain why they weren't ready yet, but I was worried the results weren't the expected good ones but something else. The phone rang, and I answered it.

"This is Dr. Simko again. I have received the results from Marcus's last bone marrow biopsy. It's not good, I'm afraid. His blast percentage has increased from twenty-three percent to fifty percent."

I was shocked to hear this news. The treatment didn't work as it should. Marcus should have been in remission by now. Instead, the leukemia had come back stronger.

"Do you remember to give Marcus his prednisone every day?" Dr. Simko asked me.

"Yes, I do. He gets it every day. He has never skipped a dose," I answered. "Do you want to change anything in Marcus's treatment plan since Marcus's blasts percentage has gone up?"

"No, you continue with the protocol, and then he will come in on Friday where we can talk," Dr. Simko replied.

I immediately called Jacob to tell him Marcus's results. He was devastated and saddened to learn that Marcus had not responded to the treatment as planned.

I felt empty inside. The previous week, it was my understanding that Marcus was doing okay. Suddenly one result changed the picture. My gut told me something in his treatment plan needed to be changed. I tried to stay optimistic. My husband and I involved Marcus in the results, as he was mature enough to understand what was going on. I assured him the doctors knew so many ways to help him. If one way didn't work, they would try another way. He shouldn't worry.

The day after the news, I decided to take Marcus to Memorial Hermann Park in downtown Houston for a lunch picnic when Lucas was in summer camp and Jacob at work. I wanted Marcus to have fun and allow him to get out of the house. I picked up Subway sandwiches on the way. Marcus had his favorite foot-long sandwich with ham, cheddar cheese, toasted, then lettuce, tomatoes, cucumbers, and ranch dressing. I had a smaller sandwich and I bought some chips for Marcus. On that sunny day, we set sail toward downtown Houston. Five minutes after we left Subway, Marcus got hungry. "I'm going to eat my sandwich now. It's too hard to wait," Marcus informed me.

"Well, why don't you eat a bit of it now and save the rest for when we reach the park?" I asked. "Otherwise, you won't have any lunch later and I'm sure the chips will not be enough."

Marcus agreed. He unfolded his sandwich and, with enormous pleasure, took some big bites of his foot-long sandwich. As expected, while he ate his sandwich, food fell everywhere on the back seat.

"Are you making a mess in the back seat, Marcus?" I asked, trying to catch a glimpse from the rearview mirror.

"Yes, I did. I promise to clean it up later," Marcus assured me.

Once we arrived at Memorial Hermann Park, Marcus and I walked around and looked at the people.

"Look, there's a rabbit!" Marcus said, pointing at the little animal.

At first, I couldn't see it. Marcus had spotted a little brown rabbit in a bush. It stopped, and Marcus asked me to take a photo of the rabbit so we could show it to Lucas later that day.

I realized that Marcus still needed a lot of food because the prednisone made him super hungry. I started to make my homemade Subway sandwiches for him, as this was cheaper and more fun than buying them at our local Subway.

I baked the mini Italian breads myself. In Denmark, we have a long tradition for baking breads, cakes, and cookies. Most people, especially from my parents' generation, know how to bake breads. Many of my Danish friends are proficient home bakers.

When Marcus's nurse, Arthur, came by to change his dressing one day upon entering our house, the smell of freshly baked bread greeted him. He walked into the kitchen and saw the pan covered with warm Italian breads.

"These look delicious," Arthur said, admiring all the breads. "I wasn't hungry before I came here, but now I'm hungry thanks to these freshly baked breads you made Marcus."

Marcus licked his lips and smiled.

"I have a surprise for you. I'm going to give you some of my breads to try," Marcus told him and hurried over to the counter where the breads were cooling off.

I found a brown paper lunch bag, and Marcus helped pick some breads for Arthur.

"Thanks a lot. I'm going fishing later today," Arthur said, involving us in his plans. During his previous visits, Arthur had shared his passion for fishing with Marcus.

"What fish are you going to catch?" Marcus asked with great interest.

"I'm going to catch catfish," Arthur explained with delight. "I fry them in the pan. I think I'll make a fish sandwich with your breads."

"It sounds really yummy. I love catfish. I wish I could go fishing with you," Marcus said with a bowed head. He became very still, building up a tense facial tension.

"Marcus, you have to wait a bit. I think Alexander wants to go fishing with you next time we go to Denmark. Remember, he loves fishing and he has promised to teach you how to fish," I said, trying to make Marcus feel better. I caressed his soft hair and let Arthur complete the dressing change.

CHAPTER NINE

Declining Health

On Friday, June 27, 2014, Marcus had his next outpatient appointment with Dr. Simko. Marcus did his lab work and later went to get his chemotherapy infusion. He wasn't getting a bone marrow biopsy that day, as this was not part of the protocol. I had a meeting with Dr. Simko in which we discussed Marcus's situation. He admitted that Marcus's test results were concerning. He had reviewed all his labs, and they showed that leukemia blasts were still circulating in his peripheral blood. I told him it was my understanding that no leukemia blasts had been seen in the labs for weeks. I was very upset to find out that the leukemia blasts had been circulating in Marcus's blood all along while I thought Marcus's blood was clear from cancer.

While Marcus received his chemotherapy, I continued to discuss Marcus's situation with Dr. Simko. I even asked him to call my husband to explain the severity of the results. I insisted that the doctors take Marcus off the protocol and offer him a different treatment. It became clearer and clearer to my husband and me that Marcus's protocol was ineffective.

"Dr. Simko, why do you want to keep Marcus on the protocol when we can all see that the treatment is not doing its job?" My head pounded.

"Marcus needs to finish his treatment because otherwise we don't know what to do next." Dr. Simko refused to go any deeper.

I didn't understand that answer. It didn't make sense to me. Why weaken Marcus by continuing to give him chemotherapy to no effect? Why would the doctors not switch him over to a different protocol? I couldn't see the point in allowing the leukemia to grow stronger. After all, the goal was to bring Marcus into remission as quickly as possible. The doctors didn't listen

Chapter Nine

to our concerns and they didn't give us the option to remove Marcus from the protocol and tailor a new treatment program specifically for his needs.

This only further intensified my concerns. My shoulders tightened. I had a desire to change Dr. Simko's standpoint, but I had no authority to do so. My mind raced through possible arguments; however, I didn't believe I was able to persuade him to consult other doctors for advice. *Why didn't Dr. Simko comprehend that keeping Marcus on the protocol wouldn't make him go into remission?* The stakes were getting higher.

"I'm not comfortable keeping Marcus at home for a whole week without a doctor seeing him and checking his labs," I told Dr. Simko. "I want to bring Marcus in early next week for an appointment. Is this possible?" I had trust issues. I hope he knew what he was doing.

"Yes, I can arrange for that. I will not be in clinic that day, but I will make sure another doctor sees Marcus," Dr. Simko replied.

I walked away. *He's making a mistake*, I thought.

That Friday at TCH CCC was awful. This was the first time I had even the slightest suspicion that the doctors at TCH could not handle Marcus's case. Coming from Denmark, Jacob and I had no experience with the US medical system, and we didn't speak up or seek a second opinion. We trusted the doctors.

When we got home after dinner, we all watched some TV. I was sitting next to Lucas in our big black couch, and Marcus was lying down on the other couch resting his head on my husband's lap. My husband carefully stroked Marcus's hair. He did it repeatedly that night. He gave Marcus all the love he had in him.

Back in Denmark, I had been in contact with my father's sister Sorella. Sorella was her nickname, and it means "sister" in Italian. She had been very shocked when she learned that Marcus was diagnosed with leukemia. Once, Marcus had made a drawing specifically for Sorella when she was sick. Marcus had used strong and vibrant colors. It sent a powerful message of love to Sorella. When I gave the drawing to her, she instantly asked me to hang it up on the wall.

"Look at Marcus's drawing!" Sorella said, forgetting for a moment how miserable she felt. "It could have been Tello who had made the drawing."

Tello was the nickname she used for my father. Tello was short for fratello, which means "brother" in Italian.

"I cannot believe Marcus picked my favorite colors—red and yellow—for the drawing. The drawing style is exactly like Tello's style," Sorella said, still beaming.

I agreed with her. Marcus was a mini artist, almost a copy of my father. He had seen my father's paintings hanging in our house. He had never met my father, just heard about him.

One day back in Denmark, when Marcus was three years old, I took him with me to visit my father's grave in Asminderød Kirkegård (Graveyard). In the car over, I had told Marcus that we were going to visit Grandpa. It was a cold and windy day, and we both wore heavy jackets. When we reached the grave, Marcus started looking around the grave and behind my father's gravestone.

"Mommy, where is he then?" Marcus asked me.

"What do you mean?" I asked, scrunching my eyebrows.

"Where is Grandpa? You told me we were going to visit him, and I can't find him. He's not behind the gravestone." His shoulders slumped. "I already looked there."

I smiled and explained to him that Grandpa was in his coffin in the grave below. Marcus asked me if Grandpa was sleeping and if he had a pillow and a duvet cover over him so he wouldn't get cold. His questions were so caring, so innocent, and so sweet. We put flowers on Grandpa's grave and left.

In June, when Sorella heard Marcus had to stay at home for many months because of his chemotherapy treatment, she had asked me to go out and buy painting supplies for him. She wanted to enrich his time with an activity he liked. That weekend, I decided it was time to get Marcus's art supplies. His health was getting poorer and his energy level decreasing. His body talked to me, and it spoke clearly.

I drove to one of my favorite art supply stores, Michaels. I spent an hour there getting a complete set of art supplies for him. I bought canvases, oil paints, artist palettes, brushes, and brush cleaners. When I got home, Marcus was thrilled to see all these professional painting items. We made the dinner table into a crafts table. We covered it with used newspapers and spread out the art supplies. Lucas was not interested in painting that day. Marcus picked

Chapter Nine

a medium-size canvas. Then he picked three colors: dark blue, dark green, and light green. He started painting on the top and painted it dark blue. It looked like a sky. Then he picked the dark green and painted the bottom of the canvas. After that, he painted light green, followed by dark green, and then light green. He took the brush and started painting dark green but suddenly stopped.

"Why did you stop painting?" I asked Marcus.

"I'm done for today," Marcus replied, no longer interested in his artwork.

"Okay, you can always finish your painting later," I told him, offering an encouraging smile. "Let's clean up the table then."

This behavior was so unlike Marcus. Before, he would never have stopped while he was in the middle of doing an art project. The painting looked like it was the sky in the top with grass on the bottom. Half of the painting was blank. It remained this way, unfinished.

Over the weekend, he also started to develop an eye infection in his left eye. His eye became red and irritated. He had no immune defense due to the chemotherapy, and the leukemia took a toll on him.

On Monday, June 30, Marcus had a morning appointment at TCH CCC. The nurse drew his labs, and we met with an elderly oncologist. The doctor looked at Marcus's inflamed red eye and prescribed some eye drops. The doctor didn't want to discuss Marcus's protocol or other available treatment options. He requested that we continue with Marcus's treatment plan until Thursday, July 3, at which time he was due for his last bone marrow biopsy.

The problem was that when I reviewed his labs that Monday, I could tell Marcus wasn't in remission. He still had blasts in his peripheral blood. This was a clear indication that the leukemia blasts were still present in his bone marrow because they start growing in the bone marrow. It seemed more and more unlikely he would be in remission by the end of the induction program.

I continued to apply the eye drops to Marcus's left eye, but it didn't clear up. On Thursday, July 3, when Marcus woke up in the morning, he was not feeling well. Slowly, he walked down the stairs to the living room complaining about stomach pain. He looked at the beanbag on the floor, threw himself in it, and lay still. I felt of his head, and it was a bit warm.

Jacob and I drove in to TCH CCC together with Marcus. I wanted to overprotect him. Marcus was tired. After his labs were drawn, we waited in the waiting area for his next appointment. Marcus lay down on the benches to sleep. I covered him with a blanket, as he was cold. Marcus was called in to meet with a nurse practitioner. Marcus's vitals were okay. He wasn't feverish and his blood pressure was fine. The nurse practitioner said Marcus was in a condition where he could have the bone marrow biopsy. Even while waiting for his bone marrow biopsy, Marcus was uncomfortable and tired. The procedure went well, but when Marcus was done and the nurse rechecked his temperature, he had a fever. The nurse called us into the recovery area. Marcus was waking up from the anesthesia. The nurse told us they had called Dr. Karen Rabin to come and see Marcus. She was the director of the Leukemia and Lymphoma Program at TCH. Marcus's situation was escalating. The doctor had to admit him to TCH and cancel the chemotherapy infusion scheduled for that day. Marcus started complaining about stomach pain.

Dr. Rabin and an oncology fellow came to see Marcus while he was still in bed in the recovery area. She ordered blood labs from Marcus to check for infections. At the same time, she ordered IV antibiotics to be started and admitted Marcus to TCH.

My husband and I discussed Marcus's leukemia status with Dr. Rabin. She had studied Marcus's case. She was aware that Marcus had not responded to the induction protocol. She was concerned but asked us to be patient and wait for the results from the bone marrow biopsy. She was very nice to Marcus and us. She talked to Marcus and tried to calm him down and find out what caused his stomach pain. The nurses struggled to draw the labs because Marcus was a hard stick. They had to poke him several times, and Marcus cried and cried; his muscles clenched.

I understood without having to think. Dr. Rabin didn't believe Marcus would be in remission, but she needed the evidence before she could draw that conclusion. This was the last time I would accept Marcus to be on a standard induction protocol that led nowhere but to more suffering. The induction therapy he had received had led nowhere, absolutely nowhere. Clearly, the doctors needed to use a different approach to Marcus's case that now presented itself with multiple medical challenges. We needed to achieve remission soon, but how would the doctors be able to do it? I looked at

Chapter Nine

Marcus lying in his hospital bed, covered with blankets, weak and exhausted. He had suffered so much hardship already, yet he was not at all near the finish line. Cancer was an evil, invisible predator with cells that invaded the body, and we had only just begun unpacking the layers of it.

CHAPTER TEN

Back to the Hospital

Later in the afternoon, the nurse told us she had located a room for Marcus on the neurology floor, the tenth floor at TCH, as the oncology floor had no available rooms. He was starting to feel a bit better, and my husband left to pick up Lucas from Ross's house.

Marcus was no longer beep-free. He was on fluids and antibiotics. We were back at TCH even though we had desired for Marcus never to go back again to the inpatient floor. If the doctors had to admit him again, we had certainly not envisioned that he would return to TCH in such a miserable condition.

When he was first diagnosed, I felt hopeful that he would be cured. Marcus's prognosis was good. The road ahead was straightforward. What I did not take into account was the situation that Marcus might not respond to induction. Still, I was positive the doctors had some alternative backup treatment plan for Marcus. We all had to stay optimistic and we assured Marcus he would be fine.

The day after he was admitted to the hospital was the Fourth of July, and Marcus had been looking forward to a day full of celebration. We had planned to have hot dogs and celebrate and enjoy the day together without friends because of Marcus's suppressed immune system. I told him we would celebrate with hot dogs at TCH instead of at home. We could watch the World Cup on the TV and watch the fireworks outside from his room.

"Marcus, I think it's better to be at TCH because you don't feel well. When you have a fever, TCH is the right place for you to be," I said, rubbing his back and trying to soothe him.

Chapter Ten

"I know, Mommy. It will get better soon and then we can go home." Marcus sighed but offered a weak smile.

He accepted our situation, and we started talking about the next couple of days. Maybe Lucas could come visit and they could go to the playroom together, I mused. Marcus found that very exciting.

When Marcus had rested, he wanted to take a walk on the neurology floor. He walked slowly. That floor didn't have nearly as nice decorations as the oncology floor. There was no Ronald McDonald House. It looked uninspiring. We only saw a few children on our tour, and they didn't even look sick compared to the children on the ninth floor.

While walking, Marcus started complaining about stomach pain again. He could not tolerate walking anymore. I was unable to locate a nurse who could get a wheelchair for Marcus so I grabbed an office chair from the closest nursing station and asked Marcus to sit on it. That way I could roll him to his room and help him back into bed. His condition was getting worse.

When he was back in his bed, Marcus could rest and watch some TV. I told the nurse that Marcus had too much pain to walk and that he should remain in bed for today.

That evening, Marcus still had a bit of energy left to charm his night nurse who was from Argentina and loved soccer. He discussed the World Cup with her and made the point that Argentina would be in the final against Germany.

On the tenth floor of the main campus, neither Marcus nor I slept well. Jacob and I were prepared to receive bad news, and we had talked it over with Marcus to prepare him as well. We needed to show him that he was going to be fine. We had followed all the directions given by the doctors, and Marcus got all chemotherapy according to his protocol. We kept him safe at home and took all the precautions so he didn't get any infections. Yet the measures were not enough.

On the Fourth of July, Marcus still had severe pain in his stomach and his right eye continued to be red and inflamed. It looked worse. Dr. Rabin entered Marcus's room.

"Good morning, Marcus. How are you feeling today?" Dr. Rabin asked, chewing on her lips.

"I'm not feeling well," he replied, rubbing his belly. "My tummy hurts."

Dr. Rabin sat down on the couch beside me. We sat in silence together. I could hear my own heartbeat. It wasn't her fault she came with bad news, but I didn't want to hear it. My mouth went dry.

"I am sorry, Mrs. Nielsen. Marcus still has about thirty percent leukemia left." She glanced down for a moment, maybe too worried to meet my eyes.

I winced at the news, then felt the sadness wash over me, as if I were a rock falling off a cliff.

"Well, it's still a twenty percent decrease since his last bone marrow biopsy. Remember, it was fifty percent last time and now it's down to thirty percent. This is good, right?"

We must have made some kind of progress in one month, I thought.

She sighed, shaking her head. "No, it's not good enough, I'm afraid. The number should have been zero percent or at least below five percent. He is not in remission, Mrs. Nielsen."

I cupped my face in my hands. Tears threatened to spill. "What do we do now?"

"We need to meet today with your husband and talk about the next step of his treatment. Marcus will need a bone marrow transplant," Dr. Rabin explained, exuding calm and focus. "When will Mr. Nielsen be here today?"

"I'll call him right now. He can be here in about an hour or so. He will need to take Lucas to a friend's house first," I said.

"Okay, let's meet at two o'clock and discuss Marcus's next treatment plan," Dr. Rabin concluded.

"We will." I started to organize my papers that were spread all over the couch.

She left the room, and I immediately called Jacob, ignoring a strong headache that had started to build up.

The nurse entered the room.

"I just talked to a nurse from the oncology floor. She has room nine-two-two available for Marcus," she informed us, and then suggested we start packing up our stuff.

At least that was a nice update for a change. I preferred to stay at the oncology floor with Marcus because the nurses there were specifically skilled to care for the cancer children.

Marcus had fatigue and could not walk, so the nurse rolled him down in his bed. At 2 p.m., Dr. Rabin showed up with her oncology fellow, a young doctor who carried a bunch of paperwork.

"Let's go next door and talk," Dr. Rabin said, gesturing down the hall while carrying stacks of papers. "Marcus doesn't need to be involved in the meeting."

"Yes, if the meeting is boring, I want to stay in my room and watch TV," Marcus said.

We went into an empty room next door. A mixture of medicine and sanitizers drifted through the air. The hospital bed was neatly made with freshly pressed bedsheets ready for its next patient.

It was the Fourth of July, and many children had been discharged so they could celebrate Independence Day at home. Marcus could not.

Dr. Rabin was leading the meeting. She presented a new protocol for us. As Marcus had failed induction, his prognosis was now poor. His leukemia was aggressive, and he would need a bone marrow transplant to survive. The goal remained the same. However, in an effort to bring Marcus into remission, he would need intensified chemotherapy. Higher intensity meant higher risks of side effects.

The first drug she recommended was a chemotherapy agent called Nelarabine. Dr. Rabin was optimistic about giving Marcus this drug because it had previously shown to be very effective against T-cell ALL. She was hopeful it would work on Marcus, but she couldn't give us any guarantees. Dr. Rabin explained that Marcus had no fever and could start the treatment the day after if he continued to be fever-free.

"Marcus complained earlier that his stomach was hurting," my husband added. "Is it safe to start chemotherapy treatment in this condition?" Jacob cleared his throat.

The circles beneath his eyes had darkened with each night he stayed up late to work and worrying about what Marcus's future might hold.

"We don't know what's wrong with his stomach. And what about his red eye? That problem hasn't been resolved, either," Jacob asked, cocking his head.

Dr. Rabin assured us that if Marcus's condition did not get any worse until the day after, he could start Nelarabine treatment. That way, Marcus would get a day to recover and rest. At the same time, the doctors would try to find out what was going on in Marcus's stomach.

"I also want to talk to you about the bone marrow transplant," Dr. Rabin said. "We need to start looking for a suitable donor for Marcus right now. It can take months to find a match for him." Dr. Rabin leaned back in her chair and crossed her legs. "Does Marcus have any siblings?"

"Yes, he has a younger brother, Lucas," I answered.

"The best donors for the bone marrow transplant are usually siblings. I'm going to ask you and Lucas to get a test done in the Transplant Unit to see if any of you could be a match for Marcus. If none of you is a match, we will have to look in the donor register."

Immediately, my husband and I agreed to the blood testing. Of course, we knew Lucas should also do the blood test. My husband signed all the consent forms, including the treatment protocol for the next months of treatment.

I folded my hands and couldn't wait to leave this room.

"When can Marcus come home?" I inquired. For a moment, I imagined leaving the hospital with Marcus in remission as he danced his way to our car parked in the hospital garage. The world looked suddenly brighter and more beautiful.

"Marcus has to stay at the hospital while he gets Nelarabine, which is a five-day course treatment. If he does well and recovers from his stomach pain, the earliest we can discharge him will be"—she glanced at the calendar—"if he starts tomorrow, Saturday, he can get home maybe on Wednesday. Of course, providing he recovers from everything and he does well with his treatment."

"Yes, I understand," I nodded. I was washed with a wave of peace and contentment.

We went back to Marcus's room and talked for a bit. We explained to Marcus that Dr. Rabin had a new plan for him and that he would start his new treatment the day after.

"Today is your resting day, Marcus. Let's celebrate the Fourth of July with hot dogs," I suggested, hoping to cheer him up.

We all agreed it was a good idea. My husband took off to find a place to buy hot dogs at TCH. Marcus was getting hungry again, which was a good

Chapter Ten

sign, so we agreed that we should all have hot dogs and celebrate as we had previously planned. Lucas was at a friend's house so we didn't have to worry about him at that moment. He was safe and happy there.

When Jacob returned with the food, Marcus ate two big hot dogs with gusto. He loved them. I had kept my promise to him that no matter how his bone marrow results looked, we would celebrate Independence Day. It didn't matter if he was in remission or not, or if we were stuck at TCH or not.

I reflected over the month I had spent at home with Marcus. Even though the past month came with emotional and physical challenges, it had been a special month for me. I had the opportunity to be alone with Marcus and experience new sides of him. He had indeed a lot of appetite for life. He made ambitious plans for his future. He trusted my husband, the doctors, and me completely. He was positive he was going to be cured from leukemia. He was a fighter and he wanted to beat the leukemia.

The future looked bright. However, we were not able to see that it was, in fact, going to get much, much darker.

Later that evening, Marcus had severe stomach pain again. It was getting worse. He could not settle down, and I had to ask the nurse to call a doctor. When the doctor came, he talked to Marcus and we discussed what Marcus had eaten for dinner. When the doctor heard Marcus had eaten two hot dogs for dinner, he concluded that Marcus probably overate and that the hot dogs were the cause of the stomach pain. I suddenly stiffened. I didn't agree that hot dogs alone could cause that type of severe pain. I wish the doctor would listen. I told him that Marcus had complained about severe stomach pain for several days and that no doctors had been able to find out what was wrong with his stomach. He had been bedridden since he was admitted to TCH and had not been able to walk around as usual.

The doctor gave Marcus pain medicine, after which he was able to calm down.

I glanced outside. The sky was covered with black clouds, buildings and rooftops wrapped in fog. The sound of rain pattered against the windows. Then thunder rumbled like an earthquake followed by lightning.

"I'm scared. I've never been in such a tall building before while there was a thunderstorm outside." He hugged his stuffed animal Wolf for comfort.

Wolf was there to protect Marcus at the hospital, and he always brought him with him.

"You're safe here at TCH, Marcus," I said in an attempt to calm him down. "Keep hugging Wolf. Mommy is right here in the bed next to you. Let's both try to get some sleep so you're ready to start your treatment tomorrow. Daddy and Lucas are at home and they're safe too." I kissed him on the forehead. "Don't worry at all, Marcus. Sweet dreams, sweetie."

On Saturday, July 5, Marcus was due to start his Nelarabine chemotherapy treatment. According to the protocol, the Nelarabine regimen consisted of five consecutive IV infusions spread out over five days. Marcus was still in bed. His severe stomach pain was unresolved. He still had a fever on and off. The doctors were eager to start the Nelarabine infusions because technically speaking, Marcus was dying of leukemia. My husband and I had to trust the doctors, and if they deemed Marcus was ready to start the treatment despite the list of unresolved issues, there was no reason for questioning their judgment.

CHAPTER ELEVEN

"This Is All So Wrong"

Marcus remained bedridden. After the first Nelarabine infusion, Marcus seemed very tired. He tried to eat some food Saturday night, but immediately after, his stomach pain returned. His left eye was getting redder and more inflamed. Two eye doctors came by to check his eye. The doctors examined him but did not come up with any specific diagnosis except for infection. As for the stomach pain, the oncologists believed Marcus's intestines had been inflamed as a side effect of the month-long chemotherapy. The inflammation most likely caused irritation and pain, but they weren't sure.

On Sunday, July 6, Marcus had his second batch of Nelarabine. My husband came to visit. Marcus was still bedridden. He had started to complain about pain in his legs and fingers. When he had to pee, he had pain and couldn't pee. He tried and tried.

"I need to pee, I need to pee!" he screamed as he tried to keep his balance. But he couldn't. We tried to help him relax and the nurse tried to calm him down, but it didn't make Marcus comfortable. He could hardly walk to the restroom. His legs started to wobble. He was not himself. His stomach pain worsened.

On Monday, July 7, the doctors prescribed the third dose of Nelarabine. Marcus was still bedridden and increasingly sleepier. When he woke up, he had pain. He started to develop high-grade fevers. The doctors had ordered that Marcus refrain from eating or drinking anything except for a sip of water for the pills he needed to swallow. They wanted to give Marcus's stomach and intestines a break to recover. My husband and I begged the doctors to control Marcus's pain. What was going on? Why does he have pain all over his body? Why isn't he able to walk? Why can't he pee? Why can't he talk normally? They called it "pins-and-needle pain." It was normal when receiving chemotherapy. The doctors continued to give him morphine for pain and Tylenol to reduce the fever in a desperate attempt to control the horrible symptoms he experienced.

What was so-called expected for the doctors and nurses was not expected for Marcus and us.

"I need to use the restroom," Marcus said, trying to reach the restroom by himself. His hands trembled.

He was falling and screaming of burning pain in his body. If I touched him, he cried and screamed. I called the nurse. She witnessed how Marcus was unable to control any movements. He couldn't control his bowel movements. There was diarrhea all over the floor. He screamed when we tried to wash him and clean him after the accident. It was as if he were burned alive. The nurse remained very cool and collected, as if this scene was completely normal.

My pulse raised, my legs weakened. This could not continue. My only thought was to stop Marcus's suffering.

Finally, we got Marcus back in bed. Anticipating this incident would happen again, the nurse left to get Marcus a big diaper. Getting the diaper on Marcus was painful, as he couldn't tolerate touch. He collapsed of exhaustion and was peaceful for a bit. Then there was no crying, no screaming, and no pain.

My husband and I saw many warning signs that Marcus didn't tolerate the treatment. We followed our gut feelings and did raise our concerns to the nurses and doctors multiple times, but they didn't take Marcus's signs or our concerns seriously. The doctors decided to stick to their initial plan to continue giving Nelarabine to Marcus. My husband and I were shocked. We replayed what we had seen; we even detailed the toxic side effects we witnessed, but the medical staff ignored our cry for help. We wanted to hit the brakes and stop the Nelarabine treatment before more harm was done to Marcus, but where could we go when the doctors didn't understand our concerns? We had nowhere to seek a second opinion. No parent caregiver was available at TCH to support us, and no one besides us was present to serve as an advocate for Marcus. Had we as caregivers no rights to be heard and understood? It was as if we took part in a play of chess and the medical team checkmated us. Clearly, there was a communication breakdown between the medical team and us as parents, which turned out to have fatal consequences for Marcus.

I demanded to have the doctor look at Marcus many times. Doctors rotated on shifts. Rarely did the same doctor see Marcus twice. One came, looked at Marcus, placed an order for the next steps in the treatment, and left. Then a new doctor came on shift. The doctors didn't know Marcus and his baseline from before he started the Nelarabine treatment.

Tuesday, July 8, Marcus was unable to swallow his pills. Since he had reached a point where he couldn't control his mouth and had swallowing difficulties, he was unable to swallow his pain medicine. The nurses had been given strict orders not to give Marcus any food or drinks.

"Mommy, Daddy, I am so thirsty. I need something to drink, please, please," Marcus begged. He was pale, and his mouth and lips were all dry and crackled. All he got were IV fluids, medicine, and Nelarabine. Nothing through his mouth. I asked the nurse permission to give Marcus some water.

"He can only have two sips of water," she said. "Remember, the doctors have ordered that he cannot have anything to eat or drink."

"But look at him," I said, gesturing to my frail son. "He's so thirsty and he's in pain." Suddenly I was yelling. "The doctors are not helping him at all!"

I had lost my patience. Marcus was so weak that I had to give him a straw so he could get the two sips of water. The nurse was hiding her feelings and acting cold in an effort to remain professional.

That Tuesday, Marcus got his fourth infusion of Nelarabine. The Nelarabine train kept rolling.

He was sliding away from us. Occasionally, he woke up, shook, and had uncontrolled movements. He couldn't get out of bed anymore. He wore a diaper, as he was unable to control his urine or bowel movements. He was like a baby, almost helpless.

Dr. Schafer, who knew Marcus from his first admission at TCH, was the attending doctor that day. He ordered an MRI, with and without contrast, with the goal to find out what was wrong with Marcus's stomach.

Jacob and I demanded he help control Marcus's peripheral pain. My son's suffering had to stop. He said he would ask around to find a pain medicine that could help Marcus better. The atmosphere changed in the room. My husband and I realized that the doctors didn't have Marcus's situation under control. They told us they had never seen reactions like this before when Nelarabine had been administered to pediatric patients. If they couldn't explain why Marcus reacted this way to Nelarabine, they should stop the treatment.

The nurse woke up Marcus because he had to be taken to the MRI room. Marcus was completely incapacitated. Every time anybody touched him or moved him, he screamed in pain. It was torture. I asked the nurses to be super careful while handling him because any touch hurt him. He was hypersensitive. I insisted that I be with Marcus all the time. My husband and I protested that Marcus was in no condition to tolerate the MRI. It would be too painful for him. The Nelarabine was frying him alive. His central nervous system was burning. His brain, his arms, fingers, legs, feet—every part of his fragile body was being fried. I cried and tried to tell the staff in the MRI room how Marcus felt. They were only interested in getting the procedure done. There was a line of children waiting for MRIs. Once in the MRI room, they attempted to lift Marcus to the stretcher that goes into the MRI machine. I told them it would be too painful for Marcus. There was no way Marcus could tolerate the procedure. They continued anyway. They also said they had to give Marcus a contrast agent. In that case, I asked them to use his PICC line. Apparently, he had to have it through a different IV. The nightmare got worse. They poked Marcus and gave him the contrast while he was crying in pain.

I held his hand.

"You're going to be all right," the nurse said, not acknowledging the level of pain Marcus actually felt. "Just relax."

He was unable to move, talk, protest, or even leave the room. What I said did not count. Their only focus was to get the MRI done as ordered. The arm with the contrast started to swell. My son was suffering so much.

I should have just stopped them.

Once back in his room, I demanded the nurse give Marcus more pain medicine. She did, and Marcus finally quieted down. The room was silent for a moment. There was no pain, no screaming.

Later, Dr. Schafer came back and told us he had asked around about controlling Marcus's pain better. He said Marcus should try a drug called Gabapentin, which could calm down his painful nerves. We agreed that Marcus needed the medicine—the sooner the better. Marcus's fever was going up and down, yet the treatment continued.

Dr. Schafer couldn't explain what happened to Marcus. My husband and I were shocked, worried, afraid, and insecure. The pain Marcus experienced was unacceptable. Dr. Schafer said it was temporary. That, to us, meant that Marcus would wake up again, the pain would disappear, and he would be our old normal and happy Marcus again. We didn't even talk in detail about the leukemia or if Nelarabine worked. Dr. Schafer mentioned briefly that from the blood work, it looked like the leukemia responded to the Nelarabine treatment. At that point, I didn't care about the leukemia. All my husband and I cared about was how we could protect Marcus from more pain and suffering. This nightmare had to stop. We wanted our Marcus back.

Later in the afternoon, a TCH social worker entered Marcus's room to talk about the bone marrow transplant. He had heard that Marcus's condition was critical and that Marcus had suffered a lot during the past days of treatment. He assured us that the transplant process would not be as intense as the Nelarabine treatment had been for Marcus. That was a relief, provided Marcus would ever get to the transplant unit.

When Marcus opened his eyes, he started shaking. He had uncontrollable cramps in his body. He talked nonsense.

"Marcus, what's wrong?" I asked him.

I received no answer. Marcus was not himself. He just lay there. He didn't talk anymore, and I couldn't get in contact with him.

He had a high fever. The nurse would come in and measure his temperature and leave. She brought some more Tylenol to camouflage the fever. Then the fever would go down. We complained that Marcus was shaking and had pain.

"I'll get him some morphine," the nurse said and came back with a syringe full of morphine.

I was crying. I witnessed the worst nightmare in my life happening to my son inside one of the best pediatric hospitals in the US.

As Marcus's condition had worsened dramatically, my husband had

Chapter Eleven

called his parents. His mother in Denmark wanted to fly over immediately. This was a great relief. I told Marcus that Grandma was coming to see him. I believe he understood what I said. He smiled a bit with his eyes closed.

My husband and I had begun to doubt the competence and professionalism of the TCH doctors. Marcus's room was like an airport where medical personnel entered and left, entered and left. Marcus had turned into a human experiment.

We assumed the doctors were aware of the consequences of continuing the Nelarabine treatment and that it was true what they said, namely that all the symptoms were temporary. They characterized the reactions as an unfortunate reaction to Nelarabine. They believed Marcus would recover.

Wednesday morning, my husband called me. The night was horrible. Marcus was sicker than ever. He had a fever and pain. He woke up trembling and he talked nonsense.

"How can he be worse?" I struggled to understand how grave the situation had become. I felt numb all over, and an unbearable sensation of emptiness overwhelmed me.

"He's worse. Believe me," Jacob said. "I haven't even dared to leave the room to get something to eat in the kitchen. You have to come in. Bring Lucas with him so Marcus and Lucas can see each other."

I found a new T-shirt for Lucas in his closet. The print on the shirt said BEST BIG BROTHER EVER.

My husband and I had explained to Lucas that Marcus was in bed and was very sick and tired. He had to be gentle with Marcus. Lucas agreed. He could sense I was serious.

When we came into Marcus's room, Lucas rushed over to Marcus's bed.

"Look at my T-shirt, Marcus," he said with a sweet voice.

Marcus recognized Lucas's voice, opened his eyes, and glanced briefly at his little brother's T-shirt. He smiled. Then he closed his eyes. This was the last time Lucas had contact with the "old" Marcus.

My husband drove home with Lucas. He hadn't slept at all that previous night. Marcus had been so unstable, had talked nonsense, and had a fever and cramps. Dr. Schafer had asked my husband if Marcus usually talked in his sleep. Dr. Schafer suggested it could be normal behavior. My husband stressed that Marcus never talked in his sleep.

On Wednesday, the doctors decided to give Marcus the fifth and last dose of Nelarabine. He did not move, did not complain anymore. He just lay in the bed while the drug dripped into his PICC line and into his traumatized body.

The emptied Nelarabine bag hung on the pole. I realized this moment was the point of no return, as once the drug was administered, there was no antidote to remedy or neutralize the toxicity associated with Nelarabine.

That night, I simply stayed as close to Marcus as possible. I prayed he would get better after he had finished the last Nelarabine dose. I wanted to be able to see him at all times. See how he was feeling, how he looked, be sure to be there if his situation deteriorated.

"One-oh-six!" the medical assistant shouted, referring to Marcus's temperature.

He was sweating; his breathing wasn't as steady as it used to be. Quickly, the nurse entered with more Tylenol for Marcus.

I wiped away his sweat on his pale forehead with a cold wet washcloth. Then I looked at the clock and realized it was time to get some sleep. I arranged a soft pillow and a blanket on the stained caregiver couch by the window and lay down. A few parents were talking and laughing outside on the hallway. Then the noise faded away. The quietness was almost tangible, no beeping machines, no crying children, no doctors talking. Marcus's breathing was slow and barely audible, but he looked comfortable.

It was 2 A.M., and the sound of something moving in Marcus's bed woke me up.

Marcus's whole body started to shake. Massive, uncontrolled series of tremors hit him like a giant tsunami. The doctors said he was going to recover, and now this happened? "Marcus, wake up!" I shouted, but he didn't respond. He appeared to be asleep, yet his whole body was convulsing with such violence I had never seen before during those past few days. There was no time to hesitate. I ran out of the room and looked for a nurse as I yelled, "Marcus is dying! Something is wrong! Come quickly!"

The nurse entered the room.

"Look at Marcus!" I screamed. "Help him! His whole body is shaking. Call the doctor! Do something!"

Unable to get Marcus's attention, the nurse leaned in on him and laid

Chapter Eleven

her hands on his body to control the spasms but in vain. The shaking continued rapidly. Her face had an alert gaze. Like a bullet out of a gun, she ran to get help.

How did a good mother stand watching her own child's suffering by his very bedside? I couldn't live through this. *Please, please let Marcus live.*

A new doctor came in and assessed Marcus. He ordered more morphine.

"Hang on, Marcus, hang on," the doctor said and left. Apparently, his job was done.

The nurse gave Marcus the morphine, and Marcus's trembling decreased. Thirty minutes after, the doctor came back to check on Marcus.

"I see Marcus is doing well again. His movements stopped," the doctor said.

Was this all he had to say? I glanced at Marcus, whose tremors had indeed stopped.

"Yes, of course it stopped because he just got morphine. The question is why does Marcus still get this trembling and how can we prevent this from happening again?" I noticed the doctor prepared to leave the room. He was clearly very evasive about Marcus's situation.

The doctor left without offering any answers.

TCH was a dark place. I was sitting in a room at night by myself bursting with anger and bitterness. I couldn't grasp a way out of this situation, couldn't make sense of how this would end, and was left without any idea when it would end. It was like being in a place with a thousand people but feeling invisible to every one of them. It was endless wonder about endless wondering. It was suffering alone.

The night continued like this. Marcus's temperature skyrocketed, the nurse gave him Tylenol, he had cramps, talked nonsense, got morphine, and the cycle repeated itself.

When it was six in the morning, I called Jacob.

"Yes, hello," he said, as if he expected my phone call this early.

What a relief to hear a familiar voice. "It's me." I tried to get my thoughts together. "Marcus is never going to get out of this hospital." I was sobbing.

"Don't say that," my husband urged, trying to console me.

"What's going on in here is crazy. They don't know *what* they are doing.

They are not helping Marcus." I paused, breathing heavily. "I'll call Dr. Brack and ask her to come in and see Marcus," I told him. "Maybe she can help—"

"Relax," Jacob interrupted. "We'll figure this out."

"I'm not sure. This is so wrong. It's all wrong," I cried as I looked at Marcus.

"Okay," my husband said with a flat, monotone voice. "I'll come in as soon as I've dropped Lucas off at summer camp. My mother is packing now. She'll be on a plane tomorrow and she'll arrive on Saturday." I closed my eyes, then dropped my phone on the couch. Thank God my mother-in-law was on her way. I only wished she was here already.

I went back to Marcus's bed and whispered into his ear that Grandma was coming soon. He was just lying there silently in his bed, poisoned by Nelarabine.

After I hung up with my husband, I immediately called Dr. Brack. Thursday was her day off from work, but she picked up her cell phone right away. I had been in contact with her throughout induction, and she was aware that Marcus didn't make it into remission. She, too, had been worried about him. I told her the situation was way out of control and that the TCH doctors didn't know how to handle Marcus. She told me she would come to see Marcus immediately at TCH.

Dr. Brack didn't waste any time. When I opened the door to Marcus's room, she gave me a big hug. I needed that. Then she went straight over to Marcus.

"Tell me what happened," she urged me. "What's going on?"

I told her about Marcus's reactions to Nelarabine, about the excruciating pain he had experienced, and his sudden inability to control his motions. I recounted his change in personality and how he slowly had drifted away in front of us all, while the doctors didn't listen to our concerns and did nothing to stop the galloping destruction.

"I'm so sorry, I'm so sorry," Dr. Brack repeated as her brows pulled together. She moved closer to me. "I don't know what to say. This is so hard, isn't it?" Dr. Brack adopted a soft tone.

She was devastated. Dr. Brack put her right hand on my left shoulder. "Let me examine him." She walked over to the right side of Marcus's bed. I followed right behind her.

Chapter Eleven

Marcus did not wake up as she listened to his lungs.

"I believe Marcus is developing pneumonia in his left lung," she said. "How long has he been in bed now?"

"He's been in bed for a week now. He's not able to do anything. He's just lying there and can't even eat anything." I teared up while I explained our dire situation. "In the night, the nurse put an O2 probe on Marcus's finger because he wasn't breathing well. The O2 alarm kept beeping and beeping because he didn't get enough oxygen. Then they gave him extra oxygen through an oxygen nose tube."

We talked for a while, and then Jacob arrived. Dr. Brack hoped Marcus would recover from the Nelarabine treatment. She couldn't offer any explanation for why he had had all those terrible symptoms and all the horrific pain. When she left, my husband and I discussed how to deal with the next couple of days. He decided he wanted to stay with Marcus overnight. I was exhausted from the lack of sleep and stress from being in the hospital. I felt Marcus kept going downhill. He had to get better soon. He just had to.

The next morning, Jacob called me. Overnight, Marcus was getting worse. He had been hallucinating. He was unstable. Dr. Schafer was in the room. He told my husband he had to transfer Marcus immediately to the pediatric intensive care unit (PICU) so Marcus could get the care he deserved.

"Why is Dr. Schafer transferring Marcus to PICU?" I asked.

"Honey, Marcus is very ill now. You have to understand this. You must come as soon as possible."

I rushed to TCH, forgetting about everything else.

Not every child who leaves PICU does so when alive. There was constant monitoring of the child. My husband showed me Marcus's bed. His chest was covered in wires, and he was hooked up to a monitor. He received oxygen. He had no clothes on, just a diaper. He had lost most of his hair. He looked fragile. His skin was pale. All his stuffed animals and personal belongings were in a bag next to his bed. The setup looked like a movie scene showing a critically ill child, except this was our Marcus lying in the bed. It smelled like medication all over PICU. Nobody was laughing.

That Saturday, I stayed with Marcus in PICU and my husband went home. He, too, was exhausted. In a way, we felt assured that Marcus would get better treatment in PICU because the nurse was there monitoring him all the time. There were always intensive care doctors present, and any emergencies would be attended to promptly. When Marcus was on the oncology floor, my husband and I dared not leave him alone in his room, fearing he would need help because of pain, fever, or cramps. In PICU, the nurse monitored his vitals and could immediately see if Marcus became unstable. Therefore, in that respect, we felt a huge relief. Dr. Schafer told me that in PICU, Marcus would get the personal attention he needed. Dr. Schafer was right, but we had begun to fear that the nurses and doctors had failed to give him sufficient attention while he was on the oncology floor.

Were we too late in getting him the care he needed?

That evening, Marcus was still breathing on his own, but he was receiving oxygen. His cramps and pain were not well controlled, as he was unable to swallow his painkillers correctly; he couldn't control his mouth sufficiently anymore. I was able to get in contact with Marcus one last time for a few minutes. He was a tiny bit alert but not comfortable. He wanted so badly to tell me something. He was shaking and could not control his movements. His big brown eyes were looking better, and his eye infection in his left eye had improved a little.

"Grandma is coming tomorrow, Marcus," I said, caressing his pale cheek. "What are we going to have for dinner when Grandma arrives?"

Marcus smiled as I told him that his beloved grandma was coming to see him.

"We're going to have rice with mushroom sauce," Marcus answered with difficulty before he passed out again. This was the last thing my son ever said.

"It's okay, Marcus. You're going to feel better tomorrow when Grandma comes." I held my hand to his cheek and did my best to keep my tears at bay.

CHAPTER TWELVE

Final Decline

Per PICU policies, visitors were not allowed to sleep inside PICU. There was only one chair for visitors next to the bed. Luckily, the Ronald McDonald House had a special unit for PICU where parents, without any charge, could sleep overnight. I had to sign up by the front desk at the Ronald McDonald House, and at evening time, the receptionist would call me to let me know if a room was available for me. If there were no rooms available, I had to sleep in the sleeping chairs in the waiting room outside PICU. It was not comfortable, and there was a lot of noise: crying parents and people watching TV or eating food.

Saturday morning, I woke up and rushed from my Ronald McDonald room to the PICU to see Marcus. He was sleeping, but he woke up a bit. Then suddenly Marcus's body stiffened; he lost consciousness, and his eyes rolled back in his head. He arched his back and began to spasm. I screamed for help. Two nurses ran over and held Marcus while counting the minutes that passed. The spasms lasted for several minutes. Then they stopped, and Marcus remained unconscious.

Marcus had had a seizure.

A seizure was one of the scariest things I had ever seen happen to Marcus. I thought we were losing him. After a short break, another violent seizure happened, and after some time yet, another one. It was awful to witness. It looked like somebody was giving him an electric shock. We could do nothing but wait for the seizures to stop. Marcus's nurse quickly conferred with the PICU doctors and came back with anti-seizure medicine for Marcus. After he got anti-seizure medicine, his activity finally ceased.

Chapter Twelve

That night and the following day turned out to be increasingly difficult for Marcus. He developed a fever, and his left arm had become inflamed around the site where he had received the contrast prior to the MRI scan of his stomach. He needed more morphine for pain. He would scream and start shaking when he needed to urinate without being able to pass any urine. The infectious disease doctor determined that Marcus had pneumonia in his left lung. Complications increased hour by hour. In the afternoon, he had more cramps and needed an oxygen mask. The doctors decided that Marcus needed continuous morphine to control his pain and cramps. If that were not sufficient to keep him comfortable, the doctors would need to sedate him.

Grandma arrived and visited with Marcus for the first time in the hospital. He wasn't awake to see her. She was devastated to see Marcus in such serious condition. She loved Marcus so much, and seeing him like this was awful for her.

Sunday night, I relieved my husband in PICU. Marcus's breathing had become more troubled, especially after the doctors had started continuous morphine treatment. I got a room in the Ronald McDonald House for the night. I talked to Marcus's young night nurse, Amanda, and let her know in which room I stayed. I had a feeling something serious would happen overnight. Amanda calmed me down and said I should get some sleep.

It was 5 A.M. in my room when the phone rang.

It was Amanda. I pressed the telephone to my ear and listened through the noise of PICU in the background.

"I want to let you know that Marcus has difficulty breathing now. The doctors have decided to sedate him and intubate him," Amanda explained. "I want to prepare you that when you see Marcus, he will have a tube in his mouth. Do not get scared when you see him."

"No, why . . . why is he not able to breathe?" I asked her. My mind spun. "I don't understand this."

Amanda hesitated. "The doctors will explain it to you when you come see Marcus. The procedure will be done in twenty minutes, so wait just a little bit before you come see him." I wanted to be with Marcus, not stay away from him.

When I saw Marcus, he looked so relaxed. It was the first time he had looked relaxed in over a week. He looked different with a tube sticking out of his mouth. The tube was taped to the side of his mouth and was connected to a ventilator that did the breathing for him. Through his nose, he had a thin feeding tube. Marcus had developed a bladder infection and now had a catheter. New complications kept arising.

My husband stayed with Marcus overnight. Tuesday morning, Marcus's body was very swollen due to excess fluid accumulation, and the doctors were concerned about his kidneys. His kidney numbers were elevated, indicating that Marcus's kidneys were unable to process the fluids, which caused his body to retain too much fluid. Marcus then started treatment to make him pee more.

Grandpa arrived from Denmark to assist our family and be with Marcus. It was impossible for him to stay in Denmark knowing how sick Marcus was. He felt helpless in Denmark and wanted to be with his grandson and us.

Many specialists were following Marcus: oncologists, eye doctors, neurologists, infectious disease doctors, kidney doctors, and intensive care doctors. The good news was that Marcus's lungs sounded better and his fever was gone. Marcus responded a bit when the neurologist tested him. The neurologist hit him with a plastic hammer—first on his arms, then on his legs—and Marcus would then move his arms and legs by instinct.

It was Wednesday, and Grandma and Grandpa were with Marcus. It was a tremendous relief that they came to be with him and offer us emotional support. The doctors' plan for Marcus was to start weaning him off the sedative medicine to wake him up again.

Marcus started to move his head a little bit and was able to breathe again by himself. He was still hooked up to the ventilator in case he didn't get enough oxygen and needed support. He made some small jerks with his body, but he wasn't waking up as anticipated by the doctors. The neurologists wanted to conduct a new MRI two days after.

On Friday, Grandma and Grandpa stayed with Marcus in PICU. The nurse reported Marcus had a good night, but his body jerked and his head moved from side to side; he wasn't relaxed like before. The neurologists conducted an EEG of Marcus's head, and it showed no seizure activity, which was good. The kidney doctors were pleased with Marcus's kidney and bladder functions, so altogether Marcus's organs seemed to be recovering. All this was

Chapter Twelve

excellent news. There was one piece of bad news. The neurologists had tested Marcus again and they were not pleased with his test results. He should've been more awake and should've responded to the neurological tests.

Next to Marcus's bed was a teenage girl. I could see she was hooked up to all sorts of mechanical equipment. One day, the whole room was full of visitors and children crying, and I asked what was going on. According to PICU protocol at TCH, a maximum of two people at a time is allowed in a room. Marcus's nurse explained to me that when a child is dying, it is PICU policy to allow all family members to be present in the room, even younger children who would otherwise not be allowed access inside PICU. The girl's family members stayed there for a while, then they all left crying. Some time after, the girl was gone and her room was empty. Cleaning staff arrived and started cleaning the empty room. Then a new pediatric patient arrived.

When death arrived next door, it affected me. It made me realize how fortunate we were. Marcus was alive, and that was all I could focus on. His room wasn't full of crying family members. It was just me sitting next to Marcus. To be honest, I felt I had to appreciate that fact and hold on to the hope that Marcus would make it back to the old Marcus. When there was life, there was hope.

On Saturday, the doctors did a bone marrow biopsy to assess the leukemia burden after the Nelarabine treatment. Marcus was still not awake after the anesthesia wore off. The day after, Marcus shivered. Those were not purposeful movements. The intensive care doctors worked hard to adjust Marcus's blood pressure medicine and treatment to get rid of excess fluid in his body. He was retaining fluids in his lungs, which made it hard for him to breathe. The oncologists, Dr. Schafer and the oncology fellow Mary, informed us that Marcus's absolute neutrophil count (ANC) was on its way up. The ANC number reflects how strong the patient's immune system is. This was the best news ever, as this indicated that Marcus's bone marrow produced healthy immune cells again.

"Marcus's body is doing what we're telling it to do, which is to recover," Dr. Schafer said as he moved around. He talked faster. "His labs are getting better, his ANC is starting to go up, and his liver and kidney levels are improving. Now we just need for Marcus to wake up." His smile grew of its own accord.

I tried to follow his excitement, but it was hard. Marcus was more than just numbers. He was still just lying there unresponsive in his bed. Marcus was reduced to a patient with lab results who was kept alive by a machine with settings. I didn't think the doctors looked at him as our wonderful Marcus with plenty of humor, a charming smile, and big brown eyes. To them, he was just another patient in PICU.

A few days after, oncology fellow Mary arranged for a meeting with all of us. Dr. Schafer had told Grandpa he had good news. It was afternoon, and we all assembled in the waiting room outside PICU. The TV was on; constant boring commercials from it was driving me insane, coffee tables with random magazines and empty paper cups were present all over. It had to be good news we were about to receive. Dr. Schafer and Mary turned up and we all sat down.

Had Nelarabine been so effective that it had eliminated all the leukemia cells? If chemotherapy is effective, it only takes a few days to a week for a course of therapy to eliminate all the leukemia cells in the bone marrow and blood. Expectations were high that Nelarabine had worked because Dr. Schafer had already mentioned that Marcus's blood test results showed evidence to that effect. Marcus's bone marrow was producing healthy blood cells.

The anticipation was a nervous kind of energy. It tingled through me like small electrical sparks from top to toe.

"We have just received the results from the bone marrow biopsy. Marcus is in remission. There are zero percent leukemia cells in his bone marrow," Dr. Schafer said with a triumphant smile on his face.

I ran over and hugged him. It was the first time since Marcus was diagnosed with leukemia that an oncologist could tell us that our son was in remission. We had all been waiting for this moment. Finally, it had come.

"This is fantastic news!" I said. "I need to tell Marcus he made it. He beat the leukemia!" I felt an intense desire to leave the conversation and hurry in to see Marcus so I could share the news with him. All the mundane worries of my life had been muted, and all there was to know about was this moment.

"Because the test results showed Marcus is in remission, we are now going to do the MRD test of Marcus's biopsy. MRD stands for minimal

Chapter Twelve

residual disease," Dr. Schafer explained. He took his time to discuss the issue further.

"We need to make sure all detectable leukemia cells are gone. Our goal is that Marcus's MRD also shows zero percent. If Marcus is MRD negative, it gives him more time to recover. It means we can wait a little longer before continuing his chemotherapy treatment."

After Mary and Dr. Schafer left, Grandma and I went straight to Marcus's bed. He looked relaxed, like a child who slept after a long day of playing. Maybe he would wake up if I told him the good news.

"Marcus, wake up. Wake up. You're in remission. I mean it. You beat the leukemia. Marcus, wake up! Please..." I shouted at him. He was unresponsive.

How could this be possible? I wanted so badly to celebrate with him. He deserved to hear this news after what he had been through.

"If you wake up, I will give you a puppy, Marcus. I promise you. I know you and Lucas want a puppy. I will give you a puppy." I took his left hand in mine and held it, then sighed dejectedly.

Still no reaction from Marcus. Nothing. The noise from the machines, the monitors, the ventilator—just hospital noises were all I heard. It is true that achievement brings its own anticlimax, but despite that, I could not let disappointment defeat me.

The day after the big news, Marcus got a new MRI of his spine and brain. His breathing was getting weaker compared to the day before. The neurologists had tested Marcus again, and he was less responsive to the tests compared to the day before. We discussed the MRI results. I called my husband over Skype at work so we could all listen to the neurologist reports. What the neurologists told us came as a knockout punch.

"Unfortunately, compared to Marcus's last MRI ten days ago, we now see some changes on the scan," the neurologist said. "This is not what we hoped to see. We're going to set up a family meeting tomorrow with Marcus's team of doctors so we can all discuss how to move forward."

My husband and I could not believe what the neurologist just said. Was Marcus's unconsciousness due to the Nelarabine treatment? We discussed the results with the PICU team, and they explained that Nelarabine had started a DNA breakdown of Marcus's body, including his brain. Only time would

Final Decline

tell us how this breakdown had affected his brain function. This was not just bad, bad news. This was *devastating* news. Nelarabine was still affecting Marcus's brain. A process had started that no one could stop. This meant the doctors couldn't do anything to reverse the damaging effects of Nelarabine. The poisoning was ongoing.

On Wednesday, July 23, my husband, Grandpa, and I met for a family meeting. I did not like the term "family meeting" when it took place in a hospital setting. We hoped to get some answers to where Marcus was heading and how he could recover. I couldn't take more bad news. I just couldn't. We were all mentally exhausted. We needed assurance that the doctors knew what they were doing and had a plan for Marcus's recovery.

Grandma and Grandpa were a huge support for us. Grandma could take care of Lucas and the household and visit Marcus in PICU. Grandpa was very involved in Marcus's care and took an active role in advocating for Marcus. He was just the type of player Marcus needed on his team along with Grandma and us.

Grandpa started to take notes on his iPad when he visited Marcus. He wrote down what Marcus was doing and which doctors had seen him. He talked to numerous doctors and he received so much medical information that it was impossible for him to remember it all. After visiting Marcus, he shared the information with my husband, Grandma, and me.

Jacob came up with the idea to create an online Google Doc diary with notes we could all share and write in in real time. He called the document "Diary for Marcus's Leukemia." This document became invaluable to us. Each of us could read it any time of the day in order to keep track of how Marcus was doing and get updates on his labs and other tests. It was also a valuable tool in that it contained medical information we could refer to when discussing Marcus's care and progress with the doctors. Marcus's diary was in Danish. We developed it to contain detailed information, including times for everything that happened to Marcus, names of the doctors we spoke to, settings on Marcus's ventilator, changes in his medicines, and other major developments and reached significant milestones. The document was technical, but at the same time personal because it contained the writer's personal accounts and observations about Marcus.

Some days passed, and finally Dr. Rabin was able to deliver the results

Chapter Twelve

from the minimal residual disease test. It was negative. No more leukemia was detectable in any tests. Wow, Nelarabine did it. It was too good to be true.

I observed Marcus lying in his bed at rest with his stuffed animal Wolf sitting next to his head. His comfy blue hospital gown, which had kid-friendly print on it, was too big for him; it designed with long length and closures conveniently located at neck and mid-back. Marcus was attached to all sorts of monitors—some secured to his skinny body with chest leads, those small painless stickers connected to wires. The leads counted Marcus's heart rate and breathing rate. A pulse oximetry (pulse-ox) machine checked his blood oxygen levels. Also painless, this machine was attached to the finger like a small bandage. It emitted a soft red light. A blood pressure cuff wrapped his bony right arm, his muscles all gone from being in bed so long. What a contrast this place was compared to the world outside this hospital.

Dr. Rabin did not attempt to leave. She had more announcements.

"We have received the results from the blood testing of your husband, you, and Lucas. Remember, the blood tests will show if any of you are a match for Marcus's bone marrow transplant," Dr. Rabin explained. "Lucas is a complete match for Marcus," she said, smiling.

An alarm from Marcus's IV pump interfered with our conversation. A nurse responded immediately, then attended to Marcus. She approached his infusion pump and tapped on the display. The alarm stopped, then she stole away to the nurses' station like a cat. Of course, I was thrilled to learn that Lucas was a complete match. It was very rare that a family member was a complete match, even for a sibling. Then Marcus could get the bone marrow transplant when he recovered, I figured. I beamed with gratitude.

But my happiness did not last long.

"However, it doesn't matter so much anymore," Dr. Rabin said, her tone solemn. She scratched her nose. "Marcus is not in a state where he can survive a bone marrow transplant."

"Other kids survive this, right? Why can't Marcus do the same?" I questioned her as I licked my lips with cautious hope.

"Fifty percent of healthy pediatric patients who go through a bone marrow transplant do not survive," Dr. Rabin said. "Unlike Marcus, these are children who are functioning and are in good health prior to the procedure.

The high-dose chemotherapy treatment leading up to the transplant is much harder than the Nelarabine treatment, and there is no way Marcus is going to survive that now." Her face crumpled.

It was as if she had given me a present just to take it away from me right after. I was denied justice. I stared off into space.

Instead, Dr. Rabin wanted to start two types of light chemotherapies to keep the leukemia at bay. Meanwhile, the neurologist team concluded that the neurotoxicity of Nelarabine without doubt was to blame for the damages of Marcus's central nervous system. The MRI showed small damages to his little brain and asymmetrical cloudy white damages to both the right and left parts of his brain. The EEG showed some activity, but it was uncoordinated activity. Over time, Marcus's nerves would heal and his brain would maybe be able to compensate for lost functions, but it was uncertain to what degree he would recover. The neurologists wanted to give Marcus time to heal and to start responding to the neurological tests. The longer Marcus didn't respond, the more likely that his damages would be severe and irreversible.

The intensive care doctors had assessed Marcus's breathing efforts. Marcus had not been able to breathe by himself and he needed increasing ventilator support. Therefore, they recommended that Marcus get a tracheostomy. A tracheostomy is a procedure used to create an opening in the neck to allow direct access to the breathing tube so the breathing tube can more easily deliver oxygen to the lungs.

The doctors had no solutions for Marcus. They could do nothing to get our old Marcus back.

At home, Jacob and I debated a million times how we should respond to the doctors giving up on Marcus.

"I can't believe the doctors can't do anything to help Marcus. They shouldn't be able to get away with this," Jacob argued as his voice raised.

"The doctors have destroyed Marcus. How can they just do that?" I crossed my arms. "Did they not know what they were doing when they gave him Nelarabine?"

"We have to insist they come up with a better plan," Jacob shouted, his fists clenched. "It can't be that they can get away with this, just expecting time to show if Marcus recovers. It's not good enough; it just isn't a good enough plan."

Chapter Twelve

To see injustice and do nothing about it means to participate in it. We could not allow the doctors to give up on Marcus. The pretended justice and arrogance from the doctors' sides were unacceptable. We couldn't fail to protest, couldn't lose our ability to defend Marcus. We had to show the doctors we expected more from them than a "we're sorry this happened to Marcus."

Days passed. Marcus got his tracheostomy. He also got a gastrostomy tube, or G-tube, because his comatose condition prevented him from being able to take adequate nutrition by mouth. This tube was inserted through Marcus's abdomen to deliver nutrition directly to his stomach. Dr. Rabin and her team still worked on putting together a maintenance chemotherapy regimen they believed Marcus could tolerate. They had to start some kind of treatment. If left untreated, the leukemia would come back. That was 100 percent certain.

It was Wednesday, July 30. Marcus had been sedated for sixteen days and had not woken up. The oncology team deemed it uncertain if Marcus would be able to recover to a state where he could tolerate lifesaving leukemia treatment. They suggested it might be better not to treat the leukemia anymore and instead allow Marcus to wake up. That also meant giving up on Marcus and letting him die from leukemia when it relapsed.

There was no way my husband and I would give up on Marcus. Never! Their recommendation was unacceptable. They ought to give Marcus a second chance. Marcus was not a quitter. The doctors messed him up with Nelarabine, and then they gave up because they could no longer go by the protocol. Now they had to consult with other hospitals and the National Oncology Group to get help. Most doctors can handle easy cases that go according to their expectations. It's when the going gets tough that the doctors are tested. That's when they have to demonstrate the extent of their knowledge, abilities, and true character.

Dr. Rabin had told us they had investigated other cases like Marcus's where Nelarabine had caused global neurotoxicity. Unfortunately, Dr. Rabin informed us that in all the similar cases she had come across in literature, the pediatric patients had died, meaning there was no precedent for how to take care of a surviving patient like Marcus.

When we discovered that Marcus's reaction was not the first in world history, my husband and I first felt betrayed by the oncologists. Both of us recalled that when Marcus developed the first signs of severe nerve pain and neurotoxicity, Dr. Schafer informed us that at TCH, the oncologists had never seen a patient react to Nelarabine the way Marcus did. Maybe they had never seen it at TCH, but they were the specialists and they should have known what dangers were involved with the use of Nelarabine. They should have been prepared. Nelarabine was *their* drug.

We learned that because Marcus presented unsolved medical problems at the time the doctors decided to start the Nelarabine treatment, it made him more prone to severe side effects. His stomach pain was unresolved, he had an infection in his left eye, and he was receiving IV antibiotics.

When my husband and I heard the reports from the previous Nelarabine neurotoxicity cases, we were speechless. The cases had been published in literature and in databases. We could read them online. Why didn't the oncologists and nurses know about the extreme dangers associated with the use of Nelarabine?

All the nurses attending to Marcus witnessed how Marcus was suffering, they heard his screaming, and they saw the enormous pain he suffered from without raising their concern to the doctors in an effective manner. We later learned that the nurses did not fully document Marcus's severe side effects in his electronic file.

A nonmedical person following Marcus during the Nelarabine treatment could easily conclude something was wrong by the way Marcus responded. Jacob and I could see it. We didn't need a medical degree to detect a human being's suffering.

On July 4, I had told Marcus that the safest place for him to be was at TCH, but it turned out to be the worst place. Had Marcus been at home presenting the side effects we witnessed at TCH, and had we taken him to CCC for outpatient treatments, I would have refused to bring him in for more Nelarabine infusions. I would have said, "Stop, this is inhumane, it is torture." When Marcus was inpatient, he was TCH property. That was how my husband and I experienced those five Nelarabine days. At no time during the treatment did the doctors deem it necessary or appropriate to cease or hold the Nelarabine treatment. They did not even suggest it to us. Why did Marcus's dignity not deserve to be honored? Does a pediatric cancer patient not have the right to be valued and respected for their sake? One should not forget that an omission is a failure to act, which in the criminal law under certain circumstances can attract legal consequences. Only, in the medical world, it apparently doesn't work that way. I acknowledge that we all wanted Marcus to achieve remission, but believing the end justifies the means is dangerous. Aiming for remission without continually discussing and considering the risks and costs as the treatment unfolds is unethical and wrong. At least it turned out to be in Marcus's case.

When Marcus was transferred to PICU, I started to develop pain in my body. I felt like my body was burning both inside and outside and I couldn't eat. I felt like throwing up. I started to become forgetful and I was extremely tired all the time. I presented classic PTSD symptoms such as trouble sleeping, angry feelings toward the doctors at TCH, and difficulty concentrating. I didn't care about anything but Marcus and, of course, Lucas. I didn't care about what was going on in the world, nor what my friends posted on Facebook. It wasn't important anymore. I was in a state of crisis. I couldn't handle other people's problems. I filtered them out. I let go of them.

Another challenge was that my husband and I were both suffering. We couldn't comfort each other. We had no energy to offer each other and we felt completely drained of hope and life energy. Mentally and physically, we had been run over by a road roller. Not just once but multiple times. Only when I was able to sleep did I feel some relief from the daily nightmares, but as I woke up each morning, reality hit me right in the face. Marcus was at TCH, nothing had changed, and my life was back to the nightmare it was.

I felt guilty for not having stopped the doctors from continuing the Nelarabine treatment. I felt I had failed to help Marcus. I had a wish to turn back the clock and do something differently. My husband and I discussed those five days repeatedly and started to blame ourselves for not having helped Marcus enough and for not having stood up for him. We shared our regrets, but it didn't help. We couldn't undo what had happened.

On Monday, August 4, the doctors transferred Marcus to PCU, the progressive care unit on the seventh floor. The PCU was a step down from PICU. The care was less intensive, and the pediatric patients were more stable than the patients in PICU. To me, getting Marcus out of PICU was a victory. Marcus had survived and needed less intensive care.

At home, after Lucas had gone to sleep, Grandma, Grandpa, my husband, and I sat in our living room discussing Marcus's situation for hours. Coping with disease can be a lonely process, but we helped each other.

We tried not to show Lucas how we felt, as it affected him to see us being sad. When Marcus moved to PCU, Lucas could come visit Marcus again. Only once had Lucas visited Marcus in PICU, assisted by his child life specialist Alyssa. Alyssa had explained to him that Marcus had a tracheostomy and G-tube and needed help to breathe from his ventilator. Lucas only stayed a few minutes next to Marcus's bed, carefully caressing his frail older brother. Lucas asked questions about Marcus's equipment and asked why Marcus had no hair. Lucas was still five years old. He didn't understand the severity of Marcus's situation.

Looking back now, from the vantage point of several years later and being much more informed than we could possibly be then, I can see several things. It would have been wise to resolve the issues Marcus was having with his stomach and eye before starting a second round of treatment. When the result of the treatment was clearly bad, it would have been wise to pause until more information could be gathered. Because it continued to have a very detrimental effect, we should have considered stopping it. The use of MRI at that time was out of line. Marcus was not well enough to endure it. I believe that the doctors and medical personnel were doing the best that they knew under very adverse conditions and we, too, did the best we could as parents. What would have been very helpful would have been a parent or caregiver specialist, who, like a child specialist, was there to help the parents understand what was happening and what choices they might have.

That is the wisdom of hindsight (or perhaps foresight for other families); but we went on—the medical professionals, Marcus, and his family—as best as we were able.

CHAPTER THIRTEEN

Signs of Hope

After Marcus was moved to PCU at the beginning of August, a new neurologist, Dr. Wolf, took on Marcus's case. Grandpa spent a lot of time discussing Marcus's neurological development with Dr. Wolf.

"Marcus's last MRI does not show severe damages to his brain. One can easily go through college with an MRI like this," Dr. Wolf assured Grandpa. "I would like to wean Marcus off some of his sedating medicines that prevents cramps and spasms. This will allow him to wake up. I need to make sure he doesn't have any seizures so I'm going to order a new EEG of his brain. Remember that it's going to take time to wean him off the medicine."

Dr. Wolf came with a fresh view on Marcus's case. She was hopeful, professional, and progressive. She seemed to be the type of doctor who was able to think outside the box and, most importantly, she assured us she was not giving up on Marcus.

A month had passed since Marcus finished the Nelarabine treatment, and in the meantime, we had received many different interpretations of Marcus's overall prognosis. One day the doctors were positive, the next day negative, then positive, then negative, and so forth. It was a roller-coaster journey. There was no comprehensive plan for Marcus. We had to wait for Marcus to wake up and, in the meantime, other complications arose.

Marcus's stomach began bleeding, and he needed urgent microsurgery. Fortunately, the operation was successful. The doctors assessed that the bleeding was a side effect from the Nelarabine treatment. They often saw stomach bleeding in pediatric cancer patients following chemotherapy treatment.

When Marcus was in PICU, Chaplain James often came to see Marcus

Chapter Thirteen

and pray for him. A young man, Chaplain James was probably in his early thirties, had plenty of humor, and displayed a warmth in personality that I responded to well. His wife just had a new baby. During our many encounters, he revealed an authentic, honest awareness of life and its struggles. He was able to empathize with me and laugh with me. I was relaxed when he was around.

Chaplain James offered emotional support and carried us through the toughest times when we didn't know if Marcus was going to make it. He continued to follow Marcus after he moved to PCU. It was nice to talk to a nonmedical person, because I knew he would not deliver bad news. He came with peace.

During the initial days in the PCU, my husband and I met with Dr. Brackett. She was an oncologist and palliative/pain management doctor at TCH. We asked her for recommendations about what we could do to help Marcus wake up and to support him in his healing process. She suggested that we could try Reiki healing, which was safe to use. Jacob and I wanted to do anything we could do to help Marcus. Dr. Brackett promised to do some research to find a reputable Reiki practitioner for Marcus. She later gave us the name of Reiki Master Xiomara Gehret Krause, who was based in the Houston area. I called her, and she accepted working with Marcus.

On Sunday, August 10, Marcus's nurse told us she had noticed that Marcus had moved his mouth a bit, as if he tried to open it. He had also made some jaw movements. These movements were a milestone for Marcus. It was the first time he had moved since he was in a coma. That same day, Xiomara Gehret Krause, nicknamed Zee, gave Marcus his first Reiki healing treatment at TCH. I didn't know anything about Reiki healing; thus, I had to do some research to find out what the deeper-leveled benefits were for Marcus.

One of the greatest Reiki healing health benefits for Marcus was stress reduction and relaxation, which triggered the body's natural healing abilities. Reiki helps bring about inner peace and harmony. It is spiritual in nature. This was exactly what Marcus deserved: a pleasant time he could truly enjoy—a private space for him to relax and trust that nobody would harm him the way Nelarabine had done.

On Monday, August 11, I was with Marcus in the morning when he surprised me by moving a bit. I almost cried. It was the first time I saw him move since he slipped away into a coma back in early July. The nurse called Dr. Wolf, the neurologist, who got so excited that she ordered an urgent EEG to be conducted while I stimulated Marcus by talking to him and trying to get his attention. Marcus opened his mouth a lot while I talked, but he did not speak. I tickled him in his armpit, and he reacted by moving his head and jaw. I massaged his feet with lotion while I talked to him. After the completion of the EEG, I was convinced Marcus was going to wake up. He would not remain in a coma even though some of his doctors had told us he would probably never regain consciousness.

Believe you can and you are halfway there—I hung on to this philosophy. I kept telling Marcus he would be okay again. I repeatedly let him know how well he did, how proud I was of him for fighting for his life, and how much I loved him.

A physiotherapist also started working with him. She stretched his legs and arms carefully and showed us how to do so with his hands by bending and stretching them. Because Marcus had been in bed for such a long time, his body was weak. He had no muscles and he had lost weight. He was so skinny, he had no hair, but he was beautiful and I loved him. No matter what he looked like, I loved him. No matter what happened to him, I loved him.

Marcus's medical team that followed him expanded. He also had a dietician and a physical therapist. He continued to have a respiratory therapist. He had a skin specialist who ensured he did not get any skin breakdown or pressure sores from constantly lying down in a bed without moving or turning by himself.

Marcus had all his stuffed animals in his bed. I made his room cozy. I brought him his own duvet cover, including his very cool *Star Wars* bedsheets. Chaplain James got excited to see that Marcus had the same bedsheets he had in his childhood.

"I can't believe Marcus has these *Star Wars* bedsheets," Chaplain James told me as he came by to visit Marcus one day. "I love them. They're so cool. They bring back memories from my childhood."

"Okay. I'm just warning you, Chaplain James," I reminded him. "If I ever come back to Marcus's room and find that his *Star Wars* sheets are gone, you will be my primary suspect."

Chapter Thirteen

We both laughed. It felt good to laugh. We should allow ourselves to have a bit of fun. I believed it would have a positive impact on Marcus if we all cheered up a bit.

We didn't know exactly how much Marcus comprehended. The neurologists believed Marcus could hear, and that was the reason why it was important to keep talking to him to stimulate his brain recovery and reconnect him with his past. From our observations, we could see that Marcus reacted to stimuli—for instance, when people talked in his room. He would start to breathe over the vent (initiating breaths of his own) and begin to slightly move his eyebrows and open his eyes a little. Mid-August, Marcus started to swallow. His movements were spontaneous, like a baby reacting to stimuli.

More days passed, and Marcus's reactions were not consistent. We never knew what to expect from him. Some days he would have a fever. Other days he would be very cold and have problems keeping his temperature stable. Then he would get an infection, after which he had to start antibiotics treatment. Every day came with new challenges. We faced those inevitable conditions with him day after day, but we fought back and dealt with them. Together. As a team.

Dr. Rabin was in charge of Marcus's leukemia treatment. She started giving him a light chemotherapy called 6-MP as a maintenance therapy. If the oncologists didn't start the maintenance treatment, the leukemia would come back. However, if they started the maintenance treatment, it would cause Marcus's immune system to decline. We understood their dilemma. Dr. Rabin told us that ultimately, it was our choice. My husband and I would not allow the leukemia to come back. You do not save a person only to kill the person after. Marcus had fought so hard. He deserved to live, and we were clear about that.

It was our choice to keep fighting. We had chosen Marcus's life over death. Our goal was to help Marcus recover. Persistence has great power and often distinguishes the strong soul from the weak. Every night I went to bed, I hoped that the next day would be better, always thinking positive thoughts. That was how I kept going.

On August 19, for the first time, Marcus woke up after having been in a coma for a month. I had been talking to him, he woke up, and he smiled at me. This meant he was still there; deep inside, it was still Marcus, he was still with us, and he was worth fighting for. It was beyond words and the most wonderful experience I had ever had. It was the first time since he fell into the coma that he opened his eyes. I talked to him, I showed him pictures of Lucas, and I played his favorite song, "Happy" by Pharrell Williams, on my iPad for him. Marcus was awake for thirty minutes, and then he slipped away again.

Marcus continued to show more improvements. He moved his head more, opened his eyes a little, and was able to breathe more and more over the ventilator, which was a good sign. He could swallow his saliva, his lips were active, and the neurologists had seen evidence that his pupils were more active.

I had decorated his room with get-well cards, posters, drawings, and other gifts from his friends at the Village School.

Lucas had started first grade. As part of a get-well present to Marcus, all the first-graders, including Lucas, had been photographed individually forming a heart with their little hands. All photos were placed on a big foldable poster board and the title was LOVE BOMB. I carried Marcus's Love Bomb up to his room and placed it at the end of his bed.

The support from the Village School, the Danish community, and our friends was enormous. A Danish friend, Mira, who was based in Houston, organized a meal train for us and started a GoFundMe page for Marcus and our family. I felt like we were on the same team.

On August 27, we had the next family meeting at TCH. The doctors presented us with all the latest results, and we discussed the next steps for Marcus. The results revealed that Marcus's leukemia biopsies and spinal taps were negative. Unfortunately, the MRI now showed global damage of Marcus's white matter in his brain versus patchy toxicity on his previous MRI scan. Dr. Wolf concluded the damages were most likely reversible, but she wasn't sure. She also concluded that Marcus was no longer comatose. He was in a vegetative state. The terms comatose and vegetative state are both types of impaired consciousness, but they are distinguishable from each other.

The word *coma* is sometimes used in a general way to cover a wide range of conditions in which the individual has suffered brain injury, leaving them with no consciousness at all or with very limited consciousness. It's very unusual for a coma to last more than a few weeks at most. People in a coma are completely unresponsive. They do not move, do not react to light or sound, and cannot feel pain. Their eyes are closed. The brain responds to extreme trauma by effectively shutting down. After a few days or weeks in a coma, a person who does not die usually "wakes up" in the sense that their eyes open. If they have only been in a coma for a few days, they may wake up to full consciousness with relatively little damage. If the person has very severe brain injuries, like in Marcus's case, they may move from a coma into a vegetative or minimally conscious state.

In a vegetative state, the person is still unconscious. They have no awareness of themselves or their environment. The main difference between a coma and a vegetative state is that at some point, the person's eyes will be open and there will be times when they seem to be awake. They may move parts of their body, but this movement is not voluntary. Movements can include grinding their teeth, thrashing, and facial movements such as grimacing, yawning, or smiling. They might jerk as a reflex response to loud noises or move a hand away from a source of pain. After four weeks, the person is said to be in a prolonged vegetative state. If a person remains in a vegetative state for several months after brain damage involving oxygen deprivation or for one year after a traumatic brain injury, the chances of recovering consciousness are very low and they are said to be in a permanent vegetative state.

The PCU team, along with the other doctors, recommended that Marcus move to HealthBridge, a rehab center for children situated in the western part of Houston, a ten-minute drive from our home.

Discharging Marcus from TCH was excellent news for us. It was a step in the right direction with the ultimate goal to get Marcus back home.

After my husband and I visited HealthBridge, we decided that this was the perfect place for Marcus. They could offer all the care Marcus needed. He could start daily physiotherapy, occupational therapy, and speech therapy. At TCH, Marcus had also started what we called "chair time" in a chair designed for special needs children.

It came as a surprise that PCU policies dictated that before discharge could happen, my husband and I needed to be certified to take care of Marcus. This meant we needed training in the vent and feeding pump. We had to learn all the work the respiratory therapists did, such as trach care, suctioning of his trach, changing of the trach, and troubleshooting when the alarms on the vent went off. We needed to learn G-tube care and manage his feedings and all his medicines. We had to do trach CPR classes and learn bathing techniques and learn how to move Marcus from his bed and into his chair. If we didn't pass all the tests, TCH couldn't discharge Marcus to HealthBridge. We also needed to learn how to flush his PICC line and change its dressing.

In the meantime, Grandma and Grandpa had gone back to Denmark. Their presence and support had been amazing for us and for Marcus and Lucas. Jacob and I were committed to completing the medical training so we could get Marcus transferred to HealthBridge. My husband had resumed work and had limited time to do medical training at TCH, but he tried hard to go to work, visit Marcus, and spend time with Lucas on the weekends. He was under tremendous pressure. He had to perform well at work, and if he underperformed, he could lose his job and visa. That would be catastrophic, leading to losing the family health insurance and coverage for Marcus's medical care.

I continued to be on a leave of absence from my job. Marcus and his recovery became my new job. When Lucas was in school, I spent time with Marcus and cared for him. I saw small new signs of improvements. He tried to make sounds and move his tongue. He moved his lower jaw as if he were chewing. We celebrated every little new thing Marcus could do. It all counted.

On September 4, Dr. Wolf and her team examined Marcus. I told her I had seen Marcus move his right arm inward. She looked excited and performed her regular reflex test with her rubber hammer on all his extremities. Since Marcus went to PICU, there had been a complete absence of reflexes. Then she did the test on Marcus's left arm, and he had a reflex.

"This is a miracle," she said and jumped with joy. "I hadn't expected to see any reflexes back so soon."

I loved how excited she was. She elaborated on her findings and Marcus's last MRI. She believed Marcus's nerve structures did not seem damaged, and that made her conclude that Marcus's damages were reversible.

As I started to do more exercises with Marcus, I could feel more resis-

Chapter Thirteen

tance in his arms and legs and could see on his face that he was hurting. The new EEGs showed more activity when Marcus was awake and moved parts of his body, or was stimulated. Marcus also started on a new medicine to wake up his brain. He got the same type of medicine pilots take when they fly long-distance flights and need to stay awake.

When Lucas visited Marcus in PCU, he was becoming less shy. He would bring cool LEGOs to show Marcus and try to get in contact with him. Sadly, Marcus didn't always respond because he was too tired from the medicine or because of his changed mental status. When Lucas got no response from Marcus, he would quickly lose patience and ask when he could go home to play with his friend Ross. Lucas was going to develop a new relationship with Marcus, and it was all on Marcus's terms. Lucas had lost his old funny brother, but Lucas still shared his love and concern for Marcus with us.

"I feel sorry for Marcus," Lucas said one day when visiting Marcus in PCU. "He can't do anything."

Lucas was right. Marcus had changed. We all felt sorry for him.

Since Marcus was about to move to HealthBridge, we had discussions with our family in Denmark about what type of help we needed the most. My other brother Christopher and his wife Susanne took a month of absence from their work as medical assistants and flew over from Denmark to help take care of Marcus. In Denmark, they specialized in elderly care and knew how to work with patients who needed care. When they arrived, they relieved us by visiting Marcus at the hospital, stimulating him, and keeping the dialogue going with the medical team. They did a fantastic job. They played with Lucas, and we enjoyed having them stay with us in our house.

My husband and I had to do "rooming-in" at TCH right before Marcus moved to HealthBridge. Rooming-in is a practice where parents and other caregivers provide total care for their child in a homelike environment while in the hospital. For twenty-four hours, Jacob and I had to take care of Marcus without any help from the medical personnel. We had to demonstrate that we could handle Marcus and manage all his needs on our own. We had worked hard to be certified. We could change his diapers, wash him, suction him, get him dressed, give him his medicines via G-tube, do G-tube care and trach care, manage his feedings and ventilator, and change his positions in his bed. We had to know the timing for all the steps, how much medicine he needed, how much formula he needed, how much free water he needed, the rate on the pump, and much more. We had received training in priming the feeding pump and troubleshooting the pump when the alarms went off, which happened often. We had to master infection control measures because Marcus's immune system was compromised due to his chemotherapy treatment.

We both passed "rooming-in." Marcus was ready for HealthBridge. A new chapter in Marcus's journey had begun.

CHAPTER FOURTEEN

HealthBridge

On September 12, Marcus moved to HealthBridge. Because he was vent dependent and could not sit, he had to be transferred by ambulance lying down on a stretcher. The transport went smoothly, and Marcus was installed in a small corner room at HealthBridge in the unit where the kids who needed the most intensive care stayed.

HealthBridge provided a range of care for those recovering from acquired or traumatic brain injuries or other complicated illnesses or injuries. It didn't look like a hospital. It was a one-story building in a residential area close to small shopping malls, only a five-minute drive from my husband's office.

Marcus started more intensive rehab to regain strength and mobility. The therapists worked on him sitting on the bedside. He couldn't sit by himself and needed support from the physical and occupational therapists. They wanted him to strengthen his back and neck muscles and maintain adequate range of motion in all muscle groups.

I was longing for a sense of normalcy and I hoped that Marcus's new life at HealthBridge would provide that. They had a vision for Marcus and launched new ideas about his recovery. Rosy times awaited.

Then, on September 18, Marcus started to develop severe breathing problems and needed additional oxygen through his vent to maintain normal saturation. Upon examination of his lungs, the doctor concluded Marcus had pneumonia and that night decided to transfer him back to PICU at TCH. He also had a fever on and off.

It's amazing how quickly your mood can change, how deep your heart can sink, and how much one person's situation can affect you. It was a

Chapter Fourteen

disappointing and somewhat worrisome beginning. Jacob, my brother Christopher, his wife Susanne, and I were taken down. Marcus had just made it to HealthBridge, and now this setback hit us like a freight train. It was unbearable even thinking about going back to the hospital, except we all knew deep inside it could happen at any minute. Marcus's condition was delicate and his recovery ahead unpredictable. Sometimes a plan is just a list of things that don't happen, but when you meet disappointment in life, it makes you stronger. The encouragement Jacob and I had through our family support made the whole difference. Christopher and Susanne had arrived with fresh energy, which helped pull ourselves up by the bootstraps.

The next day when I arrived in PICU, I thought Marcus looked better. He was resting in bed on the comfortable air mattress.

"Marcus, Christopher wants to have an air mattress like yours," I said, which prompted Marcus to smile. "He's very jealous of you, because you have such a comfortable bed. Once you get better and can eat again, I'll buy you a big Subway sandwich." I was hoping to make him more engaged and happy.

Marcus smiled. He liked what I said. He was listening.

On September 20, I brought a lovely book from my aunt Sorella. The title was *100 Wonders in the World*. I read it aloud to Marcus. I chose the chapter about the Golden Gate Bridge in San Francisco because I knew it was Marcus's dream to go see that bridge while visiting San Francisco, touring Alcatraz Island, and watching the 49ers play. Marcus listened with his eyes closed and made some small sounds as if he tried to say, "Keep going, Mommy, I like what you read to me."

Marcus moved to PCU and slowly got better as he recovered from his pneumonia. However, it was evident Marcus was still extremely weak. He was exhausted after each physical therapy session. His energy level was very low. It was hard for him to try to hold his head up. He couldn't stay awake for more than twenty minutes. He could do less than a four-month-old baby could.

We all cared for him the best we could. I loved giving him a bath and putting lotion on him after. That way, I could massage his sore muscles. He was sore from lying down in bed, unable to move by himself. He was hurting from sitting in his chair and from the exercises he did, just like we get sore after a workout.

I loved dressing Marcus after his bath. One day, I put on a US soccer T-shirt Marcus got from his PE teacher, Jeff Bond. The back of the shirt said "MARCUS." His PE teacher had ordered the official US national team jersey online when he heard Marcus got leukemia. I had showed the jersey to Marcus and told him who gave the jersey to him. Marcus looked so handsome in his new personalized jersey.

Christopher, Susanne, and I took turns visiting Marcus. Jacob also made trips to see Marcus. We all read stories to him in Danish to stimulate his brain. We played music for him, talked to him, put his favorite sports programs on his TV, and did exercises with him. However, most of all, we gave him lots of love, and he could feel it. I can't imagine any other child who was more loved than Marcus at TCH or HealthBridge. Everybody adored Marcus. He charmed the staff everywhere just by his presence alone.

Eventually, Marcus's PICC line clogged, and for some reason, the conclusion was that it was best to remove it. Later, this turned out not to be a smart decision because Marcus no longer had any IV access. In the future, whenever the nurses had to do labs on Marcus, they had to poke him and it was painful for him.

On September 25, Marcus was ready to move back to HealthBridge. Once back at HealthBridge, the doctor had to approve that Marcus could start therapy again. I discussed all Marcus's medications with his doctors and demanded to go over Marcus's new rehab plan with them. One of the goals in Marcus's plan was to learn to use a speaking valve that would allow him to practice speaking again. Marcus's rehab doctor, Dr. Tomey, was ambitious and I liked that. However, I did *not* like all her neurologic tests because they all involved pain on Marcus's part. She would hit his knees and arms with the rubber hammer and pinch his thighs to see if Marcus reacted to the pain. Marcus was incapacitated and couldn't say, "No, stop hurting me."

Marcus never cried, but his facial expressions would show us when he felt pain. Every time Marcus was hurting, it hurt me.

When Lucas came by to visit Marcus at HealthBridge, he sometimes brought cool new toys to show Marcus. When Marcus was tired, I allowed Lucas to jump into the bed with Marcus so they could watch a movie togeth-

Chapter Fourteen

er. Of course, Marcus would just be sleeping or lying with his eyes closed, but I called it movie time and Lucas loved it. Movie time was the only activity the boys used to share that they could still share together.

Throughout September and through mid-October, Marcus seemed to make more progress. I could tell Marcus to move his legs, and he was able to do so, but I discovered that Marcus's legs and arms got tighter, less flexible, and stiffer.

On a positive note, he was able to stay alert up to two hours without falling asleep. The stimulating medicine to stay awake seemed to help him. Marcus was making progress, and the team at HealthBridge decided that Marcus was ready to start physical, occupational, and speech therapy after his break due to the pneumonia. Marcus moved forward, and we had to capitalize on what came. I had faith something big was coming his way and that he was about to reach a turning point.

As Marcus started to wake up more, Dr. Baleva, one of the HealthBridge doctors, came to see Marcus. It was September 30.

Marcus's corner room had white clean walls decorated with drawings from his friends at school, and a door led to a separate restroom. The windows covered by blinds were lightly closed to allow soft sunlight to enter the room. If someone entered his room, the first thing he or she would notice on the left was Marcus in this hospital bed lying on a thick blue air mattress accompanied by his ventilator on the right side with its rhythmic hissing sound that raised and lowered in loudness as the machine cycled. His overbed table was pushed to the side, with a book placed on top of it sitting next to a white washcloth used to wipe away sweat from Marcus's face. Marcus's wheelchair was pushed aside into a corner.

"I think Marcus looks more and more like he did before he got sick. When I look at his photos on the wall, I can see he looks close to how he did before he got sick," Dr. Baleva exclaimed as she pointed to a photo of a younger Marcus hanging on the wall.

Seeing Marcus's hair grow back was a heartening sign. Some days he would have his eyes open for longer periods, giving me a chance to admire his big brown eyes. He was so beautiful.

"As soon as Marcus is ready, we're going to wean him off the ventilator," Dr. Baleva said with a cheerful voice.

I sensed Dr. Baleva had big expectations for Marcus's recovery. As soon as Marcus forged ahead with his ability to breathe by himself or with increased signs of alertness, she saw opportunities for him. She foresaw that Marcus would eventually be able to breathe by himself without any ventilator support. She also believed that over time Marcus would be able to respond to commands and interact more with his surroundings. She truly expected that later stages of his recovery could bring increased mental and physical function, and she was willing to support him with any necessary measures.

"Exactly," I said. "My husband and I like that plan. We must help Marcus get stronger and more alert. The sooner, the better."

Once again, reality hit. Later that afternoon, Marcus's heart rate was elevated and his oxygen saturation started to drop. Following an X-ray, the lung doctor, Dr. Susarla, concluded Marcus suffered from "white lungs," meaning his lungs were clogged with mucus. An intensive lung-cleaning process started with medicine to clean out the mucus. He got extra oxygen via his ventilator and avoided going back to TCH.

On October 1, Marcus seemed very alert. For the first time, he showed the speech therapist that he could blink his eye on command and he responded to different sounds. This was exciting news.

For days, Marcus still struggled with lung issues, but the team at HealthBridge, along with the lung doctor, was able to manage Marcus, giving him many different types of antibiotics and lung treatments so he didn't need to be transferred back to TCH. Over a few days, his lung functions recovered.

On October 4, when I came to HealthBridge to visit Marcus, his heart rate was 170 and his temperature was too high. Marcus's nurse José said Marcus's brain was storming. By *storming*, he meant that Marcus's brain did not function normally yet, which caused the abnormally high heart rate and rising temperature, even though Marcus was lying still in his bed. José gave Marcus medicine, and I helped cover Marcus's body with cold washcloths. A bit later, his heart rate lowered again.

Marcus moved his extremities more and more. Some movements were uncontrolled quick movements, but they also counted. In the afternoon, Dr. Baleva came to see Marcus, who happened to be awake.

Chapter Fourteen

"Marcus, show Dr. Baleva you can move your arms," I told him. I had a deep desire to share Marcus's achievements with Dr. Baleva.

He moved his arms and made several sounds as if he wanted to tell me something.

"Do it again," I said. "Did you see it, Dr. Baleva?" I bragged.

"Yes, Marcus, you impress me!" Dr. Baleva said with a pleased expression. "I told you he would make more progress. Keep up your work, Marcus."

It was a huge undertaking for Marcus to have come so far, such a fearless endeavor we could only admire but not understand. He had just demonstrated that he was recovering and becoming more alert and responsive. He was this superhuman the doctors at TCH had once given up on, and now months after, he blew away the doctors. I could tell that Dr. Baleva was vastly proud of him, and even though Marcus was unable to tell her, I think he liked her and her positive presence.

Marcus had gained about five pounds over the last months. His goal was to weigh about fifty pounds. He was now awake up to six hours. He could push his American football with his hands. On command, he could stick his tongue out of his mouth.

However, in the midst of all the progress, Marcus started to develop too much tone. Normally, healthy amounts of tone in a muscular body is good, but Marcus's tone was too much and uncontrollable to a degree where he couldn't relax his muscles. He was already wearing braces on his feet, elbows, and arms to prevent the muscles from contracting. They did help a bit but were far from enough to keep the tone at bay.

Dr. Tomey had addressed the tone with medicine, but it wasn't enough. Marcus developed involuntary movements and jerking. He was in pain, his heart rate went up, and he was sweating. The constant uncontrolled jerking of his arms caused sores on his elbows. The doctors at HealthBridge were increasingly concerned because of Marcus's repetitive jerking movements and repeatedly had to give him morphine to relax.

Dr. Toomey didn't believe Marcus was fully conscious yet, as he did not show her that he understood her commands. She believed he was still going through stages where he became more conscious and aware of his surroundings.

Mid-October, Marcus started to vomit. The doctors weren't able to find out why he started vomiting. His tone and involuntary movements were better controlled, but the trade-off was that Marcus became more tired and inactive.

On October 20, Marcus had an appointment to get a functional MRI (fMRI) at TCH. The fMRI would be able to show which parts of Marcus's brain worked normally. It would help the neurologists and the rehab doctors set realistic goals for Marcus and give a prognosis for his recovery.

On October 21, it was my birthday and we had an appointment at TCH to discuss the results from the fMRI. I hoped Marcus's birthday present to me was that the fMRI showed his brain was healing up. That was all I wanted for my birthday.

CHAPTER FIFTEEN

Irreversible Brain Damage

At 7:15 A.M., my husband and I arrived at HealthBridge and waited for the transport to TCH. When we arrived at TCH, Marcus was supposed to get an EEG, but in the EEG room, he threw up and was rushed to the ER. The doctors were worried some of the milk Marcus had thrown up had gone into his lungs. Luckily, X-rays taken in the ER showed that this was not the case.

The ER where Marcus, Jacob, and I were waiting was small with clean white walls. The room was cold with no natural light. A computer was sitting on a desk by the wall waiting to be opened and used by the next doctor entering the room. We were told Dr. Wolf, the neurologist, would come and talk to us. Even though Marcus had made great strides in his recovery, alarming symptoms had started to present themselves. The shaking, the storming, the sweating, the excess tone, the vomiting. These adverse late side effects from the brain injury were not expected if Marcus's brain damages were reversible and to some extent self-healing. Dr. Wolf arrived in Marcus's room. As soon I saw her, I started to shake; my intuition told me Dr. Wolf had bad news for us. I wanted her to leave again and never come back.

She pulled up the fMRI images on the computer screen and asked us to come look at the screen. Marcus was lying next to us resting. Then she started talking as if she were delivering a lecture to a crowd of medical students.

"Look at the MRI images here. We now see global damages on his scan. We don't get a clear picture of the parts of the brain that control functions like language, movement, cognitive skills, and so forth. We don't see any brain activity in those areas."

Chapter Fifteen

She pointed out the areas on the computer screen with a pen. I was trying to make sense of what she was telling us, but I couldn't.

"In the middle of the brain where the white matter is supposed to show activity, Marcus's white matter is completely gone or reduced. Compared to his last MRI, even areas on the outermost part of his brain have shrunk," she concluded, unaffected by what she just told us.

Everything went black; I couldn't see and almost fainted. I sank down on a chair. My husband couldn't keep himself together, either. We were speechless, but Dr. Wolf continued talking. I wanted to scream, "Stop it, stop it!" I didn't want to hear any details. No scale big enough could measure the pain I felt.

"These damages are irreversible brain damages. Marcus will have very limited chances for recovery. He may be able to stand and walk after years of training. Talking—most likely not. Making progress will not take months. We're talking about years."

Marcus's life was annihilated. I felt emotionally bankrupt. In that moment, there was nothing left to feel, nothing left to say, nothing left but complete blackness that descended on me.

I didn't know which challenge was the worst: the brain damage or the leukemia. Either condition was the most horrible condition to battle in itself. Add the two of them together, and the mission seemed impossible. How was Marcus ever going to survive this? All hope seemed to vanish.

Despite the change of prognosis, our overall goal for Marcus was for him to improve, to become more conscious, and to continue his rehab efforts. Marcus remained himself. The fMRI results didn't change Marcus. Indeed, the medical evidence changed his long-term prognosis, but it was up to Marcus and us to defy the neurological prognosis. We chose to work with the reality rather than fighting it. There was no time to fall too deep into the valley, but again we needed time to process the news. I cried a lot. Crying is a cathartic release, and it just happened. Crying it out was healthy for me.

The doctors and staff at HealthBridge were incredibly supportive during this phase of shock and grief. Their commitment to keep working hard for Marcus was evident. We also got strength and love from our family and friends in Houston who were there to help us and visit Marcus. When they arrived to visit Marcus, me, or my husband at HealthBridge, their presence spread positive energy in Marcus's room, giving us strength to keep fighting for our son.

I never lost faith in him. Despite the odds, I knew he could accomplish everything in life and I wanted to help him all the way until he reached his goals. Not one second did I consider giving up on him. My love for him was too strong. He was my son, and I truly believed that when it comes to healing, love is more powerful than anything else in life. Gradually, I became more committed than ever before to fight for my son. It took courage. The power of courage can be beautiful. I knew we could get through this regardless of how long and fearful the journey was.

The other issue was Marcus's tone that had become increasingly severe. He developed what doctors call *dystonia*. Dystonia is a neurological movement disorder syndrome in which sustained or repetitive muscle contractions result in twisting and repetitive movements or abnormal fixed postures. The condition is very painful. Dr. Toomey had to medicate Marcus to better control his pain, but the side effect of the dystonia medicine was that he became more relaxed and sleepy, making rehab routines impossible. When Marcus got relaxing medicine, he was less likely to be able to breathe by himself. It was a vicious cycle. Marcus needed to recover quickly to be able to continue his chemotherapy treatment. In terms of his cancer treatment, he was already undertreated. As time passed without him receiving proper chemotherapy, the likelihood of a leukemia relapse increased. On the other hand, the stronger Marcus got, the more likely the oncologists were to consider giving Marcus a more effective treatment for his leukemia. Maybe ultimately, they would consider Marcus for the lifesaving bone marrow transplant he needed from Lucas.

CHAPTER SIXTEEN

Choosing to Celebrate

Over the next couple of weeks in October and November, I worked intensively with a stimulation program for Marcus. I tried to keep him awake and make him do small exercises, and continued stretching him. I would bring big and small balls and cheer him on to try to hold one and let go of it. It was too difficult for him. Therefore, I would try to have him push the ball instead, and if he did so, I would hug and kiss him and show him what a great job he did. I would bring different flavors for him to smell such as cinnamon, chocolate, and lemon. I had to awaken his brain and make it rewire to remember all he had learned in his life before he got sick.

Some days, Marcus and I would throw a party in his room. I closed his door, put on loud music, and danced with Marcus, holding his hands while he was sitting in his chair. Marcus smiled. He loved it.

Then a nurse would enter his room.

"Marcus, did you just throw a party? Why was I not invited?" the nurse asked him, and immediately Marcus started smiling.

Those moments were unforgettable. They seemed to be little things, but I realized they were actually big things. What we had was life, love, and laughter—three important Ls. With Marcus, I aimed high and never set the bar too low.

Marcus deserved to have some fun and quality of life. I wanted him to feel some pleasure. He worked so hard to get better. I didn't believe it was wrong to feel happiness in times of sadness.

His days and nights were filled with medicine, noise, medical equipment, and endless treatments. He wasn't even at home with Lucas, my husband,

Chapter Sixteen

and me. The Reiki healing gave him tremendous pleasure and relaxation. He continued to receive two weekly healing sessions as he had since becoming comatose. Zee would come anywhere to work with Marcus. She would do anything for him.

Marcus's journey toward recovery consisted of many difficult parts. The hardest was to keep up hope that the situation was temporary. I could see it was temporary because Marcus changed. I knew doctors were no gods. Despite their pessimistic prognosis, I chose not to believe them. They didn't know Marcus. I chose to be stronger than the leukemia, stronger than any neurological condition. I looked only at Marcus and I chose to see his full potential. If something looks difficult, it doesn't mean it's impossible.

Some days I felt like giving up. I wished to get my old life back, to take a break, to go to work, but I couldn't. I had to be there for Marcus and my family. Being a mother is a lifelong commitment.

One of my overall goals was to reduce the long list of medications Marcus was still getting. I had Dr. Toomey review Marcus's medication list many times with the goal to eliminate anything he didn't need anymore. I discovered that it's much easier for a doctor to start a new medicine than to cease the medicine.

Ever since Marcus was in a coma at TCH, every day the nurse would give him an injection with a drug called Lovenox. Lovenox is a blood-thinning drug. In Marcus's case, it was used to prevent blood clots in his leg veins because he was on bed rest. The drug had to be given by injection, and every time Marcus got the injection, it hurt him. After Marcus became more active with his therapy and did chair time more frequently, I kept raising questions about Lovenox. Did he really need that medicine?

After endless discussions with Dr. Toomey about ceasing the Lovenox, I persuaded her to cease the Lovenox injection, and Marcus did fine. He never developed any blood clots. The medical team started to respect me and listen to me, and gradually I became more proactive.

In the fall, Katie, the child life specialist at HealthBridge, organized a fall festival outside for the patients and their families. I wanted Marcus to participate. He hadn't been outside for about four months. At first, the respiratory therapists said Marcus couldn't go outside because he was vent dependent and needed an oxygen tank. I didn't agree with them. Marcus's wheelchair contained space for all his equipment. He would be fine, I insisted. In addition, the personnel would be there if Marcus needed help. Marcus's respiratory therapist, Mary, gave in, found an oxygen tank, and prepared his vent equipment, so I was able to take Marcus outside for the festival. There were music, stalls with games, food, and gifts, and many children. It was a sunny day, and I had brought Marcus's cap for him.

When I came outside with Marcus, one of his nurses came over to us to talk. The nurse took off his Ray-Ban sunglasses. "Here, Marcus, you should wear my sunglasses to protect your eyes." He handed them to me. "You haven't been outside for a long time, and the sun is very bright today."

I put the sunglasses on Marcus. He looked way too cool with those expensive Ray-Ban sunglasses on.

"Are you sure it's okay for Marcus to borrow them?" I asked. "They're very expensive."

"Of course, no problem," the nurse replied.

It was a great idea. What a gesture from that nurse. How caring of him.

Deep inside me, I felt truly happy. There's a reason behind the saying that happiness is the best makeup. I did not need any makeup that day.

Marcus continued to gain weight, but he also started to vomit more. The doctors believed it was due to the chemotherapy treatment. His tone increased to a degree that was painful and interfered with his physical therapy. There were days when Marcus's muscles were so tight it was impossible for the physical therapists to train with him. He couldn't even bend his arms and legs. He was in pain and had to have increased doses of pain medicine to make him relax. Dr. Toomey explained Marcus was maxed out on his tone medicine.

On Halloween Day, my oldest brother Alexander and his wife Berit arrived from Denmark. When they came to see Marcus at HealthBridge, Marcus had a good day. He was awake and seemed responsive. He smiled as he saw Alexander and Berit. I guessed he recognized them.

I taught them all about Marcus's routines and medical equipment, but they already knew a lot about Marcus, his needs, and the names of most of the staff at HealthBridge from reading Marcus's online Danish diary.

Like Christopher and Susanne, Alexander and Berit were well received by all the staff. The communication was open, and there was a mutual understanding about how to take care of Marcus. It was a challenge for them to see a new and very helpless Marcus for the first time since he got brain damage. When Marcus was at home during induction, he was writing emails back and forth to his uncle Alexander, Grandma, and Grandpa. Then suddenly Marcus got silent. His flow of hopeful and innocent emails stopped.

At the beginning of November, Marcus made more progress. The neuropsychologist, Dr. Davis, tested Marcus frequently and she noticed that on a good day, he was able to focus more on objects, but he couldn't track them. Overall, she noted that Marcus had made "great improvements." His breathing got more independent. Marcus had increasing moments when he showed signs of awareness and responsiveness. He tolerated sitting in his chair for over three hours.

I would bring Lucas over to visit as much as possible, especially during the weekends. Lucas read to Marcus during Marcus's chair time. Occasionally, Lucas could not resist jumping into Marcus's bed during chair time.

"Look, Mommy, I'm Marcus in bed," Lucas said, covering himself with Marcus's blankets and stuffed animals while pretending to sleep like Marcus did.

Lucas would also pretend to be a doctor who examined Marcus's stuffed animals. One day, Lucas brought his own stuffed animal, the dog Micha, to visit Marcus. Lucas would entertain Marcus and let Marcus feel Micha on his chin. It was lovely to witness. When Lucas got a new soccer ball, he would bring it over to show Marcus and tell him that they were going to play with it when he became well. In many ways, we saw the importance of engaging Lucas in Marcus's care and daily life at HealthBridge. We would allow Lucas to push Marcus in his wheelchair when we made a little field trip with Marcus around HealthBridge's premises. Lucas felt proud to be Marcus's helper, and I'm sure Marcus loved the attention he got from his little brother.

Child life specialist Katie told me it was important to involve Lucas in Marcus's care and to make sure Lucas spent time with his brother. Katie also worked with Lucas sometimes when he came by to visit. That way, she could assist Lucas if he had some questions he wanted to talk to her about or if he had any worries. Katie would also take Lucas to the playroom to play with some of the other patients.

On one occasion, Katie and Lucas came into Marcus's room with some small toy race cars. "Katie and I are going to race with these race cars," Lucas explained to Marcus, and then he picked some race cars for him and some for Katie. "Marcus, you're going to be the referee. You have to pay attention so you can see who wins the race."

Marcus was now facing Lucas and Katie sitting on the floor so he could watch the race.

The race started. Lucas and Katie pushed their race cars at the same time. "I won, I won!" Lucas yelled, pumping his fists into the air.

"I think he agrees that Lucas won, right, Marcus?" I looked at Marcus, who was still awake. Even with limited space available in Marcus's room and by involving him as a referee, we all had fun. Marcus's room was full of laughter.

When Marcus received letters and drawings from his classmates at the Village School, I would read them aloud to him. He made sounds and moved his mouth as if he wanted to say something. One of the letters from a friend read as follows: "Get well soon. Recess is not the same without you, Marcus."

Alexander and Berit spent hours visiting Marcus. According to our schedule, I mainly visited Marcus before noon so I could spend time with Lucas when he got home from school in the afternoon. At that time, Alexander and Berit would be with Marcus reading to him, massaging him, and stimulating him all while being careful not to overdo it. When they left, Jacob would come by after work. He visited Marcus each weekend and usually every day in between work in the morning, during his lunch break, or on his way home from work. Sometimes my husband Skyped with Grandpa and Grandma so they could see Marcus and Marcus could hear their voices and listen to them telling him stories about the family and life in Denmark. The grandparents followed Marcus's online diary closely and knew everything that happened to him. They were excited about Marcus's progress, and so were we.

Things went more smoothly when Marcus's favorite nurses and respiratory therapists took care of him. His favorite nurses were José and Mercy, and his favorite respiratory therapists were Mary and Rita. They had taken care of Marcus since he was admitted to HealthBridge in September. We had a very good open dialogue with them. The challenges were still many.

Chapter Sixteen

His vomiting continued to be a problem along with the tone and storming. Marcus sometimes had rocky nights; sometimes he had good nights where he was able to get longer periods of uninterrupted sleep. Unpredictability came with the territory when dealing with Marcus.

On November 27, it was the first Thanksgiving after Marcus got sick. When we arrived for the Thanksgiving lunch at HealthBridge, Dr. Baleva greeted us. She told us that she had heard Marcus calling "Mum, Mum" all morning and didn't stop until a nurse came into his room and fixed something. Then he stopped calling. It was the first time Marcus had said anything remotely close to "Mom." What a beautiful and lovely Thanksgiving present he just gave me, not to mention a feeling of hope that lasted long after I left HealthBridge that day. At the same time, I regretted I wasn't there to hear him call my name. What a treasurable moment it would have been. I rushed to his room and kissed him.

Dr. Baleva concluded that Marcus ought to start using a speaking valve on his trach so he could learn to talk again. I wished the doctors could control the tone issues in a better manner. If that was the case, Marcus wouldn't need all the strong and sedating medicine, his breathing would improve, and ultimately, he could learn to talk again. Then he could practice saying "Mom" as much as he wanted.

The little things in life truly do matter, and we sometimes underestimate their influence. After this event, I realized that the smallest things can also take up the most room in your heart.

Be thankful you're here because you don't know when you will go. Be thankful when you get something because you don't know when you will lose it. Be thankful when you get something even if you didn't choose it. Be thankful for who you are. Be thankful you have what you have and not what you want. Be thankful for what you don't have that you don't want. Be thankful that you can thank others.

CHAPTER SEVENTEEN

Downturn

On Saturday, November 29, when I arrived to visit Marcus, José told me that Marcus had vomited five times and that his heart rate and blood pressure were too high. Dr. Baleva believed that there was pressure on Marcus's brain and had ordered for Marcus to go to TCH PICU for follow-up.

Jacob went with Marcus to TCH by ambulance. Luckily, from the CT scan, the doctors couldn't see any indication that Marcus had pressure on his brain, so they concluded his tone issues were related to his global brain damage. They did, however, find two new respiratory bacteria and one RSV virus from the tests they had run. His chemotherapy was placed on hold due to his infections and low white blood count. On top of those issues, he trembled a lot, ground his teeth, and stiffened his body, causing him to sweat and become uncomfortable. For sure, Marcus represented a challenge to all doctors. How could we ensure he had no pain and was alert at the same time while preventing the leukemia from coming back? This task seemed unsolvable.

The doctors were on new territory. Nevertheless, we felt the pain Marcus felt when he was awake and the tone kicked in. It was horrible. He would make sounds like a puppy crying. We all wanted to help him but couldn't identify any easy solution, any path not yet tried. Was it unethical to keep Marcus alive?

After Marcus became comatose, my husband and I had decided to sleep at home instead of at the hospital. The health personnel advised us to do so because it drained us to stay overnight at the hospital night after night. Also, we had a responsibility toward Lucas to maintain some sort of family life regardless of his brother staying in the hospital long term.

Every night at bedtime, I called TCH or HealthBridge to get an update about Marcus and to ask the night nurse to say "good night to Marcus from Mommy." Sometimes I got through to the nurse easily. Other nights, it was difficult to get through because the line was disconnected or transferred to the wrong nurse; sometimes, the nurse was with a different patient or was busy with Marcus. It could take me between five minutes to one hour to "say good night" to Marcus over the phone, but I always called him.

It was difficult to juggle between the hospital life and the normal life at home where Lucas needed us for homework, sports commitments, and playdates. I had limited my social activities because I had no energy to hang out with friends. If I decided to do something fun, I would do it with Lucas. We rarely did something together—just Lucas, my husband, and me—because one always had to stay with Marcus. Lucas's friend Ross and his parents Alison and Ken were wonderful friends. On the weekends, when they planned to take their son Ross on a trip, they always called us to ask if Lucas wanted to go with them. Lucas always said yes. It made him so happy to get a reprieve on the weekends from the hospital or at HealthBridge. Ross became like a brother to Lucas, and they have remained close friends ever since. Alison and Ken truly cared about Lucas and us. We were so grateful for their help and could always count on them.

When I wasn't with Marcus, I felt guilty, and when I wasn't with Lucas, I felt guilty. When talking to child life experts and counselors, they all said it paid off to get out of town or spend time with Lucas or other people. It recharged my mental batteries to take a break from Marcus and all the doctor talk and worries that inevitably came along when dealing with him. They were right. I did feel more energized when returning from such an uplifting break.

Throughout December, Marcus's tone problems remained unsolved and he had a recurring fever. The doctors couldn't determine if the fever was related to one or multiple infections, storming issues, or extreme discomfort due to dystonia. If he had a fever, the common procedure was to obtain a blood sample and a sample from Marcus's trach for testing. If the samples came back positive for a virus or bacteria, the doctors could then start antibiotics treatment or some kind of antiviral therapy. With repeated rounds of antibiotics, Marcus's digestive system took a hit and diarrhea was a common outcome.

Alyssa, Marcus and Lucas's child life expert at TCH, often came to visit Marcus. One time, she suggested getting an audiobook for Marcus to listen to while resting in bed. She went to the TCH library and returned with a CD collection.

"Look, Marcus," she said one afternoon. "I got you a *Harry Potter* audiobook collection. Your mom told me you love the *Harry Potter* books." She smiled softly at Marcus, holding up the CD.

She put on the audiobook, and immediately it seemed like Marcus started listening to the story, the tone, and the adventures of Harry Potter and his friends. From that time onward, we introduced more and more audiobooks to him. If he was all worked up from tone, we played calming classical music to him. On the other hand, if he was comfortable and in a good mood, we played pop music or other favorite music pieces he loved. I had researched and studied the benefits of music therapy and was a great believer of its healing aspects.

Despite the setbacks Marcus encountered on his journey toward recovery, we remained strong and determined to keep pushing the doctors to find new solutions to manage his dystonia. The dystonia would only be present when Marcus was awake. Once he was asleep, his brain went into sleep mode, his body relaxed, and the tone would be absent.

On December 10, Marcus got his first dose of Tetrabenazine, a newly developed medicine that was supposed to help manage Marcus's tone much better. Along with a big group of other doctors, Dr. Wolf arrived to assess Marcus and talk about the new drug.

She stood in a stoic manner, her shoulders pushed back and her followers behind her listening carefully. She had gathered information about Tetrabenazine and anticipated it would work well for Marcus.

"I want to give Marcus two doses of Tetrabenazine daily if he's not completely knocked out from his first dose," Dr. Wolf said, exuding calmness and focus.

"How long does Tetrabenazine take to kick in?" I asked her, trusting this drug would be a breakthrough in the management of his dystonia and that it would show immediate effect.

"It can take up to two to three weeks to see the full effect," Dr. Wolf explained with an emotionless attitude.

This was not good enough.

"Two to three weeks? That's a long time to wait for Marcus." I breathed a sigh of frustration, looking around in confusion. Was this the best solution she could offer? She was trying to help Marcus, I got that, but why couldn't she understand how miserable Marcus was? It was as if she had all the time in the world, too much unjustified patience. In addition, I had a hard time figuring out how Marcus was feeling and how he experienced episodes of storming and seizures. Were they harmful? What happened inside his brain? I wanted her to clarify if Marcus was suffering; I wanted her to assure me it wasn't as bad as it looked.

"What's the difference between storming and seizures?" I looked at Dr. Wolf.

"Storming isn't harmful to the brain. Seizures are harmful because they destroy neurons in the brain," she replied. I stopped to pay attention as she educated me about the brain and its complexities.

I asked her about the extent of Marcus's brain damage. She told me his brain damage was equivalent to the damage a child will get after being deprived of oxygen for ten minutes. It was so sad to hear her talk about how devastating the brain damage was. It was even more incomprehensible that the Nelarabine drug had caused such tremendous brain damage.

Initially, Marcus responded well to Tetrabenazine, but he was absent and sedated. It was a price worth paying to offer him some relief. We had no other choice than to sedate him. Keeping him suffering was wrong.

CHAPTER EIGHTEEN

Christmas

On December 17, Marcus's immune system was so strong that the oncologists deemed it was time to restart his chemotherapy. His vomiting had stopped when he got a break from the chemotherapy. Now we had to see if Marcus was able to tolerate the chemotherapy without vomiting. At the same time, the neurologist team followed Marcus's response to Tetrabenazine. So far, it had some effect but not the complete effect as expected. Therefore, the neurology team strongly believed it was appropriate to come up with a plan B in case Marcus needed more pain relief. They had asked Dr. Curry, a neurosurgeon, to discuss with us if an intrathecal Baclofen pump (ITB) could help Marcus. An ITB consists of delivering a liquid form of Baclofen into the spinal fluid, using a device called a Baclofen pump.

The benefit of the Baclofen pump was that it could deliver Baclofen (pain medicine) directly into Marcus's spinal fluid. It was made of a catheter (a small, flexible tube) and a pump. The pump stored and released the right amount of medicine through the catheter. A tiny motor moved the medication from the pump through the catheter. Marcus's treatment team could use a small computer outside his body to send messages to the pump and make adjustments in the dose, rate, and timing of the medication.

We all had a longing desire to see a profound change in Marcus's condition. I dared not believe any new doctor could help him anymore. There had been so many letdowns along the road already.

I had just made a cup of tea in the caregiver kitchen at TCH. I returned to Marcus's room and looked forward to enjoying it while waiting for Dr. Curry to arrive for the consultation.

Chapter Eighteen

I thoroughly wanted this meeting to go well. The success of the consultation depended on how well Dr. Curry and I communicated with each other. It was critical for me to establish a strong relationship and contact with Dr. Curry. That way, chances were higher that I would make him understand the hardship Marcus was going through. Not even in my wildest dreams did I expect the meeting would go as well as it did.

Dr. Curry entered the room and greeted me warmly. A traditional white knee-length overcoat covered parts of a blue shirt and fashionable tie. His full beard was neatly groomed, he listened actively to my concerns, and his replies indicated a very full understanding of the severity of Marcus's situation. His personality was hugely likable. Dr. Curry's clinical interests included treatment of pediatric movement disorders and chronic pain, and his research interests encompassed the mechanisms of dystonia. He was a complete match for the medical challenges Marcus presented.

"I believe Marcus would benefit from a Baclofen pump," Dr. Curry said. He approached Marcus, who was sitting in his wheelchair, then gently examined his resistance in his arms and legs. He squeezed his hand and carefully let go of it. "Marcus's brain damage is complex, and he should have better pain management support."

The compassion in his voice and the depths of his observations surprised me.

"What do you think about Marcus's tone level after he started Tetrabenazine?" I asked Dr. Curry, who at that point had followed Marcus for some time.

"We absolutely need to get Marcus's tone under control. If we don't, Marcus will get permanent injuries on his ligaments and bones and will suffer from pain in his muscles. To Marcus, it feels like he's constantly working out in a fitness center. That's why he's sweating so much. If his muscles remain tight, they will prevent him from growing." A worried expression stretched across his face.

I felt like crying when listening to him tell me how severe Marcus's tone was. I had no idea how harmful spasticity was. We didn't know how much pain Marcus had—he couldn't tell us. Only his body language and numbers on his monitors could help guide us.

In the midst of the ethical dilemmas we faced, my husband and I had to do our best to get into the Christmas spirit. We had to do it for Lucas's sake and for our family's sake. Christmas was such a contrast to Marcus's situation. It didn't make sense to celebrate Christmas under such terrible conditions for Marcus in December 2014. Our first Thanksgiving after Marcus got sick was not that enjoyable and, in December, Marcus was even worse. He couldn't enjoy Christmas with our family at home eating the traditional Danish Christmas dinner on December 24 in the evening. He couldn't open his presents with eagerness and shout for joy or scream aloud when he got a toy he had wished for for so long. He was trapped inside his physical body. He had red marks and bruises on his elbows and feet from the constant involuntary movements. His diaper area was also red and the skin so sensitive due to diarrhea rash and his suppressed immune system. Sometimes the nurses had to double-diaper him because the diarrhea was more than one diaper could handle. Inevitably, Marcus got painful diaper rash that needed special care. The wound team worked hard on wound prevention so he wouldn't get any deep skin breakdown or pressure sores on his elbows or feet. They put thick patches on the delicate skin areas on his elbows and heels to protect his skin. They reassessed, came with a new miracle ointment for his diaper rash, and followed up very closely until the skin issues had disappeared. He got first-class treatment.

Mid-December, my husband's younger brother Thomas, his wife Laila, and their two sons Bjarke and Niklas arrived in Houston to celebrate Christmas with us. It was lovely that they decided to come all the way over from Denmark to visit us and support us during the first Christmas without Marcus at home. Lucas and his cousins could also play and get time to bond.

I enjoyed when we had friends coming to visit Marcus and us at TCH. My work colleagues came to see Marcus and me, and other friends who lived closer by TCH came to visit. A dear friend, Alexandra, came with a jar full of homemade Danish Christmas cookies. I showed the present to Marcus.

"Look, Marcus! Look at what Alexandra made for us. Try and smell. Can you smell the cinnamon?" I let Marcus smell the cookies. He didn't attempt to sniff but sat quietly and allowed the aroma of the cinnamon to enter his nostrils.

Alexandra also carried some fresh pine branches that smelled wonderful, just like Christmas.

Chapter Eighteen

"Smell these pine branches, Marcus," I told him while letting Marcus feel and smell the pine branches.

I showed Marcus and Alexandra a video I had made of Lucas's Christmas sing-along show at the Village School. Marcus knew all the Christmas songs on the program because he used to sing them every year with his classmates. Marcus should have been there, singing with his friends, waiting for Santa Claus to join the show. It was so unfair and sad, but I couldn't cry even though I felt like crying. It didn't help him or us. Instead, I shared the joy Lucas experienced by showing Marcus the video. At least that way Marcus could get a taste of the atmosphere from the show. It looked like Marcus enjoyed watching the video sequence. That was all that counted.

One afternoon, my friend Erin arrived with a delicious homemade dinner for me to bring back home. Erin and her Danish husband were excellent cooks. They had made a light salad with strawberry vinegar dressing, a lasagna, and homemade lime yogurt and vanilla yogurt—all carefully crafted with love. Another day, she delivered lunch and cakes to us at TCH. The thoughtfulness from our friends in Houston was comforting. They knew Christmas was a difficult time for a family in crisis. When your child is sick and the future is uncertain, the importance of celebrating Christmas diminishes. The only thing in the world that counted for us was for Marcus to get healthy and strong. It was a simple wish, yet nobody knew if it was within reach.

Jacob and his brother Thomas spent hours visiting Marcus, mostly taking turns so only one of them was with Marcus. Thomas's wife and sons were also in Houston, and they mainly spent time with Lucas and me. My husband opened some Christmas presents for Marcus. One present was a Danish children's book from his cousins about the Greek gods. He read Marcus's new book aloud. He put on a CD with Christmas stories for Marcus. He did anything for Marcus. He loved him without bounds.

I'm positive Marcus felt our presence when family or friends were with him. At one point, when Marcus was sleeping, Thomas had seen Marcus smiling with his eyes closed as if he were dreaming or thinking about something funny. It was priceless to see Marcus's precious smile. He was still there. He had a right to live, to be loved, and to be respected regardless of his medical status.

On December 23, during another family meeting at TCH, all the doctors recommended that Marcus get the intrathecal Baclofen pump. The oncologists, supported by us, decided to hold the chemotherapy again to give Marcus the most favorable conditions to recover from the Baclofen pump surgery. We were grateful that Dr. Curry had assessed Marcus and believed the Baclofen pump was the right decision for Marcus. We had run out of other alternatives.

Over the holidays, Jacob, Thomas, and I took turns visiting Marcus. We read books to him, played holiday music, and arranged Skype sessions with the family in Denmark. It was important that Lucas had the opportunity to spend time with his cousins, and Laila, at home. With them living in Denmark, he rarely saw them.

Along with my husband's family who had come from Denmark, on December 24 in the evening, we celebrated Christmas at home eating a traditional homemade Danish Christmas dinner followed by the exchange of gifts. It was joyful, except Marcus was missing. Christmas wasn't the same as it used to be.

On December 27, I came to see Marcus, bringing him extra Christmas gifts such as clothes, audiobooks, and books. He had a new light-green shirt on he just received for Christmas. It fit him nicely, and he looked so handsome. I prepared to Skype with my Danish girlfriend Maja, who was based in Mexico City. Even though Marcus was a bit drowsy when I called Maja, he woke up and showed interest in my Skype session with her.

"Hi, Marcus! You look great!" Maja said, beaming with excitement as she saw Marcus in the video.

I showed Marcus the screen so he could see Maja. She smiled at him.

"I love your new shirt," Maja said, full of energy.

Over the years, Maja and I had made plans to visit each other with our families. I had invited her and her daughter to come visit us in Houston, and Jacob, the boys, and I were supposed to make a weekend trip to Mexico City. As it happens so often regrettably, none of our plans was carried out.

Skype is indeed a good invention and allowed us to stay in touch through inexpensive means. Maja and I chatted, we laughed, and we included Marcus in our chitchat. He smiled, endlessly charming Maja.

"It's getting late. Marcus, let's wish Maja a merry Christmas."

Chapter Eighteen

After my Skype session with Maja, I Skyped with Alexander and Berit in Denmark. Marcus was still going strong. He was awake and again interested in the Skype session with them. Later, on my phone, I showed Marcus a picture of Lucas standing on the deck of the USS *Texas BB-35* battleship. On the battleship, Lucas played with a big gun on the ship pretending to be shooting. Marcus smiled when I showed him the picture.

The last days of December passed with Marcus suffering from occasional storming incidents leading to sweating, pain, high heart rate, fever, and high blood pressure. As for the continual vomiting, it was probably connected to the chemotherapy treatment, but the storming could also factor in. We had tried to put on a fan to cool him down, but we discovered the best remedy was to put on his splints. The splints would prevent his muscles from cramping up so forcefully. Unfortunately, with changing shifts, new nurses were on duty and were not aware that the splints were important to apply. It was holiday season, and many of Marcus's familiar nurses were off. We witnessed firsthand the consequences when substitute nurses who were new to Marcus took care of him. Again, this emphasized how important it was for us to advocate for Marcus every day, always, and to be by his bedside. Only that way could we make an impact on his care. We were Marcus's personal medical police officers and always on duty. On December 30, Dr. Curry did Marcus's Baclofen pump surgery. The operation was successful, and Marcus did well. The following day, a nurse practitioner gave me a lecture about the Baclofen pump. Every time Marcus needed a refill of Baclofen, I had to bring Marcus to the hospital. If the pump ran dry, it was broken.

Marcus was quickly more comfortable and relaxed. This was what he needed. He was ready for a new year, a new beginning. Once again, he was on his way to recovery.

CHAPTER NINETEEN

A New Year

It was a new day, a new year, a new beginning. Despite what the doctors had told us, Marcus had surprised all of them. He was still in remission with no signs of the leukemia coming back. His body had recovered, but his brain damage had showed us its ugly side. Yet again, with Marcus's new Baclofen pump in place, the PCU team was getting ready to transfer Marcus back to HealthBridge to continue his rehab program.

On January 9, Marcus moved to HealthBridge for the third time. Marcus's nurse José and all the personnel welcomed him back. I truly hoped that the next time Marcus would leave HealthBridge, it would be to move home to us where he belonged with his family.

On Saturday, January 10, Lucas came to HealthBridge to see Marcus. Lucas had missed him. As he saw Marcus in his bed, he jumped in to be close to his brother. Lucas wanted to show him his new FIFA 15 game on his Nintendo 3DS. FIFA 15 was a soccer game Marcus used to play on his 3DS before he got sick. Lucas stayed with Marcus in the bed, and the boys watched a movie on the TV. The next day, Lucas brought his Christmas gift for Marcus.

"Look, I have a present for you," Lucas said while bouncing from foot to foot.

Lucas got no reaction from Marcus. Lucas lowered his head, his mouth falling open slightly.

"Marcus seems a bit tired," I said, rubbing Lucas's arm to get his attention. "Can you help open the present for Marcus? I think he would like you to help him."

Chapter Nineteen

Quickly, Lucas opened the gift wrap. He showed Marcus a very cool soccer kit with Ronaldo's name printed on the back.

"This is for you, Marcus," Lucas said while handing over the gift.

Still no reaction from Marcus. Lucas was used to not getting any reaction from Marcus, but it still hurt. Lucas stumbled back a step.

"I think Marcus loves his new gift. He should try wearing the uniform tomorrow. He's going to look so cool," I promised Lucas. "Let's go discuss it with José so he makes sure Marcus wears it tomorrow."

Over the next days and weeks, Marcus recovered slowly from the surgery. On January 13, my Danish cousin Stina arrived in Houston. Again, we got relief from family members. Diligently, I trained her. She spent time with Marcus, stimulated him, read aloud, and talked to him in Danish and played with Lucas at home.

Marcus's lung doctor, Dr. Susarla, was happy with Marcus's breathing progress. Marcus's goal was to one day breathe by himself. It took a lot of work for him, and his brain had to be ready to do the work. Due to Marcus's Baclofen pump surgery, his wound had to heal up first, which prevented him from doing physical therapy for eight weeks; however, Marcus could do light occupational therapy.

He did well throughout January and his tone improved. During the next family meeting at HealthBridge, it became clear that Marcus's doctors believed it was realistic to discharge Marcus from HealthBridge within a couple of months. Because Marcus needed 24/7 nursing care, there were two discharge options: Marcus could move to a facility where he could get nursing care, or he could move home with 24/7 nursing care installed in our house. There was no way we would accept for Marcus to live in a nursing care facility. Jacob and I wanted Marcus home where he belonged so he could take part in our family life. The staff at HealthBridge supported us and promised to help us get all the arrangements in place for a safe return home for Marcus.

Once again, my husband and I had to do forty-eight hours of rooming-in. We had to repeat all the trach training, vent training, feeding training, G-tube care, and CPR we did at TCH. Forty-eight hours of rooming in was four full shifts. Two shifts had to be day shifts and two had to be night shifts. We had some months to complete the training. The staff at HealthBridge were wonderful teachers. I sometimes asked the same questions repeatedly. I would ask José to come into Marcus's room.

"José, why does Marcus's monitor not read his heart rate, pulse, and O2 saturation?" I pointed to Marcus's alarm that beeped on his screen. "His meter reader on his finger keeps falling off so the monitors don't get any reading."

"Let me check it." José went over to Marcus's index finger to check the meter reader. "The tape doesn't stick well enough. Let me get a new one for him."

When he came back, he said, "Let me put it on. I want to make sure the new one works." He carefully attached the reader with tape on Marcus's thumb in an effort to get a good and steady reading.

We both looked at Marcus's monitor. The numbers came back on the screen and the alarm stopped beeping.

"You fixed it, José. Thanks a lot," I said, smiling at him.

José was a professional, caring nurse. When I knew José was on duty, I always relaxed.

One morning when I came to see Marcus on a day when José was Marcus's nurse, José had styled Marcus's hair with gel after giving him his bath. Marcus had such a refreshing look. José had a special bond with Marcus. Now and then, José rolled his computer table over in front of Marcus's room and placed Marcus in his wheelchair by the door facing the common areas. That way, José could talk to Marcus and watch him. The interactions between José and Marcus were phenomenal, and José delivered on the formula every day. Like Marcus, José was passionate about soccer. When dressing Marcus, José usually picked a soccer shirt for him, especially when he knew Lucas would come to visit. Often, Lucas brought a soccer ball with him.

One day inside HealthBridge, Lucas was already dressed in his athletic outfit and dribbled full speed toward Marcus's ward. Decorative artwork was hanging on the walls. The nurses were busy updating patient charts on their computers. A quietness dominated the area. Marcus sat in his wheelchair outside his room.

José, dressed in his blue scrubs and tennis shoes, saw Lucas dribble. He cheered up and laughed, ready for fun. "Pass the ball, Lucas! I'm ready!" José shouted and stepped away from his computer, prepared to receive the ball. The other nurses paused for a minute and watched the action with wonder.

Oh, no, what if Lucas hits the wall with the soccer ball and breaks a painting? I thought. *Or he loses control of the ball and it hits Marcus?* My heartbeat started to race.

"I'm gonna make a hard pass." A formidable kick cannoned off the legs of Lucas. I saw the ball flying in the air with high speed toward José, who mastered trapping the ball with elegance and ease. The ball was under control.

Thank God, I thought.

"Lucas and José, really! Why do you play indoor soccer when you're not allowed to do so?" I yelled while Lucas and José started laughing.

The boys couldn't help playing. Soccer does bring people together. Marcus saw them play too and, honestly, I think he liked watching this risky scene unfold.

José wasn't the only excellent nurse at HealthBridge. I had made a list of our favorite day and night nurses for Marcus. That way, the charging nurse could better accommodate our wishes and assign a nurse to Marcus who knew him. In January, Jacob ran his second Houston Marathon. I drove to downtown to see him cross the finish line while my cousin Stina and Lucas stayed with Marcus. I relieved Stina and Lucas after the marathon.

I rushed to Marcus's room to share the news. Marcus was in bed resting, not fully awake. I leaned toward him and hugged him. Then I whispered to him, "Remember, I told you Daddy was going to run the Houston Marathon today? I saw him finish the race this morning. He was awesome. I'm telling you, he really was, just like you." A happy sigh escaped my lips. "When you get stronger and older, you and Daddy are going to run a marathon together."

Marcus woke up. He gave me a big smile. I felt deeply connected to him.

"I can't run a marathon, but I know you can one day. You and Daddy make a good team." I wasn't afraid to be wrong. The more Marcus progressed, the more I rejected the idea that he was never going to recover.

My love for him and Lucas grew stronger every day. I made sure to communicate this to both of my sons every day. A child cannot hear this too often.

"Soon, you're going to move back home. You're going to get a huge room with plenty of toys for you and Lucas to play with." I tousled his hair. He looked cute.

"Once you feel better, you and Lucas can team up, get on top of Daddy, and tickle him until he starts giggling."

He smiled, almost laughed. It seemed Marcus internalized what I just told him. I hugged and kissed him, promising him he would soon be home.

It was difficult to see my cousin Stina and other family members leave to go back to Denmark. They were deeply attached to Marcus because they spent so much time with him, yet they were worried about him and what the future would bring. Would they see Marcus again?

Saying goodbye to our family members was the price we paid for not living in our home country. It was hard, and it never got easier with time. I cried a lot. Every time, Lucas affectionately said, "It's okay, Mommy. You don't need to cry."

Lucas was growing more confident while visiting Marcus. He liked to go to HealthBridge where the atmosphere was more relaxed than at TCH. One day when we visited Marcus, Lucas challenged nurse Jason to play soccer with him outside on the basketball court. Jason accepted the challenge. The two of them went outside but quickly returned. Jason was breathing hard and was almost sweating as he entered through the door.

"It looks like you got in trouble, Jason," I said. "I've warned you many times that Lucas is a good soccer player."

"Yes, I got in big, big trouble." His cheeks were burning. "Lucas is too good a soccer player, and I'm out of shape." Jason struggled to breathe while all his colleagues laughed at him.

As Lucas returned to Marcus, he was doing chair time and Lucas jumped right into Marcus's bed. He grabbed his weekend reader *Snow* by Dr. Seuss and started reading to Marcus. Marcus was sitting with his eyes closed and smiled as Lucas started to read, using intonation and all his best reading techniques. In the Danish Saturday school, Lucas borrowed Danish books and audio CDs for Marcus. Lucas showed Marcus affection and love. They were still brothers, and neither brain damage nor leukemia could disturb the sibling love they shared for each other.

The Baclofen medicine continued to sedate Marcus along with the other

Chapter Nineteen

relaxing medicines he was taking. He was unable to keep his eyes open, but he was listening because he reacted to the things we told him.

"Do you want to have movie night with Lucas when you get home?" I asked Marcus.

A bright smile formed on his face.

I took that as a yes. Sometimes, he opened his mouth in an effort to talk, but only sounds came out. He often moved his arms or legs in response to a question, but his smile was the best indication of a yes.

By the end of January, Marcus could breathe completely by himself for over one hour without vent support but with minimal supplemental oxygen. The lung doctor had evaluated his performance. He assessed that Marcus could soon try a speaking valve.

Marcus moved his lips and tongue when he was alert. Dr. Davis, the neuropsychologist, and Dr. Toomey had asked me to try to make Marcus interested in tasting different things he liked. I brought Nutella for him. I dipped a stick with a sponge in some Nutella and touched it onto his lips. Slowly, I asked Marcus to stick his tongue out to touch the Nutella. It was hard for Marcus. He couldn't control his tongue, but he managed to touch a bit of the Nutella with the tip of it. He liked the taste. His mouth was filled with saliva and Nutella, and soon the mixture started to drip out from both sides of his mouth. He tried to swallow a few times, but that, too, was difficult. I cleaned his mouth and hugged him for trying so hard to taste the Nutella. The next time, I brought Coke. He hadn't tasted *anything* since June the year before. The pleasure of eating something we absolutely love is indescribable. But Marcus did not have that pleasure. He still couldn't eat and received all nutrition through a G-tube in his stomach.

On February 1, Marcus had his first soccer practice. Recent test results showed the pseudomonas bacteria was still colonized in his trach, and the infectious disease doctors had not given clearance for him to move around outside his room at HealthBridge. Lucas packed his Brazilian World Cup soccer ball in his bag and dumped it in Marcus's room.

"If Marcus can't go outside to play, let's make a soccer field in Marcus's room! Help me, Mommy." Lucas tugged on my arm, urging me to get started.

"Okay, let's move the bed and things around," I said while helping Lucas to create a small soccer field. I opened the blinds to allow light to enter the room.

I put Marcus's foot splints on. His foot splints had a soccer design on them. Marcus was leaning back in his wheelchair. He still couldn't sit in a ninety-degree angle because his Baclofen pump wound needed more time to heal. I removed the footrests on the wheelchair so his feet were hanging down freely.

"Marcus is ready to play now," I said.

Lucas kicked the ball softly in the direction of Marcus's feet. Marcus tried to kick with his feet. He hit the ball gently. It came back to Lucas.

"Marcus, you are doing so good. You can hit the ball!" Lucas screamed with joy. "Mommy, you need to be the referee sitting in the ref chair." He pointed to the recliner in Marcus's room.

"Okay, I will be the ref." I plopped down in the chair.

Laughter filled the room, and the sun shone straight through the window. Marcus, still stiff in his body, had slid down his chair. Small pearls of sweat started to form on his forehead.

"It's halftime now," Lucas said after a few minutes of playing.

I gave the boys a lollipop. I helped hold it for Marcus. With much difficulty, he licked it a bit.

"Halftime is over!" I shouted, and the boys started playing while I fetched the staff so they could see Marcus practice with Lucas. I put pop music on. What a party! Then Marcus got tired and had to go back to bed to rest. It was Super Bowl night, and we wanted to get home in time to watch it live on TV with Jacob and his brother Søren, who was visiting from Denmark.

"You've trained a lot today, Marcus. I'm so proud of you. You should enjoy some Super Bowl now, and then rest after," I told him as I turned on the TV.

What a lovely day. Such delight to spend time with Marcus and Lucas playing together. Life made so much sense that day.

On February 2, Jacob and I had a very constructive meeting at HealthBridge. The doctors confirmed that Marcus's plan was to transition him back home. His leukemia had not relapsed for seven months. Left untreated, Marcus's risk for a relapse remained considerable. However, it was

Chapter Nineteen

impossible for the oncologists to estimate when the leukemia would return, if it did return.

Dr. Wolf encouraged us to value any progress he made and hoped that some of the neurons in his brain were in shock and not dead. That meant there was a chance some of them could "wake up" and possibly start to refunction.

The goal for his breathing trials was to do twelve hours without vent support or supplemental oxygen. The biggest risk for Marcus's respiratory system was developing pneumonia.

Despite the threat of the leukemia recurring, a new pneumonia sneaking in on him, and the enormous challenges he otherwise faced, I sensed optimism in the air. When it came to Marcus's doctors, they had a tendency to remain pessimistic about his future. Finally, the medical team gave Marcus credit for what he had achieved. They gave us credit for all we had done for him. It was almost like getting the grades after an assessment in school. This was the proof that what we had done for him were the right things. Our work, love, and support for Marcus started to pay off.

The Baclofen pump had helped decrease the tone tremendously. After the involuntary movements and tone had lessened and we had stopped the chemotherapy treatment, Marcus had no more skin issues. His energy level had increased, and his overall quality of life had improved. He had grown, gotten new healthy hair, and now weighed almost sixty-four pounds. While doing his breathing trials, he had an HME placed on top of his trach. An HME functioned as an artificial nose moisturizing the air that passed through the trach to his windpipe. What freedom Marcus must have felt not hearing the noises from his pumping vent and its frequent alarms, not to mention having tubes all connected to him!

When lying down in bed, he tried to lift up his head and body. He started to suck his right thumb like a baby who had just discovered his fingers. If his nose was itchy, he moved his hand to scratch it. He responded and showed interest when he heard sudden noises. He looked at his G-tube when the nurse came with medicine for him. At one point, the nurse directed Marcus's hand and finger on the tip of the syringe. She enabled him to push the top part of the syringe to thereby give himself the medicine through the G-tube.

On February 8, he was breathing by himself for nine hours.

"Marcus is a champion!" his respiratory therapist Mary said with a gleam in her eyes. "He's unaffected when he breathes by himself. He doesn't get stressed. Tomorrow, his trial is going to be ten hours."

Marcus was now cleared to go outside on HealthBridge premises. Lucas and I took him outside in the fresh air and warm sun. The weather was beautiful, and flowers were blooming. Marcus was wearing his sunglasses, his green cotton jacket, and a blanket around his legs. On the big playground, with full steam, Lucas dribbled the ball without looking at it. Suddenly he took off steering toward the winding paths. Pushing Marcus in his wheelchair, I followed behind Lucas. Once back at the playground, the boys played soccer and tried to score on me. Marcus enjoyed being outside. Even if he was resting in his wheelchair, Lucas and I could roll him with us out on the basketball court. This allowed me to play basketball with Lucas while watching Marcus have some family time undisturbed by medical personnel.

On February 9, Marcus's O2 alarm started beeping. He wasn't getting enough oxygen. Rita, Marcus's respiratory therapist, switched him directly over to the ventilator and increased the power. She also added seven liters of supplemental oxygen. Rita called Dr. Nicolls to come and examine Marcus immediately. Upon examining Marcus's lungs, Dr. Nicolls found the reason why he didn't get enough oxygen.

"Marcus's lungs sound a bit collapsed," he explained. "I'm going to order X-rays and blood tests to check for infections. Then I need to consult with Dr. Susarla, the lung doctor."

Søren had left to fly back to his wife and three young daughters in Denmark. We were on our own. I called Jacob and asked him to be with Marcus so I could get back and pick up Lucas from school. Marcus seemed stable and, after a while, my husband decided to leave.

It was 8 P.M. The phone rang, and my heart rose to my throat. Every time the phone rang, chances were a doctor was calling to deliver bad news. That's how it had been since Marcus got sick. With hesitant steps, I walked across the kitchen and grasped the receiver.

It was Dr. Nicolls.

"I'm sorry to disturb you," he said, reluctance evident in his voice. "Dr. Susarla has looked at Marcus's X-rays. It looks like he has pneumonia."

Chapter Nineteen

I didn't understand, as if my brain short-circuited and needed to be rebooted.

"We agree Marcus needs to go to TCH immediately for an evaluation of his lung functions," Dr. Nicolls said. I kept silent. I had heard this too many times. Marcus needed to go to TCH. I couldn't take it anymore.

"What is going on?" I asked. "Marcus just did so well. I thought his lungs were strong."

Dr. Nicolls responded slowly, "I know . . . he did very well . . . but he's very sick now. That's why he needs to go to TCH."

I was on the verge of tears. This could not be happening. He was just getting ready to move back home and then this happened. The prospect of going back to TCH was daunting. I was done with TCH, completely done. Marcus tolerated the transfer to TCH well. After examination at PICU, the doctors concluded Marcus had pneumonia and, immediately after, he started antibiotic treatment. The nurse inserted an IV port in his foot. Once again, he had to have medicine through his vein. Marcus's breathing was so compromised that he needed twelve liters of supplemental oxygen on top of vent support. He developed a fever, vocalized uncontrollably, and had many involuntary movements.

Chaplain James came to see Marcus, as did many other doctors who knew him. Marcus's oncologist, Dr. Rabin, reviewed his labs and examined him. Then she gave me an update.

"I can tell from Marcus's labs that he has an infection and that his immune system is fighting the infection," Dr. Rabin explained.

"Is that a good thing?" I asked.

"Yes, it's good for Marcus. His immune system is doing what it's supposed to do. Apart from the infection in his left lung, I think he looks good. I am very happy to see that," Dr. Rabin concluded.

After she left, I sighed and was thankful. I feared the lab work results, but at the same time, I wished to know what was going on with Marcus. I had a love-hate relationship with the labs. It felt like Dr. Rabin rendered a judgment. Did she see any signs of leukemia? When the labs yielded a good result, it was the best gift I could wish for. The world made sense. Marcus was safe.

As Marcus was feeling better and his temperature went down, he moved to PCU.

After I had picked up his wheelchair from HealthBridge and transported it to TCH, he started to do chair time again. Child life specialist Alyssa came by to visit Marcus. She had just returned from the hospital library where she had found a CD containing Mark Twain's *The Adventures of Tom Sawyer*.

"I have a new audiobook for you," she told Marcus.

He smiled at her as she showed him the audiobook.

"Have you read this book before, Marcus?" Alyssa asked.

"I don't think he's read it yet. It's a good book for you, Marcus," I replied.

Marcus showed more interest in the people entering the room. If the nurse suctioned his trach, he made some irritating sounds to signal he didn't like it. Marcus's personality was showing. His smile was the same. All the visitors noticed that he was able to hold his head and control his upper body much better. Marcus received so much positive feedback.

The next day, everything was the opposite. Marcus had had a rough night. He had vomited and was feeling uneasy. He had many involuntary movements and his blood pressure was too high. He had a wiggly tooth and he had a permanent tooth surfacing in his gum. I tried to massage his gums where I figured the tissue was irritating him. The doctors ordered more Ativan to break the storming and jerking. His whole body was jerking, and his tongue was moving around frantically. He was suffering. We urged the doctors to give him more medicine to calm him down, but it wasn't until later that evening that Marcus calmed down and was able to sleep.

Dr. Curry, the neurosurgeon, came to examine Marcus. Dr. Curry carefully explained that tone masked many involuntary movements. Once the tone was under control, involuntary movements emerged. Dr. Curry assessed that some of Marcus's movements were conscious movement, suggesting that a new layer in his brain had started to refunction. He decided to increase the dosage of Baclofen on Marcus's pump in an attempt to limit Marcus's mouth movements and his thumb-sucking habit.

Dr. Roge, who came from the physical rehabilitation and medicine department, made the point that the tone relapse Marcus had displayed the day before was caused by the pneumonia. Doctors often see tone relapsing during disease. It seemed a plausible explanation why Marcus's behavior had changed. One day, he was doing well. The following day, the tone came back tenfold. Luckily, after a few days of adjustments in his Baclofen dosage and other tone medicines, Marcus was calmer and more comfortable. He tolerated the stretching and exercises I did with him and he restarted his breathing trials.

On Valentine's Day, I picked up Lucas from school. He was in a good mood.

"I have a big Valentine's bag for Marcus," he told me with enthusiasm.

He opened his backpack and pulled out a long string with Valentine's Day cards attached to it. Every student from Marcus's class had made a beautiful Valentine's Day card for him. One boy had created a personal cartoon for Marcus. Another girl had made an amazing drawing. He even got lollipops.

The next time I visited Marcus at TCH, I read each card to him, after which I hung the string with the cards up on the wall so Marcus and everyone who entered his room could enjoy this lovely treasure. This was incredibly sweet of all his friends and the teachers who had helped organize this project.

On February 17, Marcus had recovered considerably from the pneumonia, and the doctors assessed he was ready to transition back to HealthBridge. It was the fourth time Marcus moved to HealthBridge.

"You can go home and get some rest now," José told me. "I have everything under control. I plan for Marcus to do chair time around four today. He needs to sleep first after the long transport."

With this promising turn and based on the concept of an online meal train, I came up with a new idea to make a visitor train for Marcus. The meal train organized by our friends had helped us when Marcus was in critical condition at TCH the year before. I felt that what Marcus needed the most now was company and stimulation in between his scheduled activities.

I had talked to those friends who knew Marcus well and who had expressed a desire to help us rehabilitate Marcus by visiting him at HealthBridge. I decided to create a visitor train by drafting a calendar and putting in the name and times of those friends who had volunteered to come spend time with him. I educated them in Marcus's needs and explained to them how much activity he tolerated. I informed the staff at HealthBridge who was allowed to spend time with Marcus when neither my husband nor I was with Marcus. The purpose was that mainly people who knew him from before he got sick took part in the visitor train. They had freedom to entertain him with worthwhile activities, which could be anything from reading to him, talking to him, or doing therapy such as playing with balls or other sensory games. Marcus's rehab doctor, Dr. Toomey, had stressed the importance of reawaking his memory and past life, and this was only possible through one-on-one work with Marcus. In fact, when I introduced the idea about the visitor train to Dr. Toomey, she loved it and encouraged me to launch it.

One of Marcus's visitor train members was Michele, who was the homeroom mom in Marcus's second-grade class. She read a book from class about the Chinese New Year. She had clementines in her bag and showed them to Marcus. I made clementine juice so he could taste it on his tongue. She amused him with gossip about the class. One of Marcus's friends had got into trouble in class, and she told Marcus the whole story. Marcus had big listening ears and showed great interest in her storytelling. Michele promised him to shoot a video from class and show it to him the next time she came by.

Every day had its own problems. Rarely, we experienced a full day with Marcus without some kind of drama, but we made sure to enjoy the moments we had with him when he was alert. When I figured Marcus was well, I took advantage of the moment. One Saturday, Lucas and I had a party with Marcus. Lucas had borrowed a tic-tac-toe game from the game room. He made two teams. Lucas and Marcus's stuffed animal named Wolf was on one team while Marcus and I were on the other team. We had Coke and chips and listened to music. Marcus was vocalizing loudly that day. He tasted the salt from the chips on his tongue and little sips of Coke. If I told him he needed a break with the chips and cola, he protested by making loud noises. At one point, while Lucas and I played tic-tac-toe in Marcus's bed, Lucas asked Marcus to be quieter. Marcus had become too hyperactive and too loud. The nurses applauded that Marcus was so interactive and they talked to him and asked him questions.

At the end of February, Marcus started to benefit more and more from the visitors who had signed up to be part of his visitor train. All efforts to

Chapter Nineteen

interact with Marcus helped him heal and become more conscious and aware of himself. His body and brain were waking up slowly.

One of the speech and feeding therapists, Caitlin, had started to work with Marcus. She noticed he had tone in his face muscles, and the first step in his speech therapy session was to help loosen up all the small muscles in his face. I had informed Caitlin that I was willing to take part in any training needed so I could work with Marcus independently.

It was extremely inhibiting for Marcus and us not to be able to communicate verbally. I imagined what it would be like if Marcus could talk to me again. I imagined what it would be like if he could say simple words such as "yes" or "no." If he could just call me "Mom" when he missed me or needed me. He didn't cry if he was sad, miserable, or in pain. You had to know him to be able to read him.

I had set up my first appointment with Caitlin and came in early to spend time with Marcus first. I was hoping he would be alert and able to participate in the training program. Caitlin entered the room with a pile of papers.

"I have already told Marcus you were coming," I said, hands clutched together. "What assignments do you have for Marcus and me?"

A competent, methodical therapist, she knew exactly what strategy would benefit him. "I'm going to teach you to use a program called Beckman Oral Motor Interventions." Caitlin pulled out a stack of papers and pointed to the headline on the first page.

"What's that?" Having never heard about any such program, I thumbed my ear.

"I evaluated Marcus the other day when you were not here," she said, her focus on me.

"So due to his brain injuries, Marcus has impaired oral motor skills. I noticed he has a lot of tone in his muscles around his mouth. He needs to develop strength in those muscles." Caitlin observed Marcus, the head of his bed raised to assist him in sitting up.

"I'm going to teach you hands-on techniques for tonic bite. Then you'll be able to practice specific intervention strategies for improving Marcus's facial muscle function."

This sounds difficult. Maybe it wasn't such a good idea for me to get involved in this, I thought.

Caitlin was so knowledgeable about this topic. "That will prepare him for eating and speech later." She handed me the educational sheets.

She explained five different muscle massage techniques and stretches on Marcus's small face muscles. Then I practiced on Marcus while she corrected me and gave me tips on how to improve my techniques. The exercises weren't as difficult to learn as I had anticipated. It took a few weeks to cover the entire program, after which time Caitlin told me I was competent to do the exercises without supervision.

After completion of the Beckman Oral Motor Interventions Program, I had received training in all disciplines in regard to his therapies and care except for Reiki healing training. No need to mention I was not a professional, but at least I had demonstrated enough skill sets and knowledge for the professionals to trust me when taking care of Marcus. It was time for me to use that expertise to my advantage with the ambition to help accelerate Marcus's rehabilitation. He absolutely needed to be stronger so he could get the bone marrow transplant. With his leukemia being aggressive from the onset, the only curative treatment was a bone marrow transplant. Marcus lived on borrowed time. The leukemia could relapse any moment.

CHAPTER TWENTY

Taking Charge

My self-confidence grew as I became more educated. The medical world was no stranger to me. I learned about medicine, nursing care, respiratory care, and all the therapy forms Marcus needed.

As time passed, I became less and less a passive observer of my son's care and more and more authoritative. The medical professionals came to me for advice and listened to me when I explained what I did to Marcus and how he responded to the changes in his care. We never sugarcoated our observations of Marcus. If we had a concern about him, we immediately brought it to the nurses' or doctors' attention. Jacob and I discovered that often we had to be persistent. We had to keep following up when we raised a medical issue with Marcus. My best technique was to pretend I was the president of the United States. I would say, "Marcus needs this or that *now*." If he didn't get what I asked for, I followed up until Marcus got it. I did not take no for an answer. Marcus was a very sick child, and they had to understand that. My husband and I were Marcus's voice.

I analyzed every medical professional taking care of Marcus. What type of person was the staff member? I questioned them to find out how well they knew Marcus and his routines and how interested they were in Marcus's well-being. If they showed no or little engagement in Marcus and his needs, I asked their supervisor not to assign that nurse to Marcus.

With time, it became easier and easier for me to read a person and label the person on either the "okay list" or the "black list." Jacob and I passed on information to each other so we both knew whom to go to for help. We

Chapter Twenty

found out who was professional and who did not live up to our standards at HealthBridge or TCH.

Our mantra was to be polite but insistent. We always demanded that Marcus receive the care he deserved. Always remember the patient is the weak one and that you have to speak up for them. My husband and I experienced that it worked. When Marcus had a top-notch team following him, he did much better and, consequently, we felt better. It was a matter of building up mutual trust and respect between his medical Dream Team and us. The ambiance was not serious all the time. We made sure to laugh.

It made me happy when the doctors talked about Marcus coming home. Jacob and I knew it would be difficult to have Marcus at home, as we had to build a hospital unit for him in our house. In addition, Marcus needed 24/7 nursing care. On the other hand, he would be much more comfortable at home surrounded by family and less noise.

On March 3, Marcus had his next appointment at TCH West Campus. The polite young nurse was able to draw his labs under the guidance of an ultrasound.

Worry had prevented me from eating earlier. I couldn't take my mind off Marcus's labs. Dr. Metha, the oncologist reviewing Marcus's lab that day, entered the exam room, walking with wide steps toward me.

"His labs look good," he said. "There are no signs of leukemia." He handed me a printout of Marcus's labs.

I smiled from ear to ear. An invisible knot was released from my stomach.

"Did you hear that, Marcus? You are doing so well. The leukemia is still gone!" I felt as if the whole world was on my side.

We were all aware that the risk of leukemia relapse was real. Marcus was undertreated, thus increasing the risk for leukemia relapse even more. About two months had passed since he had not received any chemotherapy treatment at all. Yes, Marcus was improving and the leukemia was gone. Would it stay gone?

On the way back from TCH West Campus, Marcus was awake. He and I looked at all the cars passing us on I-10. It was the middle of the day and traffic was light, allowing cars to drive fast on the inviting broad highways.

"Look, there's a cool car, Marcus, the red one," I said while pointing out the car for him. "And another one is coming here. It's going too fast. The driver will get a speeding ticket. Did you see it, Marcus?"

Marcus looked captivated. Spotting fast cars was an activity he liked. I had asked the paramedics to raise the head part of his stretcher so Marcus could sit a bit more upright and thereby see out through the back windows of the ambulance.

Throughout March, Marcus enjoyed different visitors coming by as part of his visitor train. On one occasion, his visitor Frances reported that Marcus had tried to say hi to her when she arrived. Our Danish friends read Danish books to him to keep up his skills.

They read books to him like my husband and I did and told Marcus stories about their own families. Marcus's homeroom mom, Michele, did some math with him so he could feel like he had a math lesson. Sometimes, I told Marcus he had a science class. I found his shark book. I read it aloud and showed him pictures.

Marcus was interested in all things science, including rocks and minerals. Zee had given Lucas a rock and mineral collection he showed Marcus one day at HealthBridge. Both boys were passionate about their interests. Marcus even had a replica of a huge black shark tooth from the prehistoric shark called Megalodon, meaning "big tooth."

In preparation of Marcus's discharge to home, I wanted him to have a dental checkup, dental cleaning, and haircut so he was well-groomed when moving home. A contact of mine was a hairdresser, and she offered to come to HealthBridge to cut his hair. After she had cut his hair, Marcus received many compliments from the staff.

I had fruitful conversations with Dr. Toomey about Marcus's rehab progress. I showed her that Marcus was almost able to keep a pacifier in his mouth just by using his mouth and face muscles. His body awareness had improved.

Before the speech therapist had started working with him and taught me the oral intervention exercises, Marcus had tried to suck a pacifier and keep it in place in his mouth. Unfortunately, the pacifier simply fell out of his mouth and onto the floor. A healthy newborn baby would be able to suck, but Marcus couldn't even do something that simple.

"I can see you're getting better at this," Dr. Toomey said, pulling out the

Chapter Twenty

pacifier, which caused Marcus to make angry noises, gesticulating his arms and leaning forward as if he was attempting to get out of his chair.

Poor Marcus. Why did she do this to him? Now he wasn't able to show her that he could hold on to the pacifier.

"I like that he got agitated," Dr. Toomey explained to me. "It's positive. It means that he responds to what I do to him. I want to see reactions. Keep up the training you're doing. You're doing a terrific job with Marcus."

Those motivating words from her meant the world to me. The encouraging feedback we got from the professionals stimulated my husband and I to keep working with Marcus and spending hours and hours by his bedside.

Even though we had already been checked off for completing training at TCH, my husband and I had to complete the same training once again for Marcus to be discharged to our home. They told us that we couldn't be sure that at home Marcus would always have a nurse; thus, Jacob or I had to monitor Marcus and take care of him. It was a huge responsibility to be Marcus's caretaker because he was trach dependent. However, self-doubt was not an option, and I had to master the job and believe in myself.

Early March, tests revealed Marcus had got on infection called clostridium difficile, or C. diff. In Marcus's case, the bacterium caused severe diarrhea. The doctors had been struggling to get rid of the persistent infection for weeks. Marcus clearly was uncomfortable due to pain and diarrhea, which led to increased tone. Mid-March, a test was negative for C. diff. Finally, Marcus had recovered from the horrible infection.

I was a strong believer that the Reiki energy had a positive effect on Marcus. A Reiki treatment feels like a wonderful glowing radiance that flows through and around you. Reiki treats the whole person—including body, emotions, mind, and spirit—creating many beneficial effects that include relaxation and feelings of peace, security, and well-being. The hospital personnel applauded Marcus's Reiki healing, as it was safe and noninvasive. The healing, combined with endless amounts of love and training, was leading the way for Marcus.

During interactive moments with occupational and physical therapy, I played Marcus's favorite pop music. I stimulated him with smells and different textures to hold in his hand. I asked him to hold small balls, big balls, soft balls, hard balls, and so forth. I even brought his big army toys from home. He had a big-size jet flyer and tank he loved to play with before he got sick. When pushing the buttons, the toys were noisy, making the sounds of guns firing. I helped Marcus push the buttons with his fingers. On his iPad, I helped steer his finger so he could enter his password. I looked up Michael Jackson music videos and soccer videos on YouTube and showed them to him. When I researched to find a new poster for his new soccer room at home, I reviewed all the options on Amazon with Marcus. I found a nice poster featuring his favorite soccer player: Messi.

"Help me order your new Messi poster," I told him while Marcus smiled back at me.

I guided his index finger on the iPad. I lifted his finger and placed it on the ADD TO CART button, and then I checked out for him.

When there were loud noises coming from Marcus's room, I informed the nurses what was going on. One day, I was standing in the doorway trying to get José's attention.

"Hey, just so you know, there's a war going on in Marcus's room. Come and see!"

New patients had arrived in the ward. A child was crying next door. No doubt, José was busy.

"Marcus is firing at the enemy with his jet flyer and tank," I said as I helped Marcus demonstrate how he was playing. This moment was too precious not to share. José sneaked a peek at Marcus.

Here José could contain himself no longer and went on, between gasps of laughter: "This is unbelievable. I love how you play with your toys. Keep going." He ceased all movement for a minute, forgetting to blink.

Then he turned toward me, changing the subject. "By the way, I would like to get a Reiki healing session with Zee one day." He paused.

"I watched Marcus's heart rate the other day on the big monitor when Zee was healing him, and I noticed he got so relaxed—his heart rate even lowered. It was incredible, hard to believe, really." A look of astonishment crossed his face.

"I told you healing works," I said with a firm voice. I knew it did.

Gradually, Marcus's lungs were getting stronger and he only needed 0.5 liters of supplemental oxygen. In his bed, he managed to use his legs and feet to play and roll the big Spider-Man ball from one side to the other side. José

Chapter Twenty

and Mercy witnessed it, and Dr. Nicolls too. Marcus coughed strongly and brought up a lot of mucus.

"If you can cough with such violent force, Marcus, I don't think you need a trach anymore," José joked.

I also showed them how Marcus had started to turn a little bit onto his side. Initially, he needed a soft push and guidance, but he used his muscles to turn. José, Mercy, Dr. Toomey—in fact, all the staff at HealthBridge—praised us for all the work we had done for Marcus. They could see how much he had progressed and how interactive he had become.

It was spring break for Lucas, and he was in a spring soccer camp. Jacob had taken a day off from work to go to the Houston Livestock Show and Rodeo with Lucas. I told Marcus that next year he could come with us and that we'd have a blast together.

I had graduated with the oral intervention protocol Caitlin taught me. I continued to do the rest of my scheduled training to complete my nursing and respiratory classes.

After several good weeks in a row, Marcus's health seemed to decline a bit. He was increasingly tired and lacked energy. He had moments of alertness but slept a lot. The doctors ran some tests and discovered that the C. diff had relapsed. Due to an allergic reaction to the antibiotic, he developed a red skin rash and a low-grade fever. Dr. Nicolls had explained that Marcus's white blood count was a bit lower than usual but still within the normal range. His other lab levels were normal, and Dr. Nicolls was optimistic that Marcus would be discharged in the near future.

"We're planning on a discharge date for Tuesday, April fourteenth. By then, we expect that you and your husband will have completed your forty-eight hours of care-by-parent," Dr. Nicolls reminded me.

"Of course we will. I can easily do my care-by-parent. It's more difficult for my husband. He's very busy at work. He needs to take time off to do the training and his forty-eight hours," I explained. "We'll figure it out. I promise," I told Dr. Nicolls.

On March 27, I did my first twelve-hour block of care-by-parent from 9 A.M. until 9 P.M. I bathed him, applied lotion to his body, and gave him all his medications. I changed him, did G-tube and trach care, and did respiratory treatments.

The diarrhea continued. Within thirty minutes, after he got his milk, I had to change Marcus's diapers four times. His skin in the diaper area was bleeding.

Marcus was heavy and difficult to handle by myself. My back ached. I had to take some painkillers. Then a new visitor train member, Miss Scavo, his second-grade teacher at the Village School, came to visit. Unfortunately, he was too tired to open his eyes. He rested with eyes closed in his wheelchair while Miss Scavo read two of his preferred books to him. She was a nice interruption in the middle of a long, demanding day.

After she left, Marcus coughed violently and vomited a lot of milk. Then with the help of his lift, I got him back into his bed and changed two diapers with diarrhea. It was messy. The diarrhea seeped all over his mattress. I called Dr. Baleva to examine his bleeding diaper rash, as I was getting increasingly concerned about his skin. She concluded he had a yeast infection in his diaper area, which he needed medicine for.

It was a never-ending story. Every time we solved one medical problem, we got two new problems to deal with. I closed my eyes and repeated to myself that we all have choices in life. I chose Marcus. I convinced myself I could do this. I had to suppress the pain, fatigue, and frustration. Times would get better. I hoped.

Around 8 P.M., I got him ready for bed and turned on some healing music, jumped onto the end of his bed, and continued to talk to him softly. He was awake. His feet were cold.

"Would you like a foot massage, honey?" I asked him while grabbing a lightly scented lotion on his nightstand next to the bed. "With Mommy, you get full service, Marcus. When you get better, you can give *me* a foot massage," I whispered to him.

Carefully, I put on some lotion on his cold, stiff feet and started massaging them. The blood circulation in his feet was bad because he couldn't move around and fluid had accumulated in them. He made sounds as if to tell me he liked the foot massage and wanted to say, "Keep going, keep going." Once done with the foot massage, his feet were soft, relaxed, and warm. I'm sure it felt good.

By 9 P.M. that night after finishing all the routines on his care plan, I cuddled him with some light blankets and kissed him good night. The day

Chapter Twenty

had been strenuous. Twelve hours of intense work and care. The reward was the satisfaction that I had made a difference to Marcus. My first care-by-parent at HealthBridge had been successful. The more time I spent with Marcus, the more I bonded with him. Now I missed Lucas. I loved him too. It was time to go home and kiss him good night.

On March 30, Marcus had a Baclofen pump checkup with Dr. Curry at TCH Main Campus. After that, Dr. Rabin wanted to see him for an oncology checkup.

It was a beautiful, pleasant day in Houston. The sun was shining, and Marcus was alert and looking out the windows in the ambulance as we entered downtown. Dr. Curry arrived to see Marcus.

"You look so much better. Your tone is better, but your arms are still tight. I want to increase the Baclofen setting to twenty-six hundred," Dr. Curry told Marcus. "Let me see the wound from the incision in his stomach." Dr. Curry lifted Marcus's T-shirt to take a closer look at the wound. "It looks perfect. I'm very happy with the healing of the incision. Marcus has no more restrictions. He can do all the therapies he wants."

We continued to the oncology floor at the CCC TCH to do the labs. In the examination room, I repeatedly glanced at the clock. Finally, Dr. Rabin arrived. Again, another exam to pass for Marcus. I wished Dr. Rabin had good news to report, but I couldn't count on it. His last couple of lab results had seemed less promising.

"How do his labs look today?" I asked Dr. Rabin.

"His ANC is two-point-eighteen, which is normal, but his platelets and white blood count are on the lower end today. It may be caused by his infection or side effects from his medications," Dr. Rabin explained after she examined him. Then she focused her attention on my sweet boy. "Marcus, you seem fine. I'm sure it's going to be nice for you to move home soon," she said with a smile.

She was right. We couldn't wait to get Marcus home. I didn't want to think about the low platelet count or white blood count. Next time, his labs would probably be normal again. I only wished for Marcus to come home.

Back at HealthBridge, Marcus impressed us with a new level of achievements. His physical therapists had reported to Dr. Toomey that Marcus was able to follow one-step commands, which was encouraging behavior. Dr.

Toomey expected that in the future he would be awake for longer periods. She recommended that he get Botox treatments at TCH to help reduce the tone in his arms. At that point, Marcus was on room air only, meaning that he received no more supplemental oxygen. Yet another accomplishment.

From April 1 until April 5, I completed five batches of care-by-parent with Marcus. I did parts of evening shifts and night shifts. It was time to make more decisions. My husband and I had chosen the company Epic Health Services as the home health provider for Marcus. The company could provide full-service nursing care 24/7 and all the pediatric in-house therapies Marcus needed. Their representative had done a home evaluation and rendered his recommendations on how to design a space for Marcus and his nurses in our living room. Marcus's room was on the second floor and, for safety reasons, Marcus had to stay on the first floor. Designing Marcus's new space became a family project of a quite overwhelming character because we had to factor in all his special needs, the nurses' requirements, and the fact we also lived in the house. The space had to be practical, walkways had to be free from obstructions, and we had to fit in a nursing station. On the other hand, it was a cheerful occasion.

Marcus was coming home.

CHAPTER TWENTY-ONE

Getting Ready to Be Home

I was getting excited to get Marcus home. I was a bit scared too. It was an overwhelming feeling. Many questions surfaced. Could we handle Marcus at home? What would Lucas say? How would the 24/7 nursing care in our house affect our family life? Could we trust the nurses to take care of Marcus? For the first time during our time in Houston, there was some comfort in knowing that the nearest fire station was just five minutes away from our house.

Jacob went to IKEA to buy a huge bookcase with sixteen squares that we could use to put all of Marcus's medical equipment in. The bookcase would serve as a space divider in our living room. Marcus's unit was going to be in the left part of the living room, and our family lounge in the right part of the room. At least at the beginning, we wanted Marcus to have his PICU unit in our living room. That way, Marcus could get used to being with us again and we could readily supervise the nurses. Epic, Marcus's doctors, and all involved in his care helped order the medical equipment and devices he needed at home. He needed many types of supplies such as diapers, disposable underpads, feeding and ventilator components, and monitors. The good news was that once Marcus was at home, he could finally get his customized wheelchair.

It was April 2. When I arrived to HealthBridge carrying newly washed clothes for Marcus, his nurse immediately greeted me with a lovely smile. As I passed the nurses who were working by their computers, they seemed more relaxed than usual, chatting, some even laughing as if they were at a birthday

Chapter Twenty-One

party. My first impression was that something was different, but I wasn't sure what it was.

Marcus's nurse told me he had slept well and that his diarrhea had stopped. When he woke up, he was smiling and the nurses put on music for him during chair time. His nurse moved toward me. With a fluttery stomach, I took a moment to imagine how it may have looked. What happened? What did Marcus do? What did I miss? She started telling me about this eventful morning when José interrupted the conversation. "Marcus then started partying in his chair."

This sounded exactly like the old Marcus when he was in a good mood.

"Really, what did it look like?" I rushed my words. I wanted to hear all the details.

"He moved in his chair—like, he danced, he swung his arms to the beat," José said while demonstrating Marcus's arm movements. "We all partied for a long time with him in his room." José laughed. I broke into a run, aiming for Marcus's room. I was longing to hug him.

Later on, I did a full night shift with Marcus. It lasted from 7 P.M. until 7 A.M. I set my alarms for every two hours during the night so I could check on him, change him, and suction him. The night nurse came in with his night medicines well in advance before they were due. The staff was friendly and supportive. On April 5, José and Mary, one of Marcus's respiratory therapists, informed me that I had graduated from HealthBridge. I didn't celebrate the accomplishment per se, but it didn't take me long to call Jacob and share the news about my graduation. It was a great morale booster for me. On top of that, it was a huge satisfaction to pass all the requirements, to get it over with, and to be assured that I could handle Marcus once he was home. I did something my future self would thank me for. Obviously, I did make mistakes during my training—who wouldn't?—but I didn't quit. It wasn't easy, but it was worth it.

Jacob took off time from work to do his care-by-parent blocks. On one of his day shifts, his colleague came by to visit Marcus. He brought a bunch of colorful balloons for Marcus, something fun to look at. My husband did his night shifts during the weekend. He was determined to complete his training. It was an amazing achievement for him. He was balancing the pressure at work, helping with Lucas, and worrying about the next chapter in Marcus's life.

The repeated C. diff test came back negative. That meant Marcus was finally done with the antibiotics treatment. The doctors confirmed the discharge date, April 14. We all shared the enthusiasm about the discharge—our friends, families, and everyone who had worked with Marcus. Even Dr. Brack called me to hear more about Marcus coming home. A new chapter in Marcus's—and our—lives was about to begin.

One day, I had signed up to be the Mystery Reader in Lucas' class. I wanted to read *The Giving Tree* by Shel Silverstein to his class. I took the book with me to show and read it to Marcus first.

"I want to be your Mystery Reader today just like I will be for Lucas," I explained.

Marcus smiled many times as I read to him. During the reading, he tasted a small amount of Coke that I had served on a teaspoon and let it drip slowly onto his tongue. When he finished tasting the drink, I let him taste some Cheetos crumbles on his tongue.

"Once you get home, you'll be able to play with Lucas every day and you can play soccer with him outside in the garden," I told him. "Presenting the new Messi," I said when Marcus's nurse entered his room.

Marcus showed off. He attempted to do some tricks with the ball involving both his legs and feet at the same time. Impressive! Joyful, happy laughter filled the room.

I spent the next days on the phone with insurance representatives and Epic, getting Marcus's room ready, buying supplies, and setting up outpatient doctors' appointments for Marcus, all while going back and forth to HealthBridge and still trying to be there for Lucas.

In order to prepare for the discharge, all insurance questions had to be resolved. Having Marcus at home with 24/7 nursing was costly. So was all his necessary equipment and medicines. One thing was to make sure the orders for equipment and medications were in place. Another thing was to make sure the insurance would cover it.

I had to take on a new role as administrator for Marcus's home PICU. My husband was busy at work, and it wasn't safe to move Marcus to Denmark. It was never an option to move him to Denmark. He was too compromised,

Chapter Twenty-One

too unstable. The doctors had rendered us their honest opinion in that matter. If Marcus were to fly to Denmark, it had to be with a medical transport costing in the range of $1 million. Adding to that fee, the risk of Marcus not making it all the way to Denmark due to his extensive brain damage was a real possibility. Marcus was a high-risk patient with a history of complex medical problems. Jacob and I weren't even sure the doctors in Denmark would be able to handle such a unique case as Marcus's. Another aspect we factored in was the fact there would be a lack of continuity in Marcus's care if we moved him to Denmark. Our overall goal was to make sure there was continuity in his care by doctors who knew him well.

Jacob and I realized that being on top of all insurance issues was critical for our family to survive financially. His income was the only one we had to rely on. Marcus had a GoFundMe page, and we used all his money toward co-payments and other non-covered medical needs he had.

The first shock I got was when a representative from Epic told me that our insurance provider, Cigna, had informed Epic that Marcus could only receive two hours of nursing care per day. That was unacceptable. How could my husband and I care for Marcus twenty-two hours per day all year round? We couldn't take him with us anywhere, and he needed to be monitored 24/7.

Emotionally, it was challenging enough to have Marcus battle cancer and global brain damage. We didn't realize the extra administrative burden that awaited on our part when Marcus transitioned back home. The reality was I had to ensure that Marcus had all the supplies he needed and 24/7 nursing care. I had to be available for questions about Marcus's care and needs all the time. I never had any days off. I had to be capable of solving all the problems at all times. Marcus's needs could not wait. When he needed medications, it was now—not in a week, not in a month.

Fortunately, I had a legal background that proved to serve me well. I could analyze a situation, identify the problem, and work my way toward finding a solution. I had the ability to follow through. If one solution didn't work, I would look for another one. Quitting was not my style.

My philosophy was that I didn't want to be part of the problem. I wanted to be part of the solution. I had to teach other people that same idea when they presented a problem to me. I had to be completely clear about my expectations for Marcus's services. Some people may have found me demanding. I preferred to use the word *reasonable* instead.

"Who did you talk to at Cigna?" I asked the Epic representative, who informed me Marcus could only get two hours of nursing care per day.

I had a suspicion he had not talked to a qualified Cigna staff member.

"I talked to somebody at customer service," he replied.

"Somebody? Who was it?" I asked.

"I can't remember the name. I called the customer service department," he said.

"Well, do not talk to a random person at customer service who has no knowledge of Marcus's case. You need to talk to the right person at Cigna, someone who is overseeing all his claims. I'll give you the contact information of Marcus's My Champion representative at Cigna. Call her." I handed him the name and phone number of Marcus's My Champion representative at Cigna.

Due to the complex nature of Marcus's case, we had arranged for Marcus to be enrolled in Cigna's My Personal Champion Program. My Personal Champion was designed for employees and their covered family members so they could benefit from the highest level of individual attention. Those accepted to the program were assigned a personal champion who provided dedicated service and administrative support. The Personal Champion Program was a heaven-sent arrangement.

A few days later, the Epic representative informed my husband that he had been in contact with the right person at Cigna, which now approved in-home 24/7 care for Marcus. Good fortune came knocking at our door.

When visiting Marcus one day, Dr. Toomey swung by with information about Marcus's right to special education services. She instructed us that once Marcus was home, our local school district had an obligation to create an educational plan for Marcus that met his needs. We agreed that it would be a great idea for Marcus to start light formalized education as soon as he was ready for it.

Finally, we all had something meaningful to look forward to. School, books, education. I fantasized about Marcus receiving education and about his first day back at the Village School. I imagined how his teachers would

Chapter Twenty-One

welcome him back and hug him. I envisioned how Marcus's friends would run over to him and exclaim, "Marcus, we have missed you. Welcome back."

Dr. Toomey made another point that Marcus should do more aggressive outpatient rehabilitation at TIRR Memorial Hermann (TIRR). Located in Houston, it was the best rehabilitation hospital in Texas. It was the second best in the nation, offering rehabilitation for brain injury, spinal cord injury, stroke, and neurologic disease.

Those were refreshing words from Dr. Toomey. Very optimistic views. She admitted witnessing Marcus making unprecedented progress lately.

Marcus and Lucas's dentist had promised to come perform a dental cleaning on Marcus shortly before his discharge from HealthBridge. She had already been by to examine his teeth. Her conclusion was that his teeth were healthy and that he had no cavities. She helped remove three loose teeth we were worried he might swallow. The tooth fairy had to pay Marcus three visits that night.

I set up outpatient appointments for Marcus's next visits to his special needs doctor, Dr. Jerrell at TCH Medical Campus, and to his lung doctor, Dr. Susarla. The specialty pharmacy that was going to deliver most of Marcus's medications at home called me. The pharmacist happily informed me that they were working on his prescriptions and that the medications were scheduled for delivery to HealthBridge. At home, his new hospital bed had been delivered and assembled. We received so much stuff at home, I had no idea where to put it. He got a concentrator to deliver ongoing oxygen. He got boxes of medical supplies and a new suction machine. All were lifesaving devices Marcus needed.

On April 14, the big day had arrived. I came early to pack Marcus's things in suitcases. My husband came by to pick up all of Marcus's clothes, stuffed animals, and other personal belongings.

At 2 P.M., the medical transport arrived. The medics lifted Marcus onto the stretcher and started rolling him out. On the way out, all the staff was waiting and ready to sing and clap their hands. It was their goodbye ritual for all their patients leaving the facility. They were all there: José, Mercy, Dr. Toomey, Dr. Davis—all the staff that had cared for Marcus since he came to HealthBridge seven months earlier.

I was overwhelmed. I cried. This time, my tears were happy tears. They kept singing and clapping their hands all the way until Marcus left in the ambulance to go home. They cared about Marcus and about our family. I truly felt thankful for all they had done. It was surreal that the moment had come when I could take my son back home. After the doctors realized Marcus was globally brain damaged, they predicted he would die from relapsed leukemia within months. Marcus had defied that prognosis and had proved that his life was still worth fighting for, even more now, as he had come so far.

CHAPTER TWENTY-TWO

Home at Last

At 2:30 p.m., we all arrived at home—home, where my son belonged. I never wanted him to be away from me again—ever. I loved him even more now than I had ever loved him. I could not wait for Lucas to come home from school and to give his brother the biggest hug ever. We could all be together at last.

Latasha, an experienced home health nurse, was waiting for us in her car outside of our home. It was a weird feeling to have a stranger in the house. The person was in our home, taking care of my sick son. I thought the best way to deal with the nurses was to make sure they respected me and vice versa. We had to be partners on this and create good teamwork.

I was the director of Marcus's home unit. My husband was mostly at work, and we agreed that only one of us was to oversee all of Marcus's care. I had a feeling that it would be a lot of work. I was wrong. It was going to be a lot of work times a million.

It was a happy day. Once home, Marcus vocalized and looked around. I was positive he could tell he was home and in the living room where he used to play with Lucas.

Marcus's respiratory therapist came to service his ventilator and go over the settings with Latasha and me. A delivery person from Southside Pharmacy came with Marcus's medications. Later, a delivery person from Medical Plus arrived with formula, diapers, and incontinence supplies. Next, a representative from Hill-Rom came with Marcus's vest for his vest treatment, which was an airway clearance system that helped Marcus breathe a little easier and prevent pneumonia.

Chapter Twenty-Two

The Hill-Rom representative proudly presented Marcus with his army camouflage vest I had picked for him. The representative demonstrated how to operate the generator. He programmed it with the settings prescribed by Marcus's pulmonary doctor.

It was confusing having so many medical professionals in our house giving directions about all sorts of things. I signed endless amounts of paperwork. I wanted to understand everything, so I asked many questions.

Around 7 P.M., Lucas arrived with Alison, Ross's mom. Lucas was over the moon to see Marcus home again and gave Marcus a big brother hug.

Marcus, Lucas, and I spent some time together. Then the night nurse Agnes arrived. Latasha had to give a report to Agnes. In the meantime, I took Lucas to bed.

"Good night, Marcus," Lucas said while kissing his brother on his forehead. "See you in the morning."

When Lucas was asleep, Agnes started Marcus's formula. I showed Agnes how I wanted trach care done on Marcus. It was a different role for me. At TCH and HealthBridge, I had been the student. Now the roles were reversed. I was the teacher giving instructions to Marcus's home health nurses. I was the experienced one and the boss.

Marcus was exhausted after his first big day at home. I was inundated too. I was tired but in a good way. When Jacob got home later that night after running, he could walk into our living room and whisper good night to Marcus. Marcus was fast asleep, ready for his first night home.

Jacob and I had difficulty sleeping. We heard when Marcus was suctioned, when he coughed, and when alarms went off. We had to get used to many new noises in our house. It was a mix of Marcus noises, nurse noises, and machine noises. Nevertheless, Marcus's first night at home was successful. There were no emergencies.

When Lucas woke up that first morning, he ran down the stairs to see Marcus, who was still sleeping in his bed. He said good morning to Marcus and talked to Agnes.

At 7 A.M., Theresa relieved Agnes. A shift lasts twelve hours unless anything else had been agreed to between the nurses. Shift change takes place at 7 P.M. and 7 A.M.

After Marcus's morning routines were completed, we moved him to his chair. It required a huge setup to roll him around in our house. He needed his vent to be rolled next to him and plugged in close by. He also needed a suction machine close by. I pushed his chair around in the living room and into the open kitchen.

Marcus had big open eyes looking at all our furniture, paintings, and pictures on the walls. I wished he could share his thoughts with me. He did not cry or make any sounds. He simply looked while sucking in impressions from his home environment.

Later that day, a representative from Numotion delivered Marcus's new wheelchair. Finally, Marcus got his customized wheelchair. It was made of blue metal and had a soccer ball logo on the front cover. When Lucas got home from school and saw it, he concluded the wheelchair was only to be used by soccer players, meaning Marcus or him.

Marcus was active when he saw Lucas, and Lucas immediately wanted to hang out with Marcus. The connection and love between the brothers was evident, and it was growing day by day.

"Lucas and I are going into the kitchen to do homework. Rest a bit, Marcus, and then you can do chair time after," I told him.

Lucas pulled up his homework from his backpack and started working on it. He needed some help from me and started working on an assignment. Marcus was loud and vocalized. He wanted to be part of the study hall. In Denmark when students do homework in their school after dismissal, they used to call it the homework café. It sounded better to refer to a homework café than study hall.

Marcus clearly wanted our attention and to be part of our homework café. Lucas and I decided to take a break. I asked Theresa to help us get Marcus into his wheelchair so he could join us in our homework café in the kitchen. We had a lovely time. Theresa stayed back in Marcus's unit and did Epic paperwork, which mostly consisted of documenting by hand all she did for Marcus.

Marcus was attentive and observed Lucas do his homework. At dinnertime, my husband came home from work. He was able to continue to help Lucas do homework while I started to cook dinner.

Marcus was part of our family life again the way we had wished he could

Chapter Twenty-Two

be. He could hear us talk and Lucas laugh. Love surrounded him from all sides. These were the best conditions for his recovery.

The remainder of April was a period of adjusting. During the short time Marcus had been home from April 14 until April 30, Marcus had fourteen different nurses taking care of him. The representatives from Epic told us it would take about fourteen days to make a set schedule for Marcus's day and night nurses. The goal was for Marcus to have the same nurses taking care of him.

It was a learning curve for me to navigate the home health system. The first thing I learned was that I needed a prescription from a doctor to make any changes in Marcus's medication administration, in any respiratory treatments, or existing feeding orders. The plan of care (POC) was the guide for all types of care Marcus needed. The home health nurses needed a written prescription to do something, but they also needed instructions *not* to do something written in the POC. The only exception to that rule was that in case of an emergency, a doctor could give a verbal instruction over the phone directly to the nurse. The nurse had to document the instruction in Marcus's chart for it to take effect. The procedure was complex and time-consuming.

The bed Marcus had gotten from Medical Plus was a simple metal bed with poor options for adjustments. The mattress was hard and didn't provide Marcus the support and properties he needed to avoid getting pressure sores. The nurses complained about the bed too because they weren't able to elevate it to a height where they could work with Marcus without bending over and causing back pain.

I contacted Medical Plus to request a better quality bed for Marcus, but my request was met with the response that I needed a prescription from a doctor stating that it was "a medical necessity" for Marcus to have a better bed. If Medical Plus didn't have that order, they couldn't get coverage from our insurance company. It was the most important mantra to learn: Nothing could become reality without a doctor's prescription.

Even though the insurance company covered all the major expenses for having Marcus at home, we had considerable extra costs. Running a pediatric PICU at home is expensive. First, Marcus's medical devices consumed additional electricity. There was extra water consumption and cleaning. Suddenly there was also an extra person in the household because Marcus had a nurse by his side 24/7.

Whenever the nurses told me Marcus needed some additional supplies, I was the person to get it. I spent a lot of time comparing prices on Amazon.com and other providers. For instance, we didn't have a blood pressure machine at home. Thus, I had to get one, as the nurses had to check Marcus's vitals a few times during each shift. We didn't have diapers for him. Thus, I had to get those. Marcus had disposable bed pads on top of his bedsheets, but those didn't cover sufficiently when he had big stools, had peed, or had diarrhea. The nurses said all bedridden patients used reusable bed pads underneath the disposable underpads. I ran out to Walmart and bought ten of those for him.

Many nurses had a bad habit of showing up twenty to thirty minutes late for every shift. It was unacceptable because the nurse who was waiting to be relieved couldn't just leave Marcus. My husband and I had one simple requirement when it came to Marcus's nurses: they had to be on time. If for some reason they were late, they had to call the Epic office or me to notify us when they would be coming.

In case a nurse couldn't stay late, I had to take care of Marcus. If it happened in the morning, it caused problems, because often my husband had early business meetings at work and I had to take Lucas to school. I couldn't take Marcus with me in my car while taking Lucas to school. If the night nurse couldn't stay longer, what could we do? Showing up late was never something we could prepare for. It was stressful and put our family under additional pressure because we needed a nurse for Marcus to be able to leave him.

I had many discussions with staff members at the Epic office about what to do with the "showing up late" issue. I informed them that I would make a plus list and a minus list of the nurses. After trying a nurse for a shift, I returned to the Epic office and let them know if I wanted the nurse to continue taking care of Marcus. If a nurse was trustworthy, punctual, reliable, and professional in handling Marcus, the nurse would make it to the plus list.

No more privacy at home, no more predictability, no more making plans. Home was not a place where we could get a break from the medical world and all the worries about Marcus.

On the other hand, having Marcus at home was still worth all our efforts, stress, and work. First, having Marcus at home was the best solution for him. Second, it was also the best solution for Lucas, Jacob, and me. The brothers could see each other every day and bond. If Lucas missed Marcus, he could go to his unit and hang out there. One day, Lucas brought a pile of LEGOs next to Marcus and started building while talking to Marcus. Even if Marcus was resting, he heard Lucas talk and felt his presence.

My husband or I could be with Marcus without any restrictions day or night, as he was now in our home. We knew exactly how he was doing, and I didn't have to call TCH or HealthBridge to say good night to him. I could whisper good night into his ears myself and smell his soft, warm hair.

One night when Jacob came home from work, Marcus looked toward the door and could see him as he entered the house. Marcus greeted him with a big smile. It was lovely and a wonderful surprise for my husband.

Another plus was that Marcus had his own nurse. In a hospital setting, he would always share the nurse with one or two other patients. With one nurse on a shift at home, it was guaranteed Marcus had personalized care all the time.

Many of Marcus's friends wanted to come visit Marcus after he got home. The moms asked me when they could come visit. We restricted any children in our house except for Lucas's close friend Ross.

Under no circumstances could Marcus get any infections; for him, they were life-threatening. If Marcus's friends came by, the risks of spreading germs increased. Another concern of ours was that seeing Marcus so incapacitated could cause a significant amount of distress. Marcus wasn't able to do the same and play the way he used to do with his friends, and it could be a traumatizing shock to see Marcus completely changed. My husband and I wanted to protect both Marcus and his friends. Having a visitor could be a cause of frustration and agitation for Marcus because he couldn't communicate. We wanted his friends to remember the healthy, strong, funny Marcus. Marcus had limited resources and energy so it was important for him to spend that on his rehabilitation efforts.

When Marcus had moved home, a mom of Marcus's school friend paid us a visit. She delivered a welcome-home present from his class. In the middle was a picture of all his classmates holding signs stating WE ARE CHEERING FOR YOU, MARCUS! Each student had made a small paper balloon that was attached to a big frame covered with canvas. This said it all. They were still thinking about Marcus.

Marcus was awake when Michele came by. She showed him the welcome-home gift. Her son Jack was one of Marcus's friends, and she explained to him what Jack was up to and what sports he did. Marcus became eager and started vocalizing. Different sounds came out of his mouth.

Michele offered an understanding nod. She listened intently while ignoring everything else that happened outside Marcus's unit.

"Tell me everything, Marcus," Michele said in a soothing tone of voice, making sure to keep constant eye contact with Marcus.

Marcus's mouth moved nonstop. He smiled as Michele talked back to him. I had never seen him so interactive before.

"Tell me more!" she said, gripping his hand and holding it gently. Marcus's eyes sparkled. Then she started telling Marcus stories about his class and classmates.

I'm sure Marcus felt seen and appreciated in his own essence. Michele was gentle with him, a very empathetic and extraordinary woman, and her responses were very supportive. She did all this not because of who Marcus was or what he would do in return, but because of who she was. She made a difference in Marcus's life that day.

I loved cooking food for Marcus at home. Lucas and I talked about what Marcus liked to taste. I made homemade strawberry sauce served with ice cream. I let Marcus taste the strawberry sauce, and he liked it. Next, I let him taste some vanilla ice cream on his lips and tongue. Marcus made a wry face like a baby who tasted some food for the first time and did not like it.

Clearly, the ice made him uncomfortable. It was too cold. This sensation was new to him.

On April 18, my husband and Lucas took off early in the morning to take part in a Fun Run in Danevang. Danevang is a community in Texas established by Danish settlers in 1895. The name Danevang was an alternative name for Denmark. When Lucas came home from Danevang, he proudly told Marcus that he finished in a good time, beating the Danish

Chapter Twenty-Two

consul Anna Holliday the same way Marcus had beaten her in the Fun Run the year before.

"At the race, I took a Gatorade for you." Lucas showed the Gatorade to Marcus.

Marcus tasted a bit on his lips.

"Let me find some calming music for you on your iPad," Lucas insisted while searching to find some quiet music.

When the nurses needed help to find some of Marcus's stuff, Lucas was the first one to volunteer as a helper. Lucas knew where all of Marcus's supplies were.

"Lucas, you are now promoted to nurse assistant," I praised him. "Congratulations on your new title."

Lucas often asked me, "When do you think Marcus will recover so I can play soccer with him again, Mommy?" or "When do you think we can go to Denmark again?"

He knew my answer and told me, "I know, Mommy, you don't know. We'll have to wait and see, right?"

Lucas was right. He had heard that answer so many times before; eventually, he stopped asking me questions about Marcus's recovery.

From the staff at the Epic office, we soon learned that Marcus and our family had become popular with the nurses. Some of his nurses were used to taking care of children born with genetic disorders and other serious medical problems. Some of these children could literally not do anything. When the nurses took care of Marcus, they discovered a sweet boy who had moments when he was alert, easy to handle, and in good condition. All the nurses were convinced Marcus would make a full recovery.

This was promising news. Marcus's recovery was going to take time, but he made baby steps in the right direction. He had started to swallow now, which was helping him have fewer secretions in his trach.

Yet again, with every day came new challenges. Administering and training the nurses was one task, but maintaining Marcus's medical equipment was another job. Suddenly Marcus's Hill-Rom generator for his vest treatment stopped working. I called Hill-Rom's customer service in Minnesota. They informed me they would send a new one that should arrive the day after. That was great except Marcus needed his vest treatment three times per day.

The nurse had no plan for how Marcus could get his treatments until the new generator arrived. Desperately, I looked in my collection of business cards I had saved from all of Marcus's health care providers. I found the phone number of Hill-Rom's representative based in Houston and called him. He didn't pick up so I left a voice mail. He returned my call.

"Hi, this is Robert from Hill-Rom," he said.

"Hi, this is Marcus's mom, Benedicte Nielsen. Listen, Marcus's generator is broken and a new one won't arrive until tomorrow. Do you happen to have a loaner generator Marcus can use until he gets his new one?" I asked.

"Yes, of course. I have a spare one in my car. I'll pop by your house with it," he promised.

Two hours after I hung up with Robert, he dropped off a functioning generator for Marcus at our house. *That* was service. I could relax for a moment.

Later that day, a respiratory therapist from Epic came to check Marcus's vent and the settings. The circuits on his vent had to be changed once per week. Otherwise, germs started to build up and malfunctioning was likely to happen. The most common problem was that the tube started leaking, causing a change in pressure in the airflow to Marcus. Any vital change in airflow would trigger an alarm to go off on the vent, and then we had a problem that needed to be fixed.

After going over the circuits to Marcus's vent, the respiratory therapist noted that a small filter on the vent needed to be changed. The nurse who had changed the circuits the week before had forgotten to change that particular filter. At that moment, I realized I had to take on a more active role in monitoring and maintaining Marcus's medical equipment. I had to be on top of it.

Then on April 24, Marcus had appointments at TCH, among others, with Dr. Rabin for routine labs. Unfortunately, his labs were on the lower side, meaning that they were not within normal range. But there weren't any leukemia cells detected in his sample. Dr. Rabin advised us not to draw any conclusions but to wait a few weeks and repeat the labs. At that time, they should be back to a normal range again.

Chapter Twenty-Two

All we could do was wait and pray his next lab results would be normal. Waiting was awful and full of vague uncertainty, but we all had to keep an optimistic attitude. I came back and back again to my fears, except I couldn't allow them to take over. We couldn't just sit back and do nothing but wait. I do believe that inaction breeds doubt and fear, whereas action breeds confidence and courage. Life had to continue. We shouldn't look back, because that was not the way Marcus was going. We had to push forward and keep supporting the recommendations set forth by Marcus's doctors. On the long list of upcoming appointments, the next one was with Dr. Susarla, the lung doctor.

His office was in Katy outside of Houston in a small office building. The transport went seamlessly, and Marcus arrived in good spirits. A little girl, a trach patient wearing a cute dress, had just finished her appointment and exited the exam room. When she noticed Marcus, she said hi to him.

Dr. Susarla was a friendly doctor with a good understanding of Marcus's many medical challenges. He listened to Marcus's lungs.

"His lungs sound really good and strong. You impress me, Marcus." Dr. Susarla took a step back. "I'm going to write a prescription to remove his supplemental oxygen, provided Marcus maintains his O2 saturation at ninety-three or above."

"That sounds like a good idea," I said while thinking about what else I needed to speak to Dr. Susarla about. It would be a while before Marcus's next appointment. I had to remember to get all necessary prescriptions during this visit to avoid any delays in Marcus's rehab. "He's going to start speech therapy soon so should he not have a speaking valve?" I said.

Using a speaking valve would be the first step for Marcus to allow him to use his voice. Even with such a valve, he could not speak right away. He had to learn how to use his vocal cords again.

"I agree with you. Marcus is ready to use a speaking valve now." Dr. Susarla stood tall with good posture.

I'll write a prescription for that too." Dr. Susarla began typing the prescriptions on his computer while I started getting ready to check out. It was as if Dr. Susarla had just given Marcus an A-plus for effort. I couldn't mask how proud I was of Marcus and how grateful I was that this visit brought peace at least for that day.

Dr. Susarla was a wonderful pulmonologist. He was patient and gentle when handling Marcus and he always understood my concerns and answered every question clearly and honestly. During this journey with Marcus, I felt privileged to meet so many caring doctors. I felt when doctors genuinely cared about him.

It was May, which meant it was Marcus's birthday month. His ninth birthday was coming up on May 27.

During the first half of May, my focus was to obtain prescriptions for Marcus's speech/feeding therapy, physical therapy, and occupational therapy. Epic required an individual prescription for each type of therapy. If I didn't make these calls, nothing would happen and no therapist would ever come to our house and work with Marcus.

The drill went like this: I called Marcus's special needs doctor at TCH to verify that she had sent the therapy prescriptions to Epic. The special needs doctor's assistant confirmed that she had faxed the prescriptions to Epic. Then I called the Epic office to make sure they had received the prescriptions and that they were working on scheduling Marcus's therapy evaluations. The Epic staff member confirmed the receipt of the prescriptions, but Epic could not use them because they were electronic prescriptions without signatures on them. The insurance company would not accept them without signatures. Why did TCH staff not know this?

I told her that I possessed prescriptions for speech/feeding therapy, physical therapy, and occupational therapy with signatures from Marcus's TCH physical medicine doctor, Dr. Roge. I had made it a habit to obtain original signed prescriptions regarding Marcus's care every time Marcus went to a doctor's appointment. They always came in handy. My plan was to email those directly to the staff member at the Epic office. Afterward, I called her again to ask her to verify that she had in fact received the prescriptions and that they fulfilled the insurance requirements from Cigna.

Days passed, and Epic did not send any therapists to Marcus. Finally, on May 12, a speech therapist was supposed to make her evaluation of Marcus. A representative from Epic called me to inform me that the evaluation was canceled because Epic had not yet obtained the insurance authorization for the evaluation. The Epic representative explained that the approval had to come from Cigna and not Cigna's agency, CareCentrix, which is responsible for the authorizations for his physical and occupational therapies. I asked her about the status on Marcus's physical therapist. I reminded the Epic staff member that Marcus had been home for about a month and had not started any therapy. Patience was not part of my repertoire that day.

"So, when can Marcus start his physical therapy? He can't wait any longer. I need immediate action." My pulse started speeding.

"We need to hire a physical therapist first. I've put Marcus on a waiting list," the Epic staff member said.

I rolled my eyes. "What? Marcus isn't supposed to be on any waiting list!"

"It can take up to thirty days before we can do his physical therapy evaluation," she said.

I was about to explode from anger. That was it. I was done.

"In that case, I will switch to a different provider. Marcus should not wait another month to start therapy."

"The new provider cannot use the authorization Epic obtained from the insurance company. Per CareCentrix policies, they have to obtain a new authorization."

I cleared my voice.

"I will follow up on this."

I had had enough of this. I found that the medical world I was involved in was a world of contrasts. Many employees who dealt with Marcus's case delivered top-notch service. They stayed on task and carried through. They felt a sense of ownership of Marcus's case. They were professional. I could count on them. Others were the opposite. They didn't seem to care that they were working with sick and vulnerable children who were dependent on them.

As family members to a very sick child, we faced a dilemma because the insurance had to cover Marcus's services before they were provided. That process delayed all steps of his care. The next problem we faced was that the competition in the industry was limited. If I wasn't satisfied with the service Marcus got from Epic, I couldn't easily find a different provider. The first hurdle was that the provider had to be in network with Cigna. Then they had to accept Marcus's case, and after that, the paperwork process awaited.

This administrative work drained me. I wanted to spend my energy on Marcus and Lucas, not worry about insurance approvals and paperwork.

I developed a new strategy when dealing with the medical providers. Whether it was a pharmacist at SouthSide Pharmacy, a staff member at Medical Plus, or a medical assistant at a doctor's office, I always got their names and contact information. When I identified a person who was efficient and did the work correctly, I recorded the person's name and contacts on my personal plus list of people I could contact again.

That way, I started avoiding all the hopeless staff members I encountered either on the phone or in-person during Marcus's clinic visits. Another strategy I used was going directly to the supervisor or manager level when possible. I only dealt with people who could master the complexity and details of Marcus's case. I tolerated no mistakes. I had seen what Nelarabine had done to Marcus. I had seen what could happen to an innocent person if something went medically wrong. I could smell negligence from a mile away, and I wouldn't tolerate it anymore. I had a zero-tolerance policy when it came to Marcus and my family.

Most importantly, I worked on refining my instructions to reach a very high standard. When it comes to health care details, they are of the utmost importance. When I sent email requests to a doctor to obtain a different dosage on Marcus's medicine, I rechecked my emails ten times before sending them to make sure they did not contain any mistakes. Marcus's care was too important. I discovered that if I gave clear instructions, I was already halfway there. Once the assignment was completed, I checked if the assignment was done to my satisfaction. If not, I made sure the person corrected what went wrong the first time. It took me months to learn from all my troubleshooting when mistakes happened, but over time, I became better at predicting when a mistake could easily happen and when it would likely not happen.

My plus list of contacts proved valuable not only to me but also to others involved in Marcus's care. If one provider had to contact another provider, I made sure to give each of him or her the names of the other. It simply saved them time not having the extra burden of calling medical facilities on its main phone number. The phone operator would most likely put them on hold or transfer them to the wrong department. Eventually, they might end up speaking to a voice message system. I had been faced with that experience so many times, and that was the exact reason I carried my provider list of Marcus's Dream Team with me every time Marcus went for an appointment.

I also faced issues with medication refills. I had expected that his special needs doctor had taken care of the refills. The doctor knew that Marcus needed those medications on a continuous basis. I was wrong. I had to call the doctor's office to ask for the refill orders. Since Marcus was G-tube dependent, the pharmacy had to provide the medicines in a liquid form. For that reason, not every pharmacy could handle the refill orders. It had to be a specialty pharmacy, and it took longer to process the refills. The medical assistant I talked to at the clinic promised me that the special needs doctor, Dr. Jerrell, would take care of the refills.

Two days after, the medications had not been delivered and Marcus had almost no more left. I called SouthSide Pharmacy, and they notified me that the pharmacy had not received any refill orders from Dr. Jerrell's office. I called Dr. Jerrell's office, and they said the refill orders had been sent. I asked the assistant to double-check which pharmacy they had been sent to. After investigating the issue, she called me back. She had found out Dr. Jerrell had not sent the refill orders to SouthSide Pharmacy but to a different one that could not handle the requests. She apologized on behalf of Dr. Jerrell and promised to have her resend the prescriptions to SouthSide Pharmacy. Finally, the following day, SouthSide Pharmacy delivered Marcus's medications.

Despite all the disappointments I encountered during the first month of having Marcus home, I was able to make some advancements in his care. I organized his visits to TCH to get his Botox treatment, which helped his muscles relax. His physical medicine and rehabilitation doctor, Dr. Roge, gave him eleven Botox injections spread out on his arms, hands, neck, and legs. The effect of the Botox would kick in after four days and peak at one month. After two to three months, the effect would stop. Marcus tolerated the injections. Dr. Roge had numbed the injection sites first. I didn't like watching him receive eleven injections. I talked to him and calmed him down in an attempt to distract him and help him relax.

At home, it was time to make some changes. Jacob and I decided to designate our master bedroom as Marcus's PICU and move to the second floor into Marcus's small bedroom instead. It was too complicated to have Marcus stay in the living room. He didn't get sufficient rest because we walked in and out of the room all the time. In the master bedroom, Marcus and his nurse could have more space. There was also a small private toilet and sinks where the nurses could clean Marcus's supplies. My husband bought a small fridge for Marcus's medications that needed to be refrigerated, and that was all that was needed to be able to shift Marcus to his new PICU.

The first night after Marcus had moved to the master bedroom, he had a little party going on. Marcus's nurse, Niso, reported that he had been awake for a long time that first night. He had been hyperactive, but in a sweet way, and had been kicking his legs a lot. He had grabbed the rail on his bed and tried to hold onto it as if he attempted to jump out of the bed. There was no doubt he celebrated that he had gotten a big new room.

Later, our lovely Australian friend Kristy came by to decorate Marcus's new room and Lucas's room on the second floor. An interior design student, she was the right person to be in charge of the decoration of the soccer rooms I had promised the boys. Her idea for each room was to cover one wall with a green plastic cover to resemble a huge soccer pitch. Lucas picked the soccer posters he wanted for his room. He also helped pick posters for Marcus's room with Marcus's favorite soccer player, Lionel Messi, and his club, FC Barcelona. Kristy put them up on the green pitch. The boys also had wall calendars from FC Barcelona to hang up. Kristy went to Target and Party City to get more supplies. She came back with soccer balls made out of paper that could hang from the ceiling and black-and-white soccer banners. She worked a whole day decorating the boys' rooms, and the results were amazing.

"You got your soccer room, Marcus," Lucas told him enthusiastically. "I got one too. Mine is the same as yours."

One night, Lucas and I experienced Marcus showing his emotions. It was a powerful experience. Lucas was doing his homework in the kitchen, and Marcus was doing chair time next to him. Suddenly Lucas noted a change in Marcus's face.

"Mommy, Marcus is crying. Look!" Lucas said, pointing at Marcus, who was indeed crying and crying.

Tears were rolling down Marcus's cheeks. He tried to open his mouth and speak. He tried very hard, but he only produced weak sounds and noises. Then he cried more. Lucas and I hugged Marcus and caressed his soft hair.

"It's all right, Marcus. Don't be sad." I pressed my lips to his forehead

Chapter Twenty-Two

and pulled him close to my chest. "You're getting better every day. We're here with you and we're helping you, Marcus."

The next day, it happened again. Upon recommendation from Dr. Roge, I had hired a massage therapist to help massage the tight muscles in Marcus's arms and legs. The massage therapist, Margo, was a friend of Marcus's Reiki healing practitioner, Zee. Margo worked once a week with Marcus, who benefited a lot from the massage. After Margo had concluded a massage session with Marcus, he started crying. Again, salty tears kept rolling down his cheeks.

"Crying is good. This proves he is capable of showing us his emotions," Margo said. "I think Marcus is becoming more conscious now. It's a gradual process for him."

"I'm so proud of you, Marcus. You're going to talk again soon. We're going to make so many cool things," I told him.

Zee continued to come and give Reiki healing sessions to Marcus. When she healed him, he reached a state of deep relaxation. He was in a different calm place. It was very intense to witness the change in his heart rate as he got deeper and deeper into the healing experience. His heart rate slowed down, and he let go of all tensions in his body.

The concept of Reiki healing interested me. What was it? How did it work? I put these questions aside for later. I didn't have the energy to dig into that world at that time, but I wanted to learn more about it. Zee told me she would teach me to do Reiki healing when I was ready.

Soon after, Marcus tried to use his speaking valve. A respiratory therapist came to demonstrate how to use the valve. She explained that it had to go on Marcus's trach. This meant Marcus was disconnected from the pressure support he received from the ventilator. He had to learn to breathe through the valve and maintain a reasonable heart rate and sufficient oxygen saturation. She suspected Marcus could tolerate two seconds the first time, but he actually tolerated breathing through the valve for one minute before it became too hard for him. His heart rate started to increase, and his oxygen saturation started dropping. Marcus was able to produce some nonspecific sounds through his valve. He did better than expected. Once he had built up more strength and technique to breathe through the valve, he could start learning to make sounds and learn to talk again long term.

Lucas played an active role in timing on my iPhone how long Marcus could tolerate using his valve. One time, Marcus did one minute, then a break to recover, then followed by another minute. Another time, he increased it to one and a half minutes while he made loud noises. His record was ten minutes when using his valve. It was incredible how Marcus kept surprising us with improvements.

When the Botox treatment kicked in, Marcus was able to control his legs and arms better. While in his wheelchair, he trained with his red Spider-Man ball and other types of small balls. If I sensed Marcus had a good day, I could work with him for up to two hours. I did stretching on him, his oral intervention program, and I asked him to do exercises such as kicking and trapping the ball. I made sure to play music during our training sessions and to praise him for his efforts. When Lucas was in school and Jacob was at work, I dedicated all my time to Marcus. I rarely made plans of my own. Marcus needed me. Only I could make a true and consistent difference in his life. It was important to me that Marcus felt assured that I was with him and that he was not alone on this journey.

Most evenings and nights, when my husband was working on his computer at home, I spent time researching nutritional articles about what I could give Marcus to boost brain cell recovery and the immune system. Additionally, I researched topics about the relationship between nutrition and cancer risk. I wanted to give him real ingredients through his G-tube, not just formula produced at a factory with artificial vitamins and minerals. I made him nutritious or healthy fruit drinks and green teas that contained many antioxidants. I made sure to consult with his nutritionist and special needs doctor at TCH before giving him anything, as some drinks could alter the medicinal potency of some medications.

On May 15, Marcus had his next Baclofen pump refill and oncology appointment at the TCH Katy Campus. I feared the visit. The labs. The numbers. Were they normal?

CHAPTER TWENTY-THREE

The Relapse

Dr. Roge did the Baclofen pump refill, and Marcus was off to a good start. Next, we proceeded to the oncology floor to complete the blood work. A staff member assigned Marcus a nice big exam room with plenty of space for his stretcher. Big windows allowed sunshine to enter the room. Dr. Brackett, who was familiar with Marcus, saw him that day. I preferred an oncologist who knew Marcus and me well, and Dr. Brackett was exactly the person we needed. I had a nasty suspicion the wave of good luck had ended.

She did a routine examination of his abdomen and neck. Then she paused. She spoke in a too-quiet voice, as if her words wouldn't take flight. "I think Marcus's spleen feels enlarged."

My mind skipped ahead to possible consequences.

"It seems he has some swollen lymph nodes on his neck, but I'm not sure," she said. "Let's wait for the lab results."

She left the exam room. We waited and waited. I was too familiar with waiting for a long time. Usually, it was a bad sign. The doctors had to talk and make phone calls. I hated it.

Dr. Brackett returned, looking despaired.

"Marcus's white blood count and platelets aren't normal as we had hoped," Dr. Brackett said. "His detailed blood test revels suspicious cells." It got worse and worse. Could the suspicious cells be leukemia?

"I've decided to send the sample to a pathologist at the main campus to get a quick review. I already discussed it with Dr. Rabin, and she agrees with me."

Chapter Twenty-Three

Dr. Brackett left to call the pathologist at TCH Main Campus. Marcus was awake and heard everything.

"You're going to be all right, Marcus," I told him while caressing his head. "We'll figure it out. Let's wait for all the results first."

Dr. Brackett returned after conferring with the pathologist.

"At first glance, the pathologist didn't see any leukemia cells, but the whole sample must be examined, and it can take several hours. I'm also waiting for other test results that I'll get later," Dr. Brackett said while tilting her head.

I drew a deep breath. "Do the suspicious cells have to be leukemia cells?"

"No, it's possible that the abnormal cells are abnormal cells for other reasons than leukemia. Besides, Marcus's other lab results are normal. I believe it's best to go home and wait for me to call you. However, I admit I am worried."

Hours of uncertainty and fear followed. I called Jacob at work to update him about Marcus's abnormal test results. It was hard news. He was very despaired.

Later that afternoon, Dr. Brackett called me. I didn't want to pick up the ringing phone. I had developed some kind of phone phobia. It was as if my phone had bad karma. Bad news always came by phone. I didn't want to talk to any oncologist. I wanted Marcus to be healthy and happy.

"I'm sorry, Mrs. Nielsen," Dr. Brackett said, her voice strained. "But I'm afraid Marcus does have leukemia again."

My heart sank. I wanted to scream and bawl my eyes out, but deep inside I had figured it out already. The enlarged spleen, the possible swollen lymph nodes, and the abnormal lab numbers all sounded too familiar. These exact same findings presented themselves when Marcus was first diagnosed with leukemia. There was no room for mistakes, and we couldn't waste any time now. His leukemia was simply too aggressive.

"What do we do now?" I wanted to make sure the doctors had a plan moving forward.

"I'll arrange a family meeting on Monday, May eighteenth, where we can meet and discuss what to do. Marcus doesn't need to be there, just you and your husband," Dr. Brackett said, her tone soft and kind. "Again, I'm terribly sorry."

The Relapse

On Monday, May 18, my husband and I had a family meeting at TCH. A social worker, a psychologist, Chaplain James, Dr. Rabin, and Dr. Brackett were there. Dr. Rabin informed us that they couldn't help Marcus anymore. There was no way Marcus could tolerate any form of treatment, and no doctor could bring him into remission. All efforts would be worthless. According to them, he would die from the leukemia.

This was their opinion, but I no longer trusted their judgment. They messed Marcus up on the oncology floor at TCH in the course of the Nelarabine treatment. How could I trust them again? I couldn't. Marcus's life was at stake. Could TCH only handle easy cases? Should children with difficult cases be left to die? We couldn't hide our disappointment, but maybe we expected too much from them.

At the same time, we honored the fact that medicine isn't an exact science. Other oncologists may have a different view on Marcus's case. When we left TCH, we were not sad but empty. We left TCH with the intention to keep digging for other options, for another place where we could take Marcus.

My husband and I carefully thought about what other alternatives we had in order to help Marcus. It had been almost a year since Marcus was first diagnosed with leukemia. During that entire period, TCH did not allow second opinions from other doctors. Gradually, we had become more involved in Marcus's care and in decisions about his medications. It had been a learning process for us, and I in particular decided gradually to take on a more proactive role in teaming up with Marcus's different medical teams. If we got involved, the doctors would take us more seriously and increasingly include us in his care. We wanted to make a difference for Marcus, and that was the way to secure maximum influence on his care. We were no longer afraid to question a doctor's judgment. Only by asking questions and encouraging the doctors to think outside the box could we help Marcus.

Nevertheless, we needed the doctors to show they were committed to Marcus's case. All along, we had been dependent on TCH's view on Marcus's case, but at the family meeting, we sensed they lacked confidence and expertise in handling a leukemia patient like Marcus. We believed in Marcus, we wanted to fight for him, and we wanted to fight harder than we had ever

Chapter Twenty-Three

fought before. Maybe in the heavy emptiness, we felt there was a solution that had not yet manifested itself.

CHAPTER TWENTY-FOUR

A New Approach— A New Hospital

Jacob and I were aware that the minute TCH informed us they would not take on Marcus's relapsed leukemia case, we were free to go elsewhere for a second opinion. We could look at other hospitals, talk to friends, and seek recommendations and base our decision on balanced feedback from many different sources.

My husband and I decided to go to MD Anderson to obtain that second opinion. For more than two decades, MD Anderson had been the best hospital in the US for cancer care. I asked Dr. Rabin for a referral to MD Anderson to see her colleague, Dr. Patrick A. Zweidler-McKay, whom a friend of mine had recommended to me. Due to his long last name, he went by Dr. Patrick.

Dr. Rabin knew him well. She had prepared a file containing Marcus's medical documents for us to take to MD Anderson. We didn't think we offended Dr. Rabin when asking for a referral to Dr. Patrick, and if we did, we didn't care about that. It wasn't the right time nor relevant to consider the doctors' feelings. It was the right time to think about how we could save Marcus's life. We had to stand up for him, and most importantly, if we didn't do anything, Marcus would die. If we didn't act, life itself would act upon Marcus.

My husband and I went straight from the meeting at TCH to the admissions office at MD Anderson, which was a five-minute walk from TCH

Chapter Twenty-Four

Main Campus. I had already contacted the admissions office by phone and requested Dr. Patrick to take Marcus's case.

From the first second I set foot at MD Anderson, I felt this hospital was something special—as if my intuition pulled me in that direction.

On May 19, the admissions officer called me to inform me that Dr. Patrick had accepted Marcus's case. Two hours later, Dr. Patrick called me. He sounded like the most pleasant and sympathetic doctor I had ever talked to. He explained that he had heard about Marcus's case already through the National Oncology Group. He wanted to see Marcus in his clinic the day after at 2 p.m. He promised to order a child life specialist to be there for Marcus during the appointment. That was so thoughtful. He already respected Marcus and cared about him.

Our first experience at MD Anderson was excellent. The pediatric clinic was smaller than the oncology clinic at TCH. The atmosphere in the clinic was cozy. Dr. Patrick was gentle and caring when examining Marcus. My husband and I had a long and productive meeting with Dr. Patrick and his fellow. Dr. Patrick had a fresh view on Marcus's case. I sensed he had a high work ethic from the way he asked questions and dug further and further into details about Marcus. Before he would render his recommendations about what he could do for Marcus, he wanted to conduct a thorough investigation of Marcus's medical status. Dr. Patrick worked with his own team of specialists at MD Anderson. He wanted a complete neurological evaluation along with genetic testing to determine what type of leukemia Marcus suffered from. Since leukemia can mutate, it made sense to study the type of leukemia that had presented itself this time. Through his research and faculty work, Dr. Patrick had connections to colleagues and genetic research companies all over the US.

I wished Marcus had had Dr. Patrick from the onset of his initial diagnosis of leukemia. It didn't help looking back in time and regretting that we took Marcus to TCH and not MD Anderson when he was first diagnosed with leukemia. Nevertheless, I couldn't help wondering what the outcome would have been if, initially, Marcus had been a patient at MD Anderson.

Over the next two weeks, Dr. Patrick coordinated and ordered several diagnostic tests of Marcus. Marcus and I went to MD Anderson to get the following testing done: spinal tap, bone marrow biopsy, MRI of brain and spine, and EEG. For easy access to Marcus's veins and to spare him from much suffering, Dr. Patrick, my husband, and I decided to give Marcus a PICC line again. Marcus had appointments with Dr. Slopis, who was a senior neurologist, and Dr. Madden, who was a skilled pain management doctor at MD Anderson. When I first met the two of them, I knew I wanted them to be part of Marcus's Dream Team along with Dr. Patrick, as I could not think of any more qualified specialists. Like Dr. Patrick, they demonstrated a sensitivity toward Marcus unlike other doctors.

Marcus remained living at home, but the consequence was long days at MD Anderson and ambulance transports back and forth between MD Anderson in the medical center and our home. Each ambulance ride would take from thirty minutes to hours depending on the traffic situation. I spent much time coordinating transport, getting transport insurance authorizations, and being on top of Marcus's appointments. Dr. Patrick monitored Marcus's labs carefully. Luckily, the leukemia did not progress.

In the midst of all this testing, Marcus's birthday came up on May 27. After the leukemia relapsed, I prayed this would not be his last birthday. It was time for celebrating Marcus's life. He deserved a party.

Three days before his birthday, I made a homemade Danish birthday cake and made hot cocoa. That's how we celebrate a child's birthday in Denmark. I made the strawberry filling, the layers, and the chocolate icing on top. We sang "Happy Birthday" to him and celebrated with his nurse Grace. Marcus tasted the strawberry filling and chocolate icing and swallowed it.

The season for flooding had started. Houston is vulnerable to tropical thunderstorms and dangerous flash flooding. It happened often, causing the city to enter into a state of emergency. On Memorial Day, May 25, a system moved over our area, causing heavy rain and flooding. Lucas's school had to close, and Jacob received orders to stay home from work. We couldn't take it for granted that Marcus's nurses would make it to their shifts on time.

Our life was stressful already, and the weather situation did not make it any better. On the other hand, an unexpected family day home wasn't bad, either. I made Danish-style crepes with Lucas, and we played a bit with Marcus. For Marcus's birthday, Lucas had decided to give him a big blue ball that was easy to kick for Marcus. Lucas had also picked the movie *The Penguins of Madagascar* for Marcus. Marcus kicked the blue ball with great force. The Botox treatment had started to work, and he had good movement and flexibility in his legs and hips. He controlled the ball very well compared to months before.

On his birthday morning on May 27, my husband, Lucas, and I entered Marcus's room singing a Danish birthday song for him. We all waved our hands and held Danish red-and-white paper flags. His nurse Niso had told him it was his birthday. Marcus was awake with big open eyes when we entered the room to wish him happy birthday. It was festive. Unfortunately, that day, he had appointments at MD Anderson. We left at 10 A.M. and returned at 7 P.M. after a long day.

Exactly one year before on Marcus's birthday in 2014, we all happily celebrated with him in Hawaii. I hadn't imagined that the year after, Marcus would be at MD Anderson brain damaged and diagnosed with relapsed leukemia. It reminded me how fragile life was. We should never take life or happiness for granted.

One thing I felt deep in my heart were gratitude and love. I felt gratitude because Marcus was still with us. I felt a love so strong for Marcus and Lucas that I had never experienced before. I had two boys who were extremely lovable and who cared for each other. My love for them—and the love they expressed toward me—was I all needed. The bond of love was unbreakable.

Lucas graduated first grade and was awarded the Citizenship Award at the Village School Award Ceremony.

At the time of the award ceremony, unfortunately, I was with Marcus at MD Anderson so my husband attended the ceremony alone. There was reason to be proud of Lucas after completing such a demanding school year when his brother was sick and his life was turned upside down. My husband and I had to balance our attention between the two boys, and that was challenging.

Some days at MD Anderson were long, and Marcus, his nurse, and I did not return home until around 8 P.M.

Dr. Patrick emailed me or called me as soon as he had any diagnostic results about Marcus. Even away on a conference, Dr. Patrick worked at night and sent me Marcus's lab results so I could get them as soon as they were available.

A New Approach—A New Hospital

Over some weeks, all Marcus's diagnostic oncology results were gathered, and the conclusions were as follows:

Marcus's bone marrow contained 56 percent leukemia cells, which Dr. Patrick described as a full relapse. From a bone marrow perspective, Marcus still had a reserve of healthy bone marrow (44 percent normal bone marrow), which should help Marcus tolerate chemotherapy.

Fifty percent of the leukemia cells were T-cell ALL, which was the same type of leukemia Marcus had when he was first diagnosed a year before. Six percent were AML, which was a new type of leukemia. That meant the leukemia had mutated during the relapse, and that it would be even more challenging to treat it this time.

Marcus's spinal tap showed that there was a small amount of blood in his spinal fluid, which was normal. However, the pathology report revealed that in the spinal tap, there were some blast-like cells, which most likely stemmed from Marcus's blood, but the doctors couldn't be sure. Dr. Patrick's first goal was to get rid of the leukemia cells in the peripheral blood, and if his next spinal tap still showed evidence of active leukemia, he would then treat that through a second round of treatment.

Dr. Patrick had created a master plan for Marcus. He listened to all our requests about treating Marcus as gently as possible. We had stressed our desire was to keep Marcus at home and bring him to MD Anderson for treatments.

The types of chemotherapies he had chosen for Marcus were the ones with the least neurotoxicity, having the least side effects on Marcus's brain and central nervous system.

Dr. Patrick had asked Dr. Madden and Dr. Slopis to develop a pain management plan, anti-nausea plan, anti-neurotoxicity plan, and anti-seizure plan for Marcus.

Dr. Patrick, the captain of Marcus's Dream Team, wanted to think everything through so Marcus could get preventative treatment against all side effects. He wished for Marcus to feel good all the time during treatment. Was Dr. Patrick going to be able to bring him into remission without using Nelarabine? Nobody knew the answer. Only time would tell.

While waiting for the results of all the testing, Marcus enjoyed some quiet days at home.

Chapter Twenty-Four

One afternoon, Marcus had a successful soccer session with me. Marcus used the new blue plastic ball Lucas had given him for his birthday. He trapped the ball with his feet, then rolled it to the sides and back and forth. We listened to upbeat music, and I did some exercises with his arms and asked him to turn his head to the right and to the left. He was able to turn it to the right side but not the left side because the neck muscles in his left side were too stiff. I told him how proud I was of him, and he smiled. Even with acute leukemia in his body, he made progress. Heading back to Marcus's bedroom, I arranged a procession with Marcus, his nurse Rudolf, and me.

"I need you to help me, Marcus," I told him. "I need you to kick your blue ball in front of you while I push the wheelchair." I placed the ball by his feet and stepped back.

Marcus understood my message and started kicking the ball softly in front of his feet. He controlled the ball remarkably well. I followed by pushing his wheelchair, and behind me, Rudolf pushed Marcus's ventilator. The procession moved, slowly of course, and while it did, Rudolf said something funny and Marcus and I started laughing.

My philosophy was that we should continue life as before Marcus relapsed. There was still hope that Dr. Patrick and his team would be able to bring Marcus into remission again. There was still hope that Marcus would continue his rehab, recover, and eventually have an almost normal life again. Really, nobody could know how his journey would end.

That night, the Epic office didn't send any night nurse for Marcus. The office couldn't find any available nurse, and there was no other solution than for me to take care of Marcus during the night.

His day nurse had left, and Marcus was in bed in his room, ready for his evening routines. I leaned in toward him and whispered, "It's just the two of us tonight, honey."

Marcus smiled. I think he enjoyed being alone with me. It was Marcus and Mommy time. For me, it was extra work, of course, and I was already tired. I had spent all my resources on Marcus and had taken Lucas to soccer practice and spent time with him too.

Marcus's plan of care was always present on the nursing desk, and I knew how to read it and sign off on it. I followed it systematically and was comfortable handling his medicines and feedings. I knew everything. Hours of training at TCH and HealthBridge paid off.

Marcus slept well but woke up twice. I had to change his night shirt a few times due to excessive sweating. I mastered all his night routines, including turning him, changing him, suctioning him, and administering his medicines. The following morning at seven, his day nurse Grace arrived and I could get some sleep.

During the weekends, Lucas, Marcus, and my husband were able to watch soccer together in the living room. It was a good activity for the three of them. Lucas found pleasure in reading books to Marcus, showing him cool toys, and simply hanging out with his big brother.

Marcus's nurse Niso reported that she had witnessed more progress with Marcus and was happy to see how he slowly got better and better. She had noticed that Marcus produced more sounds even without the use of his speaking valve. She had been able to get Marcus ready for the night without any problems. She could ask him to open his mouth and jaw, and he would let her brush his tongue with his toothbrush.

She and I discussed how unfair it was that the leukemia had relapsed. It didn't make sense to have Marcus and us go through that horrible year fighting back to a new life only to discover that the cancer nightmare had to start all over again. The more we talked about it, the more we tried to find some meaning behind all that happened to Marcus. There was no meaning. The only way forward was to accept the circumstances and be grateful that Marcus was stronger and had recovered so well after he had received his Baclofen pump. We had to look for all the positive things about the situation. I especially was grateful that Dr. Patrick had accepted Marcus's case.

Finally, from his research colleague, Dr. Patrick had received the reports with Marcus's test results, but they were not what we had hoped for. The researcher hadn't found any genetic problem in Marcus's leukemia cells that he was able to treat. There was still one option left that the genetic testing from FoundationOne Heme would render some treatable results. Again, more time was needed to finalize the testing and research into Marcus's leukemia cells.

On June 9, Marcus scored his first soccer goal after coming home from HealthBridge. I had rolled Marcus's wheelchair into our kitchen and placed

Chapter Twenty-Four

it in front of the sliding door to our back garden. I had opened the door and placed his outdoor soccer goal at a little distance from the sliding door. He kicked his big ball hard and right into the goal. He gave me a big smile after scoring. I recorded a video of him scoring. It was a huge accomplishment.

Marcus continued to practice talking with his speaking valve, making powerfully loud sounds. He improved all aspects of his physical training skills. I trained him to lift the big blue ball between his feet. For it to be easier for him to lift the ball, I placed Marcus in his wheelchair in front of the back of our couch so the ball could touch the back of the couch as he tried to lift it up high. He was able to lift the ball multiple times. I instructed him in Danish and English, and he followed all my commands.

"I have never seen Marcus so active before," his nurse Lee said with excitement.

"It's incredible how mobile and flexible Marcus's legs have become," I agreed. "He can control his lower body much better now. His upper body is still a challenge for him, but he'll get there."

I showed Marcus a school photo of him.

"Who is this?" I asked him.

He smiled. He could recognize himself in the photo. I kissed him.

The day before starting his chemotherapy treatment, Marcus and I had an appointment with Dr. Patrick. I had to obtain all orders for his new medicines and his preventative medicines for seizures, nausea, and pain. Dr. Patrick wanted to monitor Marcus's labs twice a week. First, he wanted to see if the leukemia blasts disappeared in his labs. Second, Dr. Patrick's concern was that Marcus's organs and electrolytes would be affected by the treatment. For that reason, he had to monitor closely how Marcus responded to the treatment. The conclusion was that once a week, Marcus's Epic nurse supervisor, Lisa, had to come to our home, draw his labs, and drive to MD Anderson to drop them off at the outpatient lab. For the second labs, I had to bring Marcus into MD Anderson. On top of that, either Dr. Patrick or another pediatric leukemia oncologist had to examine Marcus to assess how he did.

On June 16, flooding was expected in Houston and surrounding areas. Tropical Storm Bill was going to make landfall in Galveston, Texas. In anticipation of the flooding, Lucas's summer camp at school had been canceled. My husband had a meeting at work he couldn't cancel and thus could not take care of Lucas at home. Lucas wasn't allowed in the ambulance, as he was neither a patient nor a caregiver. This was the first day of Marcus's chemotherapy treatment at MD Anderson, and I could not cancel that appointment, either.

Luckily, Lucas was able to stay at Ross's house and play so I could go with Marcus to TCH and MD Anderson without having to worry about him. We were vulnerable because all our family was back in Denmark, but we were lucky to have such wonderful friends who helped us in our time of need.

Marcus had two types of IV chemotherapies. He had to receive extra hydration for four hours following the treatments. I arranged for Marcus to return home with IV fluids and a pump that I could return to MD Anderson the following week.

Marcus did well during his chemotherapy treatment. He had no seizures, and no complications arose.

At 3:30 P.M., Marcus was ready to go home. Tropical Storm Bill had not developed or moved into the Houston metropolitan area; therefore, it was safe to return home.

In the evening, Marcus's O2 sats dropped. Oxygen saturation is sometimes referred to as O sats, or simply, sats. O2 sat is a measurement of oxygen in the blood, or hemoglobin. It gives a picture as to how the body is oxygenating itself. I decided to add 0.5 liters of supplemental oxygen, which caused his sats to stabilize to a normal level again.

According to Marcus's chemotherapy plan developed by Dr. Patrick, Marcus needed some chemotherapy to be administered at home. His nurse and I had to give him IV syringes with Cytarabine and Mercaptopurine tablets.

Dr. Patrick had given permission for all of Marcus's therapies to continue as tolerated. I scheduled Reiki healing and massage sessions. I found it important to continue his wellness regiment, as this would strengthen his overall well-being and reduce the stress level from the chemotherapy. I also made appointments for his other therapies that were yet to start.

The day after on June 18, it was my and Jacob's tenth anniversary. We

Chapter Twenty-Four

had decided not to celebrate the day with dinner at a restaurant, as we didn't want to leave Marcus at night.

It should have been a happy day with celebration and joy. It started out as a good day, but during the day, Marcus had been more tired than usual and skipped chair time so he could rest.

Later in the evening, Niso wasn't relieved by the night nurse. She called the Epic office, and it turned out they had put Lee on as night nurse but had forgotten to tell him. I told them to find a new night nurse ASAP, as Niso needed to be relieved. At 9 p.m., a representative from the Epic office called. They had found a new nurse who could come at 11 p.m., so Niso had to stay an additional four hours. She was tired and had already worked for twelve hours, but she insisted she could stay. I helped her administer the chemotherapy and assisted with Marcus's night routines.

This was a good example of how the reality was in a family dependent on home health nurses. We never knew for sure if Marcus's nurses would turn up for their shifts.

On Monday, June 22, Marcus had his first appointment with Dr. Patrick after starting his leukemia treatment. Did Dr. Patrick's treatment work or not? We had placed all our trust in him and his team.

After getting the labs drawn in the pediatric clinic, we proceeded to get Marcus's PICC line dressing and caps changed in the IV center and the flushing of his PICC lines completed. We returned to the pediatric clinic and waited for the lab results. It was nerve-racking to wait. Was the chemotherapy effective? Was Marcus going to live or not?

Dr. Patrick entered the exam room. A relaxed smile crossed his face.

"All Marcus's blasts in his peripheral blood are gone," Dr. Patrick said. What joy he must have felt bringing Marcus and me such amazing results.

"Are you sure?" I couldn't believe what he just said. It was too good to be true. If I had had the space, I would have run a victory lap.

"Yes, I'm sure," he said and showed me the printouts of Marcus's lab results. "Look at these two other numbers here," he said while showing me some other printouts. "The two other numbers confirm that the leukemia blasts are reduced compared to before he started his treatment. Marcus has responded beautifully."

I looked at the numbers Dr. Patrick had highlighted on the sheets. Wow!

A New Approach—A New Hospital

It was indeed a spectacular triumph. The treatment worked. I enjoyed the communal energy of the room.

I was hoping for even more updates. "Did you get the report from FoundationOne?" I asked.

"I just did." Dr. Patrick pulled it out from his stack of papers.

"The report reveals that Marcus has three mutations, of which one can be treated with targeted therapy on children. I have an ongoing trial regarding the second mutation, but Marcus has to be eighteen years old in order to participate," Dr. Patrick said. He looked thoughtful for a moment.

"For now, I don't want to change anything in his treatment plan because his current treatment seems to be effective."

Marcus was awake and heard the discussions about his results. He wanted to talk to Dr. Patrick. Marcus's home nurse Remota and I raised the back of the stretcher so Marcus could sit up. Marcus vocalized and tried to get eye contact with Dr. Patrick. Marcus must have understood the good news but could not let us know how he felt.

It was a wonderful moment to witness the relief and excitement we all felt following the first lab results. I called Jacob at work to share the good news. Nothing could beat that feeling I experienced and hearing the relief in his voice when he heard Marcus had responded to the treatment.

"So the downside of Marcus's situation now is that his white blood count is zero-point-two, which means he has close to no immune system protecting him. You have to be extremely careful that Marcus does not get any infection from Lucas or anybody else. If there is the slightest sign of fever or infection, you have to call the clinic," Dr. Patrick said.

I wasn't intimidated by his instructions. Of course, we had to be on top of infection control measures at home.

"We will be extra careful watching Marcus for signs of infection. I promise I will instruct all his home health nurses about the increased risk," I said.

Once home, we celebrated the good news with Lucas as he returned from school. Marcus was in his wheelchair in the living room. Carefully, Lucas caressed Marcus on his hair and chin.

"Marcus's leukemia is all gone in his blood," I explained to Lucas while he started jumping up and down from excitement.

Chapter Twenty-Four

"Does that mean Marcus has no more leukemia, Mommy?" Lucas asked me.

"We hope so. It means the treatment he got works. Dr. Patrick is helping Marcus, and he'll soon feel better."

Marcus smiled. He enjoyed Lucas caressing him and the two of us discussing the good news.

"Time for celebration!" I clapped my hands together. "Please get Marcus's ball, Lucas. Let's play soccer."

Marcus, Lucas, and I played a bit of soccer. When Marcus got tired, I found a cartoon on the TV and let the boys hang out together. It was as if Marcus had finished a marathon and was resting after celebrating his results. There was a sense of completion in the air. A tremendous satisfaction that something great and amazing had been achieved. Once again, Marcus was on his way to recovery.

CHAPTER TWENTY-FIVE

New Hope

We celebrated life. With Marcus, we had experienced both sides of the line. At one end, there was cancer, while at the other end, there was life. Now we were at the end where life once again was close to becoming reality. We celebrated that Dr. Patrick had given Marcus a second chance. He had believed in Marcus, in us, and in himself. It took a great deal of risk and self-confidence to take on Marcus's complex case, and only Dr. Patrick possessed that level of self-confidence.

We celebrated. Dr. Patrick had given our family a gift so special that there was no way we could ever thank him with words—only a celebration could do. I wished we could freeze this moment so we could remain in that bubble of time when life was so present and made so much sense.

Jacob came home early from work. He had a conference call but was able to spend some precious moments with Marcus before continuing working in his home office.

Lisa from the Epic office called to inform me that the nurses were not allowed to administer chemotherapy via G-tube or by IV route. This meant that I had to give Marcus all chemotherapy from now on. I didn't understand how a professional and licensed nurse was unauthorized to administer chemotherapy while I, without any medical or nursing degree, was competent to do so. Marcus's home health nurses hadn't raised any concerns. They were fully proficient and knew how to do it. I guessed Epic policies didn't have to make sense. My husband used to say that if you don't understand it, then memorize it. Therefore, I did exactly that.

Some days later when Niso arrived in the morning for her day shift, she

Chapter Twenty-Five

brought a birthday present for Marcus and a present for Lucas. Marcus got a Messi jersey and shorts, and Lucas got a stylus with his name engraved on it. Niso put on Marcus's new Messi set, and it fit him perfectly. Immediately, Lucas tested his stylus. He loved it. Niso truly cared about both boys. She was a single mom with a teenage daughter, and I think she enjoyed spoiling the boys a bit.

Marcus continued to do well even though we noticed he became increasingly sleepy. He started to develop some reddish rash that we suspected was an allergic reaction to his prophylactic antibiotic treatment. His labs continued to show promising results. His leukemia blasts were gone in his peripheral blood, but his immune system was completely gone too. Along with Marcus's nurses, we decided that Lucas could only stay at the end of Marcus's bed. Lucas was in summer camp and could easily bring home germs that could be deadly for Marcus.

Optimism continued to dominate our spirits, as well as Marcus's. After we received good news about the recent labs, Marcus and I missed no chance to celebrate again. Marcus was sitting in his wheelchair in the kitchen, and we both looked inside a new science book Grandma had given him. I read aloud and we studied the pictures. Suddenly Marcus began to move his hands and arms. He let his arms and hands rest on the tray attached to his wheelchair and moved them toward the middle of the book. He smiled. I smiled too, and then Marcus smiled more.

"What a good job!" I told Marcus.

He had been able to move them earlier on during the recovery phase, but due to the intense tone, for months he hadn't been able to control his arms and hands at all. This was like a new beginning for him. He looked surprised at his own movements.

When Jacob and Lucas returned home, Marcus could sometimes hear it and vocalized loudly to get their attention. He started to listen to new audiobooks I had bought for him with money Marcus had received from friends. I had bought an audiobook series of *The Magic Treehouse* for Marcus. I also bought a CD with music by Colombian singer Shakira, whose song "Waka Waka (This Time for Africa)," was the official song of the 2010 FIFA World Cup in South Africa. The boys loved "Waka Waka."

On Sunday, June 28, Marcus's day nurse didn't show up. I called the

Epic office, and the representative assured me he would try to find a nurse but prepared me that he might not be successful.

Two hours after hanging up with the Epic representative, no nurse had arrived and Marcus had started to develop a fever. I was scared and angry, and my husband was very upset with the Epic office for not prioritizing Marcus's case. All staff at the Epic office knew Marcus was battling relapsed leukemia and had no immune system.

By 10:30 A.M., still no nurse had arrived. Marcus had a fever of 102. He had developed a red rash on his thighs and in his armpits, and his cheeks were flushed. I believed the rash was due to an allergic reaction, but I was unsure. I called the pediatric clinic at MD Anderson and asked what I should do. The nurse told me to bring Marcus into the clinic.

Once admitted to MD Anderson, he was assigned a nice and spacious room in the PICU with a TV and a separate bathroom. I called it Marcus's Presidential Suite.

At MD Anderson, the nurse did all the workup. Labs were drawn and X-rays were taken of Marcus's lungs. The PICU doctor ordered Marcus's home antibiotic treatment to be stopped, as the doctor suspected the antibiotic was indeed causing the rash.

The testing revealed that Marcus needed extra fluids with electrolytes and a different type of antibiotic. Marcus was very neutropenic, meaning his immune system was extremely low, his white blood count being 0.1. Marcus also needed a blood transfusion and possibly platelets. The X-rays of his lungs suggested a possible slight infection in two areas of his lungs.

Some hours after Marcus started his treatment, his fever dropped and he clearly felt better. He showed interest in watching TV and vocalized when the doctors came to examine him. Later, my husband and Lucas arrived.

The week before, I had arranged a guided tour for Lucas at MD Anderson's pediatric facilities. Marcus's child life specialist Brittney was automatically Lucas's child life specialist. I wanted Lucas to feel safe when coming to MD Anderson for the first time. Lucas liked Brittney, who had given him a child-friendly introduction to MD Anderson. Now Lucas took on the role of showing my husband around the floor, including showing him the Ronald McDonald kitchen. I made popcorn for them to enjoy. Despite being a cancer hospital, it was a place that was safe for Marcus and a place that was welcoming to our family.

After being admitted to MD Anderson's PICU, which was called Rainforest, Marcus quickly got stable. His electrolytes returned to normal, and he felt better after receiving blood and platelets. All his labs were negative for infections, and the only detected bacteria was pseudomonas in his trach, the one that had been colonized in his trach for a long time. Marcus received the last chemotherapy called PEG-ASP, which was safe to give him because the medicine didn't affect his immune system. After that chemotherapy treatment, Marcus was due to recover to allow his labs to normalize again.

The team in PICU was progressive and eager to set up goals for Marcus. I discussed several initiatives I wanted implemented for Marcus so he could improve and feel better. They listened very carefully to all my requests; they made notes and made them become real. They wanted Marcus to improve as much as we did. The attitude of the hospital staff was positive, and Marcus got individualized and qualified care as if he were their only pediatric patient. He got that much personalized attention. What a difference it made that they treated him with dignity and respect.

A physical therapist and an occupational therapist were assigned to him. They had reviewed Marcus's case before coming to make the evaluation. How prepared they both were impressed me. Usually, I had to tell everyone the full story about Marcus's condition.

Ray, the physical therapist, asked me to bring in Marcus's wheelchair, as the PICU doctor had approved for Marcus to do chair time again. The therapists did bedside balance exercises, strengthening, and stretching exercises with him. They talked about sports to Marcus, and he cheered up.

"Everybody at MD Anderson talks about your soccer videos," Ray said to Marcus. "You really know what to do with a soccer ball." He directed his attention toward me. "I'd like to see the videos. Can I?"

"Of course you can," I replied. "I'll show them to you next time you come. I have to get Lucas soon from school, so I need to leave the medical center before rush hour starts."

"Sounds great. So does Marcus do physical and occupational therapy at home?" Ray asked.

"No, Lucas and I do all the training with Marcus. The Epic office hasn't been able to organize any therapists to work with him yet." I grimaced a bit. "To be honest, I'm very disappointed. They know it's extremely important for Marcus to get strong and do rehab so he can better tolerate the leukemia treatment."

Ray crossed his arms over his chest, his brow furrowed. "I can't believe Marcus has been home for that many months and still hasn't received any therapy yet." He shook his head in dismay. "I'm glad we can help him now. He needs to start immediately. The PICU team has ordered it."

"Thanks for your efforts, Ray," I said, reaching out to shake his hand. "You are now part of Marcus's MD Anderson Dream Team."

Marcus needed support to sit on the bedside, but he was able to hold his head a bit. Ray got a stool for him to place his feet on. He directed Marcus to let his hands rest on the bedside for support. He also ordered some special boots for Marcus to wear that prevented his legs from "frogging out" and causing drop foot. Foot drop, sometimes called drop foot, is a general term for difficulty in lifting the front part of one's foot. "Frogging out" referred to Marcus's inability to keep his legs together, especially when lying in bed. His legs fell to each side, opening up as a frog's legs.

The PICU doctor entered the room. Contrary to what the PICU doctor did at TCH, the MD Anderson PICU doctor actually looked at Marcus and assessed him in person. The doctor did not rely on a fellow or resident to do the examination. The PICU doctor explained that the X-rays of his lungs contained no signs of infection. All labs remained negative, but he had a small urinary tract infection that could easily be treated with an ointment.

"Marcus is back to his baseline. He's actually my healthiest patient," the PICU doctor stated.

"Really?" I scoffed a bit. "Nobody ever said that about Marcus after he got leukemia."

"Yes, I mean it. If Marcus hadn't been ventilated, he would've been in the regular pediatric unit down the hall. It's just that the regular unit doesn't have any respiratory therapists. That's why Marcus has to stay in PICU."

It made me so happy. I couldn't believe what she said. Marcus was her healthiest patient in PICU!

"I love the way you put it," I said, beaming with pride.

Chapter Twenty-Five

"And I mean it." She reached out and squeezed my arm. "He's doing very well."

The next day, I brought a big box of Merci chocolate for the PICU team. I liked them already. They respected Marcus and showed commitment to his progress, and I wanted to honor them for that attitude.

It was July 1, and Marcus's labs had started to recover. Before they could discharge him, the PICU doctors needed to see a trend in his labs that indicated his immune system showed signs of improvement.

Meanwhile at home, my husband and I had a meeting with two representatives from Epic, one being the manager of the Katy office who was in charge of Marcus's case. We asked them to provide better service and communication, and we shared the problems we had experienced when no nurses showed up for shifts. Based on the meeting, the Epic Katy office representatives promised to improve.

The following day, Marcus had a good day trying for the first time to stand up with the help of his therapists. That was an immense challenge for him. The respiratory therapist was present monitoring his breathing efforts to make sure his heart rate didn't increase too long. He also gave Marcus additional oxygen to fuel his muscles during the workout. They didn't want him to be stressed out. It was meant as a test to see his current performance level. I had picked up his blue training ball from home and suggested to Marcus that he do a little ball show for the staff. He did so while sitting comfortably in his wheelchair. I recognized the smile on his face, that very charming smile showing the world that he rocked what he did.

He enjoyed being the center of attention in a positive way. He had always been a performer and a true entertainer. He was never shy of showing off, and he proved it again this time. His therapists cheered for him, clapped, and smiled big.

However, it was not all fun. The side effects of the chemotherapy treatment and low immune system had started to affect Marcus. His bottom became red and irritated. The PICU doctor ordered a barrier cream for him to apply on the sensitive skin. The nurses and I also experimented by blowing concentrated oxygen directly onto the irritated skin area. To our surprise, the method accelerated the healing dramatically.

Lucas came to visit Marcus too. As a surprise, I had organized Brittney to do some activities with Lucas in the kids' playroom. Brittney also had a special treat for him.

"Lucas, do you want to go to the observation deck on the twenty-fourth floor with me?" Brittney asked Lucas. "You can see the whole city from the deck!"

His eyes bulged as wide as saucers. "Yes, yes, I would like to do that!" Lucas replied.

"Only very few people are allowed to go up there. You get an impressive view," Brittney explained. Lucas rushed out the door with her.

When he returned, he was eager to tell me all about his little excursion. He believed he could see all the way to our home in West Houston. Then he had popcorn and lemonade while watching a cartoon on the TV alongside Marcus, who rested quietly in his bed.

After Lucas and Marcus had enjoyed some movie time, I took Lucas to our friends' house. Rikke babysat for Marcus and Lucas when they were younger. She was Danish and had married Brian, who was American. Lucas had been invited over to play and have a sleepover.

After dropping Lucas at Rikke and Brian's place, my cell phone rang. A tightness expanded in my chest. It was the PICU doctor.

"I'm calling you because Marcus has had some kind of attack and is unconscious. I will take him down to do a CT scan right away," the PICU doctor said. It sounded as if she called me from Marcus's room. Background noises indicated they were hastening to take him to the CT scan.

I turned off the radio in my car.

"No! What happened?" I felt sick, wishing it wasn't true that Marcus had had an attack. I needed to give myself a few moments for my rational brain to take over.

"He was sleeping, and then the alarms went off. When the nurse checked on him, she couldn't wake him up," the PICU doctor said.

I shook my head in denial, praying he would be all right.

"It may have been some type of seizure or cramp," I suggested. "I'm on my way back to MD Anderson now. I'll be there in fifteen minutes."

"Okay, we'll talk when you get there." The PICU doctor hang up.

It was difficult to pay attention to the busy traffic. Cars were everywhere, and it seemed like I hit all the red lights. How could I get to MD Anderson faster? Was there a quicker way to get there? I felt trapped in traffic.

I was worried. This was the first time the PICU doctor had called me about Marcus. When I arrived at Marcus's room, the nurse told me he had woken up. Thank God. The doctor had decided to carry through with the CT scan to rule out any signs of stroke.

It was three in the afternoon, and Marcus returned to his room. The CT scan didn't show any signs of stroke. Marcus was awake but seemed confused.

"You're fine, Marcus." I was at his side, holding his hand. "Mommy is here with you. You had a big cramp, but it's over."

Days went by as Marcus recovered at MD Anderson and his blood counts improved. We experienced some victories. Marcus's therapy at MD Anderson yielded more results. Marcus could lift his legs while sitting at the bedside. Without stressing his heart rate, he could tolerate bedside sitting for five to ten minutes with support.

On July 10, he was discharged. I made sure to have Marcus's PICU doctor sign prescriptions for Marcus to start physical, occupational, and speech therapy at home and fax them directly to the Epic office. I had experienced unnecessary delays on TCH's part in sending those prescriptions to the Epic office, so this time I made sure that all paperwork was completed and received by the Epic office before Marcus left MD Anderson.

Once again, Marcus was home where he belonged. Thanks to MD Anderson and the fantastic attitude we met there, Marcus was off to a new start, hopefully this time without leukemia.

At home, Marcus slept a lot. He started his home-wellness program. When cold, I massaged his feet to warm them up and improve blood circulation. We listened to music and played with Lucas.

On July 16, Marcus went in to get his spinal tap and bone marrow biopsy done. It was like going to a college exam with Marcus. Did he pass or not? Was the leukemia really gone?

In the evening, Dr. Patrick's nurse practitioner Lisa called.

"I got the results from his spinal tap. There are no leukemia blasts in his spinal fluid!" she said, relieved.

A sigh of relief escaped my lips. "That's perfect. I remember Dr. Patrick said the first spinal tap was infected by blasts from his peripheral blood. He was right!"

"Yes, his spinal tap is clear," Lisa confirmed.

"I need to call my husband," I said. "When will you have the final results from the bone marrow biopsy?"

"Probably in four days," Lisa told me.

I had a good feeling about Marcus's response, sensing amazing news was on its way.

One night at nine, Marcus was alert when I walked in to say good night to him.

"Let me tell you a story," I said to Marcus, who looked like he was up for some fun. "At MD Anderson, they can enroll a child in a program administered by the Make-A-Wish Foundation. So you can wish for something, and then maybe a representative can help organize it for you. I have enrolled you in the program already." Marcus smiled at me. "I heard that five years ago, the Barcelona soccer team visited MD Anderson. Squeeze my hand if you want that to be your first wish."

I held his hand, and he squeezed it hard.

"Okay, I got it. I think you should have a second wish just in case your first wish is not possible to fulfill. Before you got sick, you told me you wished to go to San Francisco to watch the 49ers play a game. Do you want that to be your second wish?"

Once again, he squeezed my hand hard. He was adorable. I implanted some dreams in his head. He deserved to have something to look forward to once all his treatments were completed. It was still possible that Marcus could recover, and I wanted him to keep that dream alive.

It was Monday, July 20, and Marcus was due for his appointment with Dr. Patrick. It was time to get the results from the bone marrow biopsy. Marcus and I waited in the exam room. Dr. Patrick knocked on the door and entered the room with a smile on his face.

That was it. It was enough for me. I sensed he had good news printed on his papers.

His cheeks going lightly pink with pleasure, Dr. Patrick did a quick recap of Marcus's status.

"I am thrilled about the spinal tap results, but on top of this, the final

Chapter Twenty-Five

pathology report shows that Marcus has only point-nine percent blasts left in his bone marrow."

I paused a moment for the words to sink in and to fully appreciate the consequences of this result. Then everything changed. I felt ultra-awake.

"Yes, yes, yes! Thank you, thank you, Dr. Patrick! I don't know how to thank you. It's incredible." My level of happiness rose to ecstatic.

"I cannot believe it. Marcus, you did it again!" I said while kissing Marcus and hugging him nonstop.

"I know. It's a fantastic result. To be honest, I had hoped for a result around thirty percent blasts left after the first round of chemotherapy, but point-nine percent is unbelievable," Dr. Patrick said, a broad smile overtaking his face. "This blast result is low enough that Marcus can continue to the stem cell transplantation unit for evaluation."

"What do you mean?" I rubbed the back of my neck. Did Dr. Patrick just talk about the stem cell transplantation?

"I want the transplant team to meet with Marcus and you for an evaluation. I already told them Lucas is a match. In the meantime, I'll design the second round of chemotherapy for Marcus to start in about a week or so." Dr. Patrick pushed up his sleeves.

He was way ahead of me, and I loved it. This was even better than expected. It was almost too much awesomeness for one day. Marcus was due to get a stem cell transplant evaluation. He had never reached that step at TCH. A stem cell transplantation would give Marcus a chance to recover permanently from the leukemia. It was unreal. Marcus could possibly survive this. He could become an adult with Lucas, get married, and have children one day. The future looked bright and open. A powerful seed of optimism was implanted inside my heart.

There was no way back now. Marcus was gaining momentum. His home therapists started working with him and made goals for him to speed up his recovery. The occupational therapist made him work with balls and tools. He could hold and let go of his hands and control his hands and finger movements much better. He could push buttons on a tool panel and showed progress with his fine motor skills. I recorded all his progress on my iPad so I could show it to Marcus's Dream Team at MD Anderson.

As Marcus got a break without chemotherapy, his hair grew healthy, shiny, and very long. In a sweet manner, nurse Niso teased him that he had bushy hair.

I organized Marcus's hairdresser Sarah to come and cut his hair at home. Marcus got a stylish short look, ready for a new beginning. With the unbearable Houston summer heat, he sure needed it too.

It was summer vacation time for Lucas, but we hadn't been able to make any trips with him yet that summer. All our focus was directed on Marcus, but with the new results from Marcus's testing, my husband could plan a short getaway with Lucas. This would be Lucas's summer vacation this year. Jacob planned to take Lucas on a road trip to New Braunfels, located close to San Antonio. They explored caves together, and Lucas had a blast. Jacob could focus entirely on Lucas, resting assured I was on top of the situation at home.

One night, I had a dream about Marcus. I dreamed that Marcus had started school again. He had played on the school playground—just him alone. It was a warm summer day with blue skies and a soft breeze. Marcus ran around on the playground completely normal as he did before he got sick. Part of the dream was that I had been to the first parent-teacher conference. All Marcus's teachers were sitting there around the table telling me about how Marcus did in school. They told me Marcus was a sweet student, very calm, and loved by all. Then I woke up. It was morning. I realized it was just a dream. I ran down to Marcus and shared my dream with him. He reacted to my retelling with eagerness and impressions as if he was ready to get out of bed and go to school right at that moment. I was sure that was his deepest desire. It was everyone's desire, and now it was realistic.

I showed Marcus how he could start practicing with his big blue plastic ball himself. If I rolled his wheelchair in front of one of the kitchen walls, he could kick the ball against the wall at his own initiative. With his legs, he could lift the ball up high, holding it tightly between his legs. His nurse Remota was cheering him on as I recorded it on my iPad.

"Come on, Marcus. Lift the ball, lift the ball." Her eyes glowed with delight as she kept cheerleading.

Then he did it, and Remota jumped and danced with joy. I absolutely loved that most of Marcus's nurses were so engaged in his progress. Their

Chapter Twenty-Five

desire for Marcus to heal was so strong that Marcus felt their positive energy too. They were also part of Marcus's Dream Team.

On July 28, Marcus started his second round of chemotherapy. His lab results had improved sufficiently, and he was strong enough to continue the next phase of his chemotherapy regiment. Dr. Patrick had to monitor Marcus's liver numbers, as they were too high. Again, time was of the essence. With leukemia treatment, the doctors seldom have the luxury of allowing excessive time for the patient to recover fully. The cancer is always lurking around the corner. I always joked with Dr. Patrick about his research. I told him he had to work much faster in finding a cure for leukemia.

At home, Marcus had a steady group of nurses that took care of him, but on and off, the Epic office representatives were forced to send new nurses. A cancer patient, Marcus was a challenge for many of his new nurses. They were specialists in home care, not cancer care; thus, it was important for them not to be thrown into a shift with Marcus without proper training first. One of those new nurses was a man named Emmanuel who was supposed to come train with Niso. When he came, he arrived ten minutes early and sat waiting outside in his car until it was time to come in. I liked that.

He was talkative and nice. I was curious to know why he came that early and waited outside in his car. He explained that he received his nursing training in Russia where he attended college.

We were in Marcus's room, and Emmanuel was sitting in the office chair in the nursing station. He looked up, rushing his words.

"When I studied and did my training in Russia, the first thing our professors told us was that if you come late, the patient was dead." Emmanuel continued with animated gestures. "This taught us discipline. After that, I never came late—ever! I am always ten minutes early."

I could take inspiration from this story.

"Early is good!" I said. "This is my motto from now on when it comes to Marcus's nurses. Early is good. Let me tell you this story I once read about former Prime Minister of Denmark Anders Fogh Rasmussen. Later he became Secretary General of NATO." Emmanuel was all ears.

"So, once he was asked why he had had such a successful career. One of the things he mentioned was that he was always ten minutes early for meetings. Apparently, one time another person had tried to show up early for a meeting in an attempt to be the first one." I covered my smile with a hand.

"What happened?" Emmanuel fidgeted with his pencil.

"When he arrived, to his surprise, Anders Fogh Rasmussen was already there, ready to start the meeting."

"There you go," Emmanuel said.

I had many interesting conversations with most of Marcus's nurses. The shifts were twelve hours, and there were often long periods when Marcus was resting or sleeping. I enjoyed engaging with the nurses and having them entertain me about their backgrounds, their career paths, their families, and dreams about the future.

On July 31, the conference with the transplant team at MD Anderson took place. Lucas was off to play in the kids' playroom while Marcus, my husband, and I met with the transplant doctor. Marcus had another exam to pass. Would the team approve him as a candidate for a bone marrow transplant? If so, when would it happen?

The conclusion of the meeting was that Marcus could be a bone marrow transplant candidate once he functioned better and had completed an intense rehab program. He needed aggressive rehab for two to three months, and the best place to get that was at TIRR at Memorial Hermann Hospital in Houston.

On a positive note, the transplant doctor stated that Marcus had a donor match in Lucas, and had he not had Lucas, it could easily take the transplant team five to six months to find a suitable donor. Summing it up, Lucas could save Marcus's life.

The next plan of action was for Marcus to start rehab at TIRR. First, Marcus's neurologist, Dr. Slopis at MD Anderson, had to see Marcus again due to our concerns about Marcus's cramps. His primary goal was to control the cramps or seizures with medications, specifically with a medication called Keppra.

At Marcus's next appointment, I showed Dr. Slopis all my iPad recordings of Marcus's latest top performances at home. Dr. Slopis listened much more than he talked. He asked questions about Marcus. He wanted to know everything about his progress.

"This is exciting. Cognitively, Marcus is more engaged and interactive

Chapter Twenty-Five

with his surroundings. This is a good trend. I like that Marcus laughs at his funny audiobooks," Dr. Slopis said while analyzing Marcus's different facial expressions. He took his time.

I asked Dr. Slopis numerous questions. He was a tremendous resource and contained such a wealth of information and knowledge.

"Why does Marcus get these cramps and seizures? Do they hurt?" I asked.

"Marcus's brain damage is complex, and more factors play a role. Marcus's brain changes as it tries to repair itself. It's important that I change Marcus's neurological treatment as his needs change."

Dr. Slopis had a perfect blend of warmth and confidence. An elderly doctor with grayish-white hair, he had the wisdom and intelligence that only comes with age. No doubt, this was something that could only be acquired through many years of practice in his field of expertise. Dr. Slopis was enthusiastic about serving Marcus; he let the spotlight shine on him. Dr. Slopis swallowed before he spoke.

"I don't think his cramps and seizures hurt him. His facial expressions and bodily expressions don't correspond to what they appear to be like. We can't interpret them as we interpret expressions on a normally functioning person." Dr. Slopis seemed to have a narrowed focus that allowed him to solely concentrate on Marcus. He laid his hand on Marcus, telling him he would be fine.

"Okay, I understand," I said. "Thank you for clarifying. I feel better now knowing that he doesn't feel pain as much." I stroked Marcus's hair.

"I'll put pressure on TIRR to make sure Marcus gets neurologically ready for a bone marrow transplant." A respected neurologist, Dr. Slopis could pull some strings for sure.

He also reassured me that he would do anything possible to help Marcus. This level of trust was a great compliment. As Marcus's other Dream Team members, he was a fine person with high integrity, and that was exactly why he was part of his Dream Team.

Marcus continued his next round of chemotherapy, and Dr. Patrick was very hopeful that the regimen would remain effective. At the same time, I wondered how I could be even more valuable to him as he prepared to go through rehab and the transplant process.

CHAPTER TWENTY-SIX

Gearing Up for the Bone Marrow Transplant

The Reiki healing had fascinated me ever since Marcus had started receiving treatments from Zee. I recalled that she had told me she also did classes and taught all the levels I would need if I ever considered becoming a Reiki master.

I had my doubts that Reiki was a cure-all, but I couldn't deny the fact that it was a gentle and safe way to induce relaxation and a wonderful experience for the person who received it. I was skeptical as to whether I would be able to feel the energy or be competent in the discipline of holistic and alternative care. Without any comparison, it was different from the legal world I mastered.

On the other hand, Zee kept saying that everybody had the ability to learn healing and she encouraged me to enroll in level one of the Reiki curriculum. I studied more and more about the Reiki philosophy and its ramifications.

I longed to experience the benefits of Reiki myself—the relaxation, immune system boost, and help with sleep. The Reiki sessions Zee did were expensive because she had to drive to get to Marcus, adding costs to her healing fee. It would be so much easier if I could heal Marcus myself. I could do it any time when he needed healing and I could give him multiple sessions during the week with no cost on our part.

In August, I completed two full days of Reiki training conducted by

Chapter Twenty-Six

Zee with a group of other students. Those two days were very intense but in a good way. I felt boosted with energy and confident after my training. I was ready to practice at home. I knew I could do it. I just had to believe in myself. Negative self-talk was a no-go.

I wanted to give it a few days before trying to heal Marcus. He had just started his second round of chemotherapy. I selected the nighttime for his healing session while he was lying in bed. I put on some soothing Reiki healing music and started my session. I did all the rituals as taught by Zee and as described in my Reiki study book. I placed my hands floating on top of Marcus's body. I grounded myself, remained focused, and felt the energy flowing from above, through my body, and out through my hands into Marcus's body. It was beautiful and very powerful. Marcus lay quiet and enjoyed it. He was so relaxed. I worked about thirty minutes and finished my session when I felt Marcus had received enough energy. I kissed him good night and went to bed.

While healing him, I felt this strange connection to him, like a reassuring and silent communication through energy waves. This positive experience laid the foundation for a completely different level of relationship to Marcus. The Reiki healing became an outlet through which I could give Marcus valuable strength and calmness. I couldn't cure Marcus's leukemia with healing, but while healing him, I could gently lift him up and place him in an invisible space where he was free and at peace.

I introduced Lucas and Jacob to Reiki by offering them a session. They happily agreed and both responded very well to their treatments.

As Marcus finished his second round of chemotherapy, he got increasingly tired, which was the reaction we all expected. The most important goal was that Marcus did not suffer from seizures or feel pain. To prevent that from happening, Dr. Slopis adjusted his Keppra medication while Dr. Madden was in charge of Marcus's tone and pain medicines. I communicated sometimes daily with Marcus's Dream Team to assess if any changes had to be made in any of his medications.

As always, some days were good and Marcus was alert and energized and participated in his therapy. At other times, he needed rest and was not up for any interaction or activities. We adapted any routines according to Marcus's needs. My goal was for Marcus to have active and meaningful days while he waited to be ready for his next bone marrow biopsy.

He had exciting sessions with his occupational therapist, Jade. She had bought an electrical toothbrush for Marcus to try. She worked diligently to help Marcus hold on to the toothbrush with his right hand and make small circles with it in his mouth as he tried to brush his teeth.

On another occasion, Lucas had invited Ross to come over for a playdate. Ross and Lucas had reached an age when Nerf guns were a big hit. Marcus had Nerf guns too and used to love to create a Nerf gun war by setting a battle scene in our house. When Lucas and Ross played with the Nerf guns in the living room, I made sure to have Marcus sit in his wheelchair in the kitchen facing the living room. That way, he could follow the boys as they played and could hear them talk and shout at each other—all while the Nerf gun darts flew all over the house. It was a nice distraction from all his daily routines.

The summer was ending. On August 24, Lucas turned seven and we celebrated him in school and with friends. On Lucas's actual birthday, I baked homemade muffins for his schoolmates. After school, Lucas invited Ross over to play and continue the celebrations at home with Marcus. The intensity of Lucas and Ross playing and talking caught Marcus's attention. It was kids' playtime and, even though Marcus was in his wheelchair watching, he benefited from being part of this joyful kid time.

Jacob and I had talked to Grandma and Grandpa about them coming to visit us in the fall to help us take care of Marcus and Lucas. It was evening, and Marcus was awake while the rest of the house was asleep.

"Mommy and Daddy have talked about inviting Grandma and Grandpa over in the fall to visit us again. They miss you and Lucas so much," I told him. "Squeeze my hand if you want them to come visit you and Lucas," I encouraged him.

Then Marcus squeezed my hand hard. This was a clear answer. Grandma and Grandpa should come soon. Marcus missed them.

On August 31, Marcus was due for his next bone marrow biopsy. Continually, he had gained weight, reaching almost seventy-seven pounds and growing at full speed.

On September 3, Dr. Patrick emailed me that he had received the results

Chapter Twenty-Six

from the bone marrow biopsy. Marcus had now only 0.7 percent leukemia blasts left in his bone marrow. The last biopsy showed 0.9 percent leukemia blasts left, so this was a reduction. On the other hand, Marcus had not completely reached 0 percent. He was in remission but not in full remission, which would have been preferable. Marcus's leukemia was aggressive, and Dr. Patrick now had to design a maintenance chemotherapy regiment that could keep the leukemia at bay while Marcus finalized his rehab efforts at TIRR.

Dr. Patrick made a block consisting of Methotrexate and PEG-ASP. He could give Marcus a high dose from the beginning, or start out on a lower dose and then escalate the dose to the maximum tolerated one. Because Marcus faced serious neurotoxicity issues, Dr. Patrick decided to start on a low dose. Before giving a green light to start the maintenance treatment, Dr. Slopis wanted to do a repeat MRI and EEG to make sure the first two blocks of chemotherapy hadn't caused further damages to Marcus's brain.

Based on the repeat MRI and EEG, Dr. Slopis concluded the chemotherapy rounds had not caused further visible damages to Marcus's brain; thus, on September 21, Marcus started his maintenance chemotherapy.

Unfortunately, one of the side effects of the Methotrexate was that it was hard on the skin. Marcus dealt with skin breakdown in his diaper area, and aggressive use of ointment was needed to prevent further sores from developing.

Tirelessly, his rehab continued at home while he waited to start his intense rehab program at TIRR.

His home physical therapist Jessica, occupational therapist Jade, and speech therapist Amy were eager to see Marcus move to higher levels of achievements. When Marcus participated actively in his training, Amy gave him an A-plus for effort. As a reward, she allowed him to pick soccer videos on her iPad to watch. At the dinner table, Marcus tried to get our attention by vocalizing. Occasionally, he would make some drama or start coughing if he got overly eager. We saw these moments of drama as signs of more intentional involvement from Marcus's side. He could not literally raise his voice, but he could make a point that he was there among us at the dinner table.

After being active for a while, Marcus sometimes got a cramp or a seizure. It was hard work for his brain to process and follow instructions.

His brain had to rewire for him to coordinate all movements and process impressions quickly.

Now and then, after a little cramp, he laughed, then he got tired after. How I wished Marcus could speak and tell us how he really felt. So many thoughts of his were trapped inside him. I hoped that one day he could reveal what it was like for him during this process.

One night, Marcus got involved in a bit of drama with Lucas who had a wriggly tooth he had decided to pull out himself. He had a hard time doing it but eventually pulled hard enough. Then the bleeding started. Lucas rushed to Niso to show her the bleeding.

"Lucas, it's normal for you to bleed after pulling out a tooth," I said while Lucas felt sorry for himself. "The bleeding will stop quickly, right, Niso?"

"Yes, it will," Niso said.

"Mommy, are you going to be the tooth fairy?" Lucas asked.

Marcus laughed.

"I might be the tooth fairy's assistant," I answered him.

We all laughed together.

Later in September, Marcus and I went to TIRR for his physical and occupational therapy evaluations. Marcus and I got a tour at the impressive facility. It was busy, with therapists working with patients of all ages—some with legs, some without, some in wheelchairs, some without. Some patients had been in car accidents; some had had strokes. The environment was well-suited for Marcus, as there were equipment, space, and facilities that we could not provide for him at home. They had a pediatric gym with all the newest technology, and most of all, I sensed the staff was qualified for the job.

Marcus worked hard to show what he mastered. I showed them the home videos of Marcus's best performances and top soccer goals. Marcus impressed the therapists. According to them, the fact that he could move his arms, legs, and head was huge. The fact that Marcus had arms and legs in the first place was huge too.

To me, Marcus had enough medical problems already, but to them, Marcus was manageable, not overly challenging.

We agreed that Marcus was going to start outpatient therapy at TIRR three times a week while he continued therapy at home. As soon as Marcus

Chapter Twenty-Six

was ready, three times could be increased to five times a week at TIRR. Later, Marcus could do an inpatient rehab program in Dallas at Baylor's Pediatric Center or at TCH. There were many possibilities for Marcus to graduate his rehab program. I congratulated the therapists at TIRR for officially becoming part of Marcus's Dream Team, which was always open to accept new members. Together, Marcus's Dream Team magnified his strengths.

At home, Lucas picked cool books, jumped into Marcus's bed, and started reading to him. I especially enjoyed when Lucas read *Frog and Toad* to Marcus. Marcus used to read them to me as he practiced his reading. Now it was Lucas's turn to make Marcus and me laugh.

At the end of September, we had a meeting at home with Sarah and Alex, who were representatives from Make-A-Wish Foundation. They interviewed us about Marcus's interests and wishes in regard to a trip they were willing to organize once Marcus had recovered. Fortunately, Marcus could wait months or even years before getting his wish fulfilled. We circled around something about a soccer wish in relation to Barcelona and Messi. Marcus was heading for great adventures. Make-A-Wish Foundation was now also part of Marcus's Dream Team. There was no end to the Dream Team. It grew bigger and bigger every day.

At the beginning of October, Marcus was in full swing with his dual rehab program: one at TIRR and one at home. When he was awake, he showed increasing progress during his sessions. At home, his speech therapist Amy worked with his mouth and tongue muscles to obtain better control. His therapists at TIRR had asked me to buy new tennis shoes for Marcus to use during training. I liked the thought of buying Marcus his first new pair of shoes after he fell ill. The therapists wanted Marcus to wear his orthopedic braces on his feet to help realign his foot and ankle. Once wearing his braces, he was to wear his tennis shoes on top, which would allow Marcus to have a better grip on the floor while standing. It was a milestone for Marcus to get new shoes. I felt almost the same as when I bought his very first baby shoes when he learned to walk.

Dr. Slopis was working on adjusting Marcus's Valium dosage to allow him to be more awake during the daytime. He had suggested that Marcus try a new drug called Onfi, which had multiple benefits. It could help reduce tone and prevent seizure activity. The downside was that it was expensive;

thus, our insurance company might object to paying for it or put restrictions on its doses.

It occurred that Marcus had a full week without visits at MD Anderson, during which time he could entirely focus on his therapy. He had now developed the strength to sit on the bedside with the help of only one person. He impressed his physical therapist Jessica. Additionally, during occupational therapy, Marcus could fold his hands and lift them folded to his head while Jade held his elbows up high.

During a training session at TIRR, for the first time Marcus tried to use the stander. The therapists went very slowly, carefully observing him for signs of increased stress or pain. They went gradually and at a low angle first. Marcus cried a bit and then came down again. It may have hurt because his muscles were weak, or he may have been frightened. It was hard to tell, but his body language signaled that he was uncomfortable. I caressed him and hugged him to comfort him. I was so proud of him.

In Denmark, Grandma and Grandpa were finalizing their plans to come visit us. We usually Skyped with them every Sunday, which allowed them to keep up with the boys from a long distance. The correspondence could not replace a real visit from them, and none of us could wait for their arrival. The excitement was building up day by day.

Marcus responded well to his new medication, Onfi. His nurses reported that Marcus seemed to be more relaxed than before he started Onfi.

Mid-October, Marcus was due for his second batch of IV Methotrexate, which Dr. Patrick had planned to escalate. Marcus's immune system had to be at a certain level before Dr. Patrick could escalate the dose of Methotrexate. As expected, his immune system was suppressed, but we had hoped that his counts were better. The consequence was that Dr. Patrick could only give Marcus the same dose as the first time, and he would be undertreated.

Dr. Patrick also gave Marcus a spinal treatment with hydrocortisone in order to prevent leukemia from developing in Marcus's spinal cord. At the same time, the doctor did a spinal tap, and once again, the result was negative for leukemia. Marcus rocked it! He remained in remission at his spine level. He also got PEG-ASP that Dr. Patrick had described as a starvation drug, meaning that it starved the leukemia cells without affecting Marcus's immune system. Most other chemotherapies had the unfortunate side effect

Chapter Twenty-Six

of suppressing the immune system while also damaging the patient's healthy cells. Marcus did well during both treatments.

On October 13, Grandma and Grandpa arrived from Denmark. They had rented a small apartment nearby as their base. They were worried about getting sick, and if they did, they had to stay away from Marcus. It was a good plan. That way, they had their own space to rest. They were elderly, and it was rather intense to be in our house with nurses, machine alarms, and Lucas running around claiming attention.

We were all so extremely excited to see them again. They brought gifts from Denmark for all of us. Lucas got soccer trading cards, and Marcus got books and audiobooks.

Grandma read books aloud to Marcus and could tell him stories about the family in Denmark. She even played soccer with Lucas outside in our backyard. Lucas teased me.

"Mommy, did you know that Grandma is better at playing soccer than you?"

"No, she isn't. I'm better. I can do tons of soccer tricks Grandma doesn't even know," I replied.

"No, Grandma is also faster than you." Lucas loved teasing me.

"What?" I protested. "That can't be true."

Grandma listened while Lucas laughed. I knew Grandma was better at so many things just because she was Grandma. Nothing could change that, but Lucas knew just how to tease me in particular when we talked about sports. I always claimed to be better at sports than Grandma, and he knew it. For the record, I was better and faster than Grandma was at soccer!

As Grandma and Grandpa were in town, I trained them to become confident around Marcus. They went with Marcus and me to TIRR and MD Anderson. They met Marcus's nurses at home and participated in Lucas's after-school activities and picked him up from school. We even went out to dinner at a restaurant called Sweet Tomatoes with Ross and his family. On a Sunday, Lucas, Jacob, and Grandpa went off to watch the Houston Dynamos play a soccer game against Seattle Sounders at BBVA Compass Stadium.

Marcus reached many goals. He demonstrated increased strength and coordination. All his achievements helped elevate everybody's spirits. He was in this game to win.

Gearing Up for the Bone Marrow Transplant

On October 21, it was my birthday and I had decided that this year, I didn't want to have a depressing and miserable birthday. The year before, I spent my birthday at TCH getting the awful news about Marcus's brain damage. I will never forget that day—never.

I invited a few friends for a birthday brunch at home. It was wonderful to hang out with my friends for a change. It was a successful day.

The day after, Marcus was due for his next Methotrexate block, but once again, his counts were too low. We hoped this was because the chemotherapy worked and that his body needed more time to recover.

On October 23, Jacob and I made a trip to Washington, DC, where my husband was set to run the Marine Corps Marathon. While we were gone, Grandma and Grandpa moved into our house and took care of Lucas and Marcus. After Washington, DC, we went to New York and Connecticut to visit some friends. We returned to Houston on October 28 after a relaxing break away.

The whole family back home was in good condition. Grandma and Grandpa had done an amazing job with the boys. They updated Marcus's on-line Google Doc diary so my husband and I could easily follow how Marcus did while we were gone.

When we returned to Houston, I told Marcus that next time, he and Lucas were going with us to New York. It made Marcus so hyperactive hearing this that out of joy, he almost jumped out of his wheelchair. Lucas stood next to Marcus and calmed him down. Lucas showed so much affection toward Marcus, caressing him and promising him they were going to have fun together in New York and see the Empire State Building and the Statue of Liberty.

I increased the number of healing sessions with Marcus as I saw fit. I had started healing the entire family. I think we were all flying high, spiritually speaking. In addition, on Halloween night, we had a big party at home with Grandma, Grandpa, Ross, and his family. A great month had ended. I wondered if the next month would be even better.

Early November, Marcus was due for his next visit with Dr. Patrick. Marcus weighed almost eighty pounds and was a big, strong boy. Lately, he had developed an annoying rash in his diaper area so we discussed with Dr. Patrick the best way to treat it. Dr. Patrick prescribed a wonder cream

Chapter Twenty-Six

called NDX cream. It was a compound cream they mixed in the pharmacy at MD Anderson. He explained that he often saw skin problems with his other patients following Methotrexate.

Dr. Patrick noted that Marcus's labs were better than the week before and he reassured me that Marcus's skin, once treated with NDX cream, would improve over the next couple of days. Four days later, Marcus received his next round of Methotrexate. For the toxicity, Dr. Patrick could give Marcus folinic acid, also known as Leucovorin, a medication used to decrease the toxic effects of Methotrexate. Dr. Patrick referred to it as a "rescue medicine." I loved that Dr. Patrick always had a plan for all my concerns.

At home, Marcus started to roll a bit in his bed. I witnessed that once he lay on his right side, he was able to roll over to his back with no further help. He held on to the rail of his bed and tried to lift himself up. He looked around more. Occasionally, he started crying, but we quickly comforted him. We believed Marcus understood his situation better and was frustrated that he was unable to move around as desired.

At TIRR, Marcus and his home health nurse practiced how to move Marcus from his bed to his wheelchair and back again without using the lift. It was promising to see how engaged the nurses were. They were deeply invested in supporting Marcus and they carefully followed all the advice from the TIRR staff.

While Grandma and Grandpa were still visiting, we arranged a sleepover for Lucas at their apartment. That evening, my husband and I decided to go to the movies to watch the new James Bond film, *Spectre*. The day after, we made a family trip to the Houston Zoo, and after that, we went to the Japanese chain restaurant Benihana for my belated birthday dinner.

Marcus impressed everyone at TIRR. Even though he had days when he was more tired than others, he had proved he could stand in the stander in a ninety-degree angle and tolerate being upright for thirty minutes. While standing, he could look around, fire a Nerf gun, and hold a ball and other objects. The TIRR team monitored his blood pressure and other vital signs to make sure he remained comfortable.

Mid-November, sadly, it was time for Grandma and Grandpa to fly back to Denmark after having spent one month with us. That month had been a happy month when they witnessed firsthand Marcus grow stronger and more capable through hard work and dedication. They had been part of that journey and they could be proud of themselves for all their efforts and support they had given us. They had bonded with Lucas and they could leave us behind with the sincere hope that soon Marcus would get his bone marrow transplant and be leukemia-free forever. He was heading that way, and they knew we would all support Marcus until he reached that goal. Nothing could stop him or us now.

After Grandma and Grandpa left, it became somewhat empty. Dr. Patrick wanted to see Marcus in the clinic and move on with the Methotrexate treatment. Mid-November, Marcus's labs showed that his bone marrow was not ready for the next block. Dr. Patrick strongly believed that the Methotrexate treatment did the job while I, on the other hand, was not so certain. Dr. Patrick had been unable to give Marcus the escalating doses, which meant Marcus was undertreated. There was too much uncertainty about Marcus's leukemia status; therefore, Dr. Patrick decided to do a bone marrow biopsy to get a clear picture of Marcus's response.

On November 19, Marcus had his next bone marrow biopsy and spinal tap. Once home, Dr. Patrick called me with the preliminary results.

CHAPTER TWENTY-SEVEN

Bad News Comes in Waves

Dr. Patrick was hesitant to speak. "Unfortunately, Marcus has sixty-six percent leukemia blasts in his sample. This means the Methotrexate has not worked."

I let out a heavy sigh, full of despair. At the same time, I had reached a point where I was used to getting bad news over the phone. Once you enter the unpredictable world of cancer, you get used to dealing with grave medical results, devastating side effects, and new complications arising just as you hoped for closure. I tried to compose myself.

"This is such sad news." My heart hurt. This was so unfair. Marcus was a sensation; he was getting so close to the bone marrow transplant.

"On the other hand, I had a feeling Marcus didn't respond well to the treatment. You expected Marcus's counts to recover, and they didn't," I said as my body tensed. Reality condemned me to acquiesce in the horrible scenario that Marcus had to start all over again. "What's the plan now?" I bit my cheek. I refused to let leukemia take over again.

"Marcus needs rest and time for his bone marrow to recover. His immune system is very low."

He continued in a comforting voice, "On a positive note, there is still thirty-five percent healthy bone marrow left. Let's meet after Thanksgiving to discuss the next steps."

I appreciated his optimism in the face of this pessimistic situation.

"Should we let Marcus take a break from TIRR?" I couldn't bear the thought of pushing Marcus to do rehab if his body was this weak.

"Yes, that will be a good idea at least until Marcus's immune system gets

Chapter Twenty-Seven

stronger." Dr. Patrick already had my full respect, but his fearless attitude and logical mind kept surprising me. He was not ready to give up on Marcus. He was a fighter like Marcus.

The following day, Marcus's heart rate was too high and he was warm. I contacted MD Anderson, and the nurse asked me to bring Marcus into the clinic. Once arrived, nurses and doctors assessed Marcus and told me he had to be hospitalized. They started fluids and antibiotic treatment. They told me that PICU at MD Anderson was full and that they were working on finding a PICU bed for Marcus at Children's Memorial Hermann Hospital in the Houston Medical Center.

I felt completely hopeless, defeated. Marcus had relapsed, and now they told me there was no bed for him at MD Anderson. Late afternoon, the nurse came back.

"I've been in contact with a hospital in Galveston, and they have a bed in their PICU for Marcus," she explained.

"Galveston? That's so far away. It takes two hours to get there by car," I said.

"We've tried everything, and that's the only option. It's flu season, and all the PICUs in the medical center are full," she stressed.

I let go of my anger. The nurse had tried everything, and it wasn't her fault there were no PICU beds available. I had to do the next best thing for Marcus.

"Okay, let's go to Galveston, Marcus," I told him. "They can't take you anywhere else. We'll manage."

Late that night, Marcus and I arrived at the hospital in Galveston. It wasn't like being at MD Anderson. Things went a bit slower. It wasn't a cancer hospital, and it was evident that the resources were not the same as at MD Anderson. The sense of security I felt at MD Anderson was not the same in Galveston. The staff at the hospital promised me that as soon as they had a free PICU bed at MD Anderson, Marcus would be transferred back there.

Jacob and I had to get familiar with a new hospital, which took some time. Lucas thought it was cool Marcus was in Galveston, because to him Galveston was a vacation destination.

Marcus got stable, but again the testing revealed the bacteria pseudomonas had colonized in his trach.

Days went by, and there was still no available PICU bed at MD Anderson. Late November, the hospital in Galveston had received a number of very sick children and needed to get some free beds in PICU. His nurse called me to let me know that she had to move Marcus over to the regular pediatric unit. The nurse had five patients instead of two in PICU. His room would be smaller too. The respiratory therapist was still responsible for Marcus's respiratory needs, but it was a downgrade for him to be moved over to the different floor. On the other hand, Marcus was more stable, and that was good news.

It was Thanksgiving Day, and Marcus's Galveston team had informed us that Marcus would soon be ready to be discharged home, as he was too well to be admitted to MD Anderson.

It was depressing to sit in the hospital with Marcus on Thanksgiving Day. I felt nostalgic watching Macy's Thanksgiving Day Parade from New York with Marcus. I had begun to have the first inklings of fear that this might be the last Thanksgiving with him. With the relapsed leukemia, the future didn't look so certain any longer.

On November 28, Marcus was discharged home. In the meantime, Dr. Patrick had worked on Marcus's next chemotherapy block, which was designed to bring him into remission. He was getting closer to his bone marrow transplant, and we wanted to give him another chance to get there. Dr. Patrick got Marcus into remission once. Could he do it again? Most importantly, could he keep Marcus in remission until he was approved for the bone marrow transplant? Those were the important questions to ask. We couldn't direct the wind, but we could adjust the sails.

On November 30, Marcus started his new chemotherapy block. Dr. Patrick decided to repeat the block from the summer because it brought Marcus into remission and he tolerated it well. We discussed what went wrong with the Methotrexate. He didn't believe Marcus's leukemia was resistant to Methotrexate; rather the issue was that he didn't get enough of it to eliminate the leukemia. Marcus got severe skin breakdown and seizures due to the toxic side effects of the drug. The escalation of the drug didn't happen,

Chapter Twenty-Seven

and Dr. Patrick had to cease the treatment prematurely, which was the reason we didn't get the desired effect from the treatment.

December arrived, and Marcus continued his chemotherapy block. He had started to develop more and more seizures, and new nurses had difficulty dealing with that.

In desperation, I emailed Dr. Slopis daily to ask him to guide us in dosing the seizure medicine. Dr. Slopis explained that most likely Marcus had breakthrough seizures because his usual tone and seizure medicine didn't work as expected due to the chemotherapy. It was an established fact that the chemotherapy decreased the effect of the tone and seizure medicines, but no one could predict how much.

On December 7, Marcus was admitted to MD Anderson. He had tone, a temperature of 100.4, and his seizures were not under control. His white blood count was 0.1 and his ANC was 0. They suspected Marcus had contracted an infection. He needed blood and platelets. His lung X-rays indicated he had pneumonia. One issue after the other surfaced. I feared that this time Marcus would stay a long time at MD Anderson. I was right.

Brittney, Marcus and Lucas's child life specialist, was the sunshine of the stay. She did a wonderful job trying to cheer up Marcus and Lucas. She brought a big gift sack with presents for the boys, including a small American football with four famous football players' names on it. The football players had visited MD Anderson, and she had secured this special autographed football for Marcus and Lucas.

Marcus slept and rested most of the time. The seizures were damaging his brain. A seizure was like an earthquake and volcano happening at the same time.

Marcus often just sat with his eyes closed, listening. I missed looking at his big brown smiling eyes. He went into hibernation.

Mid-December, the PICU staff informed us that Marcus could possibly be discharged before Christmas, provided he finished his antibiotic treatment and was stable. We desperately wanted Marcus to be home for Christmas but only if it was safe. I told them we had had many problems with changing nurses and sometimes nurses who didn't show up. If Marcus's seizure activity was uncontrolled, I didn't feel it was safe for Marcus to be at home. They agreed that all aspects of Marcus's health should be stable before discharge.

Due to concerns about his increased seizure activity, the infectious disease doctors wanted to do a spinal tap to rule out any infections or leukemia in his spine. The spinal tap was negative for leukemia but low positive for a herpes virus HSV-2 in his central nervous system. That could possibly partly explain the increased seizure activity. The team clarified that they often saw this infection with patients who hadn't had any immune system for a long time, so they weren't surprised. Marcus needed IV HSV-2 treatment for two weeks, and after those weeks of antiviral medication, he needed antiviral maintenance treatment because his immune system was suppressed. Christmas at home with Marcus was ruled out. On top of that, I got sick and couldn't visit Marcus at the hospital. He was in protective isolation.

With the antiviral medicine on board, Marcus seemed to improve. Though he was tired and mostly slept, he had small moments where he was alert. When Remota and Niso came to visit Marcus at MD Anderson, I arranged a small Christmas party for him. I made homemade gingerbread and brought delicious chocolate. Marcus seemed better, and we celebrated with Dr. Patrick and Dr. Slopis. Lucas played chess with me in Marcus's room in an attempt to have some fun. After all, it was Christmas time, which meant family time.

On Christmas Eve, I prepared a traditional Danish Christmas dinner at home. The three of us had been with Marcus most of the day. The big day was on December 25, which was when Santa was going to come to MD Anderson with gift bags for Lucas and Marcus.

I had secretly been to a Santa Workshop at MD Anderson with Brittney to select gifts for the boys from the hospital's gift storage room filled with donations.

On Christmas Day, MD Anderson Pediatric Unit hosted a Christmas lunch for patients and relatives, and we attended that with Lucas. When we got back to Marcus's room, Santa had already been there with bags of presents for the boys. Lucas helped open Marcus's gifts, and Lucas was thrilled when he discovered he got an iPad mini for Christmas. Marcus got a combined TV/DVD player, and my husband promised Marcus to install it in his "Presidential Suite" at home when he was discharged.

We looked forward to Marcus's return home, but obstacles continued to emerge. Even though his labs slowly improved, other issues needed attention.

Chapter Twenty-Seven

Marcus got a new bigger-size trach and was switched to his home vent but didn't tolerate all those changes. He desaturated and was switched back to the more powerful hospital vent. When checking the placement of his new trach, the PICU doctor noticed on the X-rays that Marcus's PICC line had become too short. He had grown a lot since the summer before and needed a PICC line replacement in his arm. It was as if Marcus had grown into a little man. Everything had grown on him, and he needed new medical equipment to fit his needs. His vent supplies needed to be adult size, and his oxygen concentrator had to go from one liter to five liters to accommodate his needs.

Over New Year's, Marcus remained at MD Anderson to recover further and for Dr. Patrick to get the bone marrow biopsy results before discharge.

Marcus had almost been at MD Anderson for a month. I was exhausted and ready for him to come home. I wanted him so badly to be in remission.

On January 4, Marcus got his spinal tap and bone marrow biopsy. Later that afternoon, Dr. Patrick and his nurse practitioner Lisa had exciting news. Dr. Patrick had been in the lab himself to see the pathology results, and overall, Marcus's cells looked normal. The preliminary results later revealed that he had 2 percent blasts. Marcus could go home!

On January 8, Marcus was discharged. New nurses were assigned to Marcus.

Some of the new nurses made us laugh. A new nurse had seen my husband one time in his running outfit, and as she entered Marcus's room, she noticed the Messi posters on Marcus's wall.

"Is that Marcus's dad on the posters?" she asked me.

"No, it's not," I said, giggling. "If it were, we would not be living in this house," I explained. "Messi is the best and most famous soccer player in the world. He can afford to live in a palace."

Now that Marcus was home, we had the grand opening of his Presidential Suite with his own TV and DVD player. Lucas was jealous that he didn't get a TV like Marcus, but he enjoyed jumping into Marcus's bed to have movie time while Marcus did chair time next to him. We celebrated the new toys Marcus received for Christmas, the new DVDs, and balls Marcus could later use for his therapy.

On January 11, Marcus started his second block of outpatient chemotherapy. Soon after, Dr. Patrick emailed me that he had ordered a minimal residual disease test. Unfortunately, the lab had missed the order and had consequently trashed Marcus's bone marrow sample.

That meant Dr. Patrick wouldn't know if Marcus had 0 percent leukemia blasts left in his sample or somewhere between 0 to 2 percent.

Mid-January 2016, the side effects of the chemotherapy started to show their ugly face. Marcus's seizure activity increased. The treatment and seizures made Marcus tired, simply too tired to open his eyes. We called it Marcus's "hibernation phase" just like a bear that sleeps away the winter months.

His skin in the diaper area got inflamed again. I simply felt that too many side effects and problems piled up. I was overwhelmed and needed support. I was at the point of crying because I felt left alone with so many issues. I wished I had a reliable and knowledgeable person who could help me with administrative and medical work.

On Monday, January 25, Marcus had an appointment with Dr. Madden, his pain management doctor. I had a fruitful meeting with him about how to secure Marcus's comfort better at home with changing nurses and medical issues. I noted we didn't have access to Marcus's MD Anderson Dream Team 24/7, and that was a problem with Marcus's current level of issues.

Dr. Madden listened carefully to my points and mentioned that MD Anderson worked with an agency that could be contacted 24/7 and could come to our home and assist Marcus and me and the home health nurses. They sent reports back to MD Anderson, and I could rest assured that they did a fantastic job. What Dr. Madden told me sounded great. I appreciated any support I could get. Dr. Madden promised to talk to the rest of Marcus's MD Anderson Dream Team and get their approval to enroll Marcus in that program. We agreed for Dr. Madden to set up a meeting for my husband and me to learn more about the advantages of the program.

Then Epic called and offered to send a new evening nurse named Victor, who was supposed to be good. I agreed to have him train and work with Marcus, and we immediately liked him. He was a big, strong man who brought laughter into our home. He was the perfect fit for Marcus. He was confident, cool, and calm. He started to work night shifts for Marcus on a regular basis. Victor was resilient and never complained. He was a great asset to us.

February arrived, and Marcus's seizure activity turned violent; in fact, so violent that we all became concerned. Dr. Slopis ordered MRIs, EEGs, and all diagnostic tests possible.

Early February, an EEG documented that Marcus had multifocal epileptiform discharges, which were abnormal patterns of brain waves. That was bad. That meant Marcus was not back to his neurologic baseline. How was Marcus going to be fit for rehab again? He was weak and tired, and the seizures made it worse. Based on Marcus's MRI results, Dr. Slopis explained that Marcus's white matter had not healed up yet, which was why Marcus continued to have seizures.

On February 8, Jacob and I had a meeting at MD Anderson with the agency Dr. Madden had suggested. The agency was a pediatric hospice under Memorial Hermann Hospital. A lovely nurse named Sasha was going to be working with Marcus and me, and Marcus's doctor would be Dr. Jones.

"How can Marcus be qualified for home hospice services when he's not dying?" I asked Dr. Jones.

"We work under the philosophy of concurrent care, which means that Marcus can continue to receive services from MD Anderson and TIRR while getting services from us at home," Dr. Jones explained.

That calmed my husband and me down. We didn't want to be in a situation where we had to give up on Marcus in order to enroll him in the hospice program.

"The same does not apply to adults. If an adult enrolls in a hospice program, that means the doctors give up treatment and the hope for a cure. For pediatric patients, it's different," Dr. Jones said. "As part of the program, we even have a child life specialist who can come to your home and work with Lucas."

Upon listening to all the benefits and meeting their wonderful team, Jacob and I were convinced it was the right program for Marcus and us. In the afternoon, Sasha came home to meet with Marcus and nurse Remota. Sasha and I discussed all of Marcus's needs; it turned out that the program offered the possibility to cover certain expenses we had for Marcus's diapers, disposable underpads, and wet wipes—all related to his incontinence care. Sasha promised to order those supplies for Marcus.

In February, Lucas and I got sick and had to stay away from Marcus, who was about to start Mercaptopurine and steroid maintenance treatment.

It was difficult when any of us was sick, as we had to keep Marcus in his room and avoid any contact with him. It was hard to be isolated from Marcus. Only my husband and his nurse could be with him.

Dr. Slopis tried to wean Marcus off some of the sedation medicines, but the effect was that he developed more tone, seizures, and involuntary movements. His arms were shaking. Due to the frustration among Marcus's Dream Team—which, by the way, had expanded to include the hospice team members—they concluded they needed to order a prolonged video EEG to get a thorough analysis of Marcus's neurological status.

We had increasing worries about Marcus at home. At some point, Niso and I decided not to give Marcus his vest treatment out of fear that it would trigger a seizure. The slightest jerk or loud sound could trigger a seizure.

It was April, and Marcus was back on his maintenance treatment with Mercaptopurine and steroids. Marcus's Dream Team was waiting for the video EEG report to shed light on how serious Marcus's neurological state was.

On April 4, Marcus had his next follow-up appointment in the morning with Dr. Patrick. Marcus had now reached eighty-eight pounds. Dr. Patrick wasn't satisfied with Marcus's labs, as his white blood count was only 1.0, which meant Marcus needed a one-week break from Mercaptopurine.

In the afternoon, Dr. Patrick called me. He had devastating news. Marcus had 7 percent leukemia blasts in his blood.

"Mercaptopurine isn't working and the steroids aren't working, so Marcus needs to stop that treatment," he told me.

Marcus had met doom. This time, we had hoped the maintenance treatment would work as planned. Dr. Patrick sounded like he was giving up, but he promised he wanted to do everything to look for trials with patients like Marcus whose leukemia was resistant. One major problem we faced was that Marcus wasn't a good candidate for a pediatric trial due to his severely compromised neurologic status. Chemotherapy is chemical warfare that destroys to save, and in Marcus's case, the destruction had proved too calamitous. Another question was if it was right to subject Marcus to further treatment.

CHAPTER TWENTY-EIGHT

The Big Decision

In the evening, Jacob and I talked about what we could possibly do. We both knew it was over. The more times the leukemia relapsed, the more aggressive it got. Dr. Patrick explained to us how the nature of Marcus's leukemia was. We agreed that we had reached a point with Marcus when we could not justify continuing to treat him. The suffering on his part had become too high, mainly due to the neurotoxicity side effects. It was unethical to push Marcus any further, as his leukemia clearly had developed resistance to the limited maintenance treatment options available to Dr. Patrick. Dr. Patrick could get Marcus into remission, but it was impossible to *keep* him in remission. That meant it was impossible to get him ready for the bone marrow transplant because he would keep relapsing in the meantime.

We also got the devastating results from the video EEG report. Marcus had severe subclinical seizure activity with over one hundred seizures a day even while he was on all the best and newest seizure medicine on the market.

On April 7, Jacob and I had a family meeting with Dr. Patrick and Dr. Slopis. They explained to us that there were no more treatment options available for Marcus. This time, Marcus had relapsed while being on Dr. Patrick's best maintenance protocol; continuing with more chemotherapy would no longer benefit him. I asked how long Marcus had to live. It could be weeks or months, I was told. Dr. Patrick couldn't know for sure. In fact, nobody knew. Marcus was the boss, and his body would tell us.

Accepting this time that Marcus was going to leave us for good was so painful and impossible to grasp. It was surreal. Marcus's Dream Team would never have given up unless there was no way out. I trusted them in their

Chapter Twenty-Eight

judgment, as they had followed Marcus for months. They understood firsthand how vulnerable he was and that it wasn't fair or ethical to ask more of Marcus. His record of achievements, his name, and his story had already become history in oncology circles across the US.

I think it was easier to accept the circumstances because we had literally tried everything possible for Marcus. Unless somebody invented a miracle treatment for cancer Marcus could tolerate, our dream of curing him was never going to become true. When you truly love a person, you should know when it's time to let go. Marcus's body and soul talked to us, letting us know that we had pushed him to his maximum capacity. He could take no more, and we could not ask him to fight any longer.

We made a plan that together we would make sure Marcus had the best time possible until the end. My husband and I agreed that we wanted to keep Marcus at home. The hospice team consisting of Sasha and Dr. Jones promised to guide Marcus's home nurses and us in keeping Marcus comfortable and relaxed. They promised to provide us with all their services in our home, including Chaplain Darla and the child life specialist Meghan for Lucas.

Together with Dr. Patrick, we decided to follow Marcus's labs on a weekly basis. That way, we could determine if the leukemia progressed and we could support him with blood products from MD Anderson. If Marcus's platelets were too low, a bleeding could start inside him and he would then bleed to death. If his hemoglobin numbers were too low, he would have trouble breathing, causing him to feel as if he was suffocating. Those scenarios sounded horrible; there was no way Jacob and I would let Marcus go through that.

We didn't desire this last portion of Marcus's journey to be nothing but crying and pain. Marcus deserved dignity and comfort.

As Marcus no longer took Mercaptopurine or steroids, he slowly felt better. In April, his energy level increased, and he had become so strong he almost pulled himself up to an upright sitting position in his bed. His arms and legs were active, causing him to move more around in his bed. He even attempted to get out of bed. Therefore, we asked Sasha to get a bigger bed for him. She quickly arranged for that, and Marcus ended up getting a broad bed suitable for a six-hundred-pound person. The bed was so big that Victor called it a "brother bed" because it could fit both boys. Marcus also attempted to get out of his wheelchair, making it dangerous for him to sit unless he was wearing his seat belt.

May was Marcus's birthday month, and my oldest brother Alexander had planned to come visit Marcus and us. On May 13, Alexander turned fifty, and on May 27, Marcus would turn ten. We decided to make a combined sixtieth birthday party for the birthday boys. Alexander was supposed to come in early May but was rejected boarding on his airplane in Copenhagen, as he had been to Libya for a work assignment. Due to new US regulations, he had to apply for a visa to visit us in the US. What a disappointment that he couldn't come as planned. We were all worried Marcus's situation might deteriorate and he would miss his opportunity to see Marcus one last time.

I continued Marcus's wellness program at home. I wanted him to experience the best I could offer him. He got the deluxe wellness package. I healed him, gave him footbaths, and massaged his feet with lotion for better blood circulation. I let him taste small samples of food and drinks he liked. I borrowed cool library books for him and spent many hours reading with him.

As death approached, I loved him more and more and didn't want him to go, but I also wanted him to be at peace. I could ask no more of Marcus. My gift to him was no longer life. My gift to him was my love and his gift to me was his love. That sufficed because, unlike life, love is eternal and nothing could interrupt or change the mutual bond and love Marcus and I had. Nothing could change the love Marcus had for his family, and our love for him would always stand.

On May 10, Marcus's blasts had increased to 80 percent in his blood while all other lab values had decreased. It went downhill. However, the plan remained unchanged. We continued to monitor him and respond to his needs quickly.

The Houston heat started to become a challenge. Marcus sweated a lot, and his room was incredibly hot because his equipment and heater produced heat. As his blood quality decreased, his breathing got weaker so we increased his supplemental oxygen to three liters. With leukemia invading his vital organs and body, his pain level increased and he needed more and stronger pain medicine.

Sasha and her team were amazing, assisting Marcus's nurses and me in

Chapter Twenty-Eight

getting medication supplies and helping us with any questions that arose related to Marcus's care. They were on standby at night. No doubt, the Memorial Hermann Hospice team had become part of Marcus's Dream Team.

Ever since Marcus relapsed, I had thought about which wish he would like from the Make-A-Wish Foundation. A trip to San Francisco was out of the question, and arranging for the Barcelona soccer team to show up at MD Anderson with short notice was impossible. Instead, I talked to Marcus's Make-A-Wish representative, Sandra, about a brand-new idea. Marcus's wish could be to get something personal from his idol Messi. I could send the PowerPoint presentation about Messi that Marcus created in second grade, pictures of Marcus's Messi soccer room, and other background information related to Marcus's interest in soccer. I figured maybe Messi could sign a T-shirt or something else and send it to Marcus. Marcus's Make-A-Wish representative loved the idea and instantly started working on it. Then I didn't hear back from her. Marcus got weaker, and I asked about the status on Marcus's wish. She had sent the assignment to Make-A-Wish Brazil, but Messi was from Argentina and played professionally in Barcelona. I suggested she send the assignment to Make-A-Wish Barcelona and accelerate the process, as Marcus was getting weaker.

On May 18, I received a notification that a package was on its way from Messi in Spain to Marcus. Would it arrive in time for Marcus to get it? It didn't contain a tracking number, and it was impossible to do anything but wait.

CHAPTER TWENTY-NINE

Wishes Do Come True

On May 19, my brother Alexander finally arrived. We believed Marcus recognized his voice. My brother had a T-shirt for both boys in his suitcase. It was the official Danish national soccer T-shirt in white and red. A few days later, we celebrated the sixtieth birthday party for Marcus and my brother. I made a Danish birthday cake from scratch with strawberry filling, vanilla sponge layers, and chocolate icing on the top and decorated with fresh whipped cream. We sang "Happy Birthday" and the Danish birthday song for the birthday boys.

Marcus slept more and more. The goal wasn't to keep Marcus awake; rather it was for him to feel good and to feel relaxed. It didn't mean that he was out all the time. He had moments of alertness.

On May 27, it was Marcus's tenth birthday. He received many wonderful gifts. What do you give the sweetest little boy on the planet who is dying? You give him anything that makes his life joyful. We decorated Marcus's room all over with Danish and American flags. In Denmark, we use the national flag every time we want to celebrate. Marcus received cards, gift cards, and cotton tank tops to wear in the heat. He got new Danish books, audiobooks, and music. Grandpa and Grandma gave Marcus bamboo bedsheets. Bamboo sheets are known for their cooling properties and are light and soft to sleep in. We pampered him.

After Marcus's birthday, my brother left to fly back to Denmark. Marcus's next visitor from Denmark was my husband's brother, Thomas.

On Saturday, June 4, Marcus got his Make-A-Wish fulfilled. Sandra had gotten to the post office to collect his package, and right after, she was on her

Chapter Twenty-Nine

way to our house. I arranged an improvised party for Marcus to mark the event. At noon, Sandra arrived with the package and Lucas helped open it. Not even Sandra was aware of its contents.

Marcus was in bed, and this was where Lucas opened his package. There was an adult-size home Barcelona T-shirt where Messi had written "Para Marcus con afecto" in black ink, followed by Messi's signature. Messi also gave him an official Barcelona DVD containing all his goals for Barcelona. Marcus was heavily medicated and drowsy, but we believed he noticed what was going on and appreciated the gifts. In the afternoon, I baked a chocolate cake and invited Ross and his family over to celebrate that Marcus had his wish fulfilled. Once again, we celebrated Marcus's birthday that time with Thomas, Ross, and his family.

Later that same day, Marcus received a letter from my dear friend Susanne in Denmark. To honor Marcus, she had picked a star in the universe and named it Marcus. It was a real star with coordinates for its location in the sky. Marcus got a certificate for it, and from that date onward, that was Marcus's star. It was a beautiful and personal gift from her.

Marcus's blasts percentage fluctuated. On June 6, they were 90 percent. Marcus had attacks of fever. Since he needed blood, Dr. Patrick organized for Marcus to have platelets and blood transfusions.

At home, our care for Marcus was aimed at cooling him down. The fever came as a result of the inflammation the leukemia caused inside his body. His skin got red and inflamed as it heated up. We had washcloths, big clothes, ice packs, and anything cooling on Marcus when he had aggressive episodes of fever.

On June 11, Marcus's "new normal" got more dramatic because his monitors' alarms kept going off when his numbers skyrocketed. It was scary, and the hospice team said it was appropriate to turn off the monitors. We started giving him Methadone every six hours for pain. The hospice team and Dr. Jones helped increase the doses as Marcus's condition progressed. He continued to do chair time because it helped his breathing. He listened to soothing classical music.

With the assistance of Chaplain Darla, we made a family art project with a tree and branches. With the fingerprints from Marcus, Lucas, my husband,

and me, we decorated the tree with beautiful, colorful leaves. Lucas helped Marcus direct his fingers onto the paper.

It was Copa America time. Copa America was a soccer tournament between the Americas. Lucas and Marcus had brother time watching the soccer games together. Sometimes they hung out in Marcus's room watching a movie. Marcus was more and more quiet.

The transfusions Marcus received at MD Anderson helped him and relieved some of the symptoms from the progressing leukemia. When Argentina played in the tournament, we made sure that Marcus was ready to listen to the game in front of the TV.

On June 19, Lucas was off to Camp Star Trail: Camps for All, which was organized and sponsored by MD Anderson. Participants were pediatric cancer patients and their siblings. All the staff at MD Anderson had convinced us that it would be great for Lucas to go away and play with other siblings whose brothers or sisters had cancer. We told Marcus that it was his gift to Lucas to go to that camp.

The morning before Lucas left, he went in early to Marcus's room. He spoke so sweetly to Marcus in Danish:

"Marcus, I'm going to camp now. I'll be back again on Friday. I'm going to miss you, Marcus." Lucas caressed his big brother and kissed him goodbye. It was the last time Lucas saw Marcus alive.

It was Monday, June 20. In the morning, I noticed Marcus's toenails and fingernails were bluish. He seemed colder. Sasha came to draw his labs. She noticed his stomach sounds were quiet.

At 1 p.m., I gave Marcus a long, wonderful healing. I felt strongly connected to him. I made sure I left him in a wonderful place, a place full of calmness and love, a place without fear.

At 4 p.m., Dr. Patrick called. Marcus's white blood count had exploded from 9.1. to 46.7. This meant we weren't talking about months anymore. Most likely, we were talking about weeks.

CHAPTER THIRTY

Letting Go

That morning, Marcus had some minor seizures and cramps. One time after a cramp, he opened his eyes and smiled at me. Then he closed his eyes. At 10 p.m., I gave him a light massage in his neck and shoulders. His hair was so soft. He was calm, tired, and so limp.

At 11 p.m., I peeked into Marcus's room. Niso had covered him with his *Star Wars* blanket. She never did that. She said he was cold.

At 2:09 a.m., Niso called me and I rushed down the stairs. She was calm, but her voice sounded worried. Something was wrong. She explained she couldn't get Marcus's blood pressure or pulse. It started around midnight. His numbers got weaker. He lay on his back, which was his best position. He was pale and cold. He was peaceful, then gasped. I immediately called my husband, who was still upstairs. He ran down the stairs and, with his right hand, held on to Marcus's left hand, which was resting on Wolf, his favorite stuffed animal. Niso was in the background and had called Sasha, who was on her way. Marcus had no cramps and he was just completely silent. My husband had placed his left hand on Marcus's heart and could feel as it slowed down. It all lasted a few minutes. Then it was over. Marcus was gone forever.

Niso said he expired at 2:26 a.m. Marcus's story was over, and he was now a beautiful shining star called Marcus in the sky.

The situation did not offer any room to think or feel because it was so intense. Jacob and I were just there with Marcus. We couldn't stop the process, death was inevitable, and we could only be bystanders. Because I knew this moment was bound to come, I believe I was prepared for it mentally and

Chapter Thirty

was ready to accept it. At the same time, there was consolation in knowing that Marcus's suffering was over. Watching someone you care about suffer is hard work. In that sense, my tremendous sorrow was mixed with a feeling of incredible relief that it was over. Jacob and I had been maxed out at all possible levels for two years, which is a long time to be under constant stress. Marcus's death represented closure and, with that, came relief. Marcus's death was neither traumatic nor surprising. This made the situation less painful to cope with in the moment because the element of shock was not present. It was not until long after that Marcus's death truly entered my consciousness and emotions.

I was worried if Jacob and I were able to be present when Marcus died. Being present for this transition to death was very special. Dying is something we all must do, and to miss this life passage of those you love most seems like the ultimate instance of not being there when someone most needs you. Marcus's passing was peaceful and gentle just as we had hoped for.

Sasha arrived shortly after. She walked us through the next steps such as choosing a funeral home for Marcus. Lucas was away on Camp Star Trail, and we discussed with Sasha how we should break the news about Marcus. We agreed it would be best to drive up to the camp and deliver the news personally to Lucas. Child life specialists and other professional staff would be available to guide us in how to organize the following days for Lucas.

Early in the morning, the body removal service arrived to pick up Marcus's body. Marcus looked so majestic, his skin and hair so fine. He didn't look sick at all. They put him on a soft stretcher and tugged a thick red blanket around his body. They made his bed so nicely with all his stuffed animals and put long-stemmed red roses on his pillow. As they took Marcus into their car, it was light outside and all the birds were singing for him. It was a beautiful, still morning. Then they left. It was time for Marcus to leave.

Again, I felt empty and sad but relieved that it was over. Marcus was not meant to be with us any longer. We didn't understand why, but I felt grateful for all he had given us. I felt grateful that I had had Marcus in my life, even though it was too short. I felt privileged to have created him. I would've rather had him and lost him than never have had him at all.

He chose me as his mother. It might sound strange, but I felt like I had been a successful mother to him. I was there when he was born, I was there throughout his short life, and I was there holding his hand when he died. I never failed him.

Among sadness and sorrow, I felt proud for all I had done for Marcus. I had dedicated these last two years of my life to him. I couldn't have done more for him, and most importantly, he knew I loved him and I knew he loved me. That was all I could ask for, and what a gift it was! His heart had stopped beating, but his love survived.

EPILOGUE

I'm Free

I'm finally free.
Don't grieve for me,
For now I'm free.
I have left behind some misery.
My days of youthful mobility
Were no longer a possibility.
My hurting body and tired eyes
Were longing for the heavenly skies.
Don't grieve for me.
You have set me free.
Just remember how I used to be.

Marcus's home health nurses and I often joked that everybody asked us how Marcus was doing, but no one asked us how *we* were doing. Many times, I said that the question is not if Marcus is going to make it. The question is if his home health nurses and I are going to make it. Marcus got all the controlled substances, but we were the ones who truly needed them.

When your child is well, it's easy to think that you would go to any length for them—and you would—but when it actually happens, you have no idea how hard it will be on your own body, mind, and spirit. No matter who tries to teach you lessons about life, you will not understand it until you go through it on your own.

Epilogue

You don't know how you're going to react to a crisis with your child or if you're capable of coping with it in a positive and healthy manner. Nevertheless, the good news is that you always have choices in life and you can choose how you cope with life's many challenges.

The stress and tremendous worries we carried inside us disappeared the minute Marcus expired. It was a relief for all of us that his sufferings ended because we had witnessed so much suffering on Marcus's part, and that was gone. His sufferings were never to return. I didn't have to fear any phone calls from doctors calling me with bad news about Marcus. No alarms would go off anymore. Marcus was gone, and this journey was never to be repeated. In that respect, Marcus's death represented a conclusion.

Mixed with the relief was the grief that his journey ended the way it did. I was never going to hold him, hug him, or see his big brown eyes or his smile anymore in this life on planet Earth. Grieving is a never-ending healing process. I don't think the grieving will ever stop. I don't ever get over the loss of Marcus, but I can choose to move on, which is what I did. I chose to find my own way to deal with the loss of Marcus.

Because Marcus's leukemia journey was so unusual due to his brain damage, I felt that I had lost him many times. The new Marcus was ever-changing. Even the doctors didn't know what to expect from a medical point of view. Marcus surprised us repeatedly, and that was his true nature. I, along with our family, had grieved ever since he fell into a coma, ever since we had lost the old Marcus, the healthy, active child we all knew before he got sick. In that context, it was fair to say that the grieving process had started two years earlier and that we had slowly lost him during that period.

I miss all my different "Marcuses" every day, and that will never change. Why does it have to change? Missing someone you have loved who is not here physically anymore is natural. The important part is how I decided to deal with this fact. Throughout Marcus's journey, I learned the very important lesson to take charge of my mind. Leukemia had destroyed Marcus, but I would not allow it to destroy my life or any other family member's lives. Leukemia had done enough harm to our family already.

There are as many legitimate ways to grieve as there are losses, and no one way is "good" or "the best." If it's possible to find some small breathing space in the grief, there could be some choices about how to move forward, one being to be thankful for what you've got and not focus on what you can't get (your child's health and life).

Besides, I didn't feel sorry for myself. I felt proud of myself for all I had been capable of during those last two devastating years. I couldn't have done anything differently. I had gained medical knowledge, learned Reiki healing, and had gained much valuable information about life and myself. Most importantly, Marcus's story contained wonderful moments and victories along the road, the biggest victory being that my husband, Lucas, and I were still sound, healthy, and not to mention together as a family after having lost Marcus. There were many tears shed, but laughter was present too.

One piece of wisdom I deduced from my Reiki healing was guiding me in the right direction during Marcus's disease process. It was that I could achieve so much in life if my intention to do it was strong enough to take me there. I had a strong intention to complete the journey with Marcus and survive it myself. I learned how to accept the circumstances I couldn't change and let go of unrealistic expectations about Marcus's recovery. I had hope and dreams, but the hope was never to overshine the acceptance of the reality when reality hit. Hope and acceptance had to go hand in hand. Where there was life, there was hope. Nobody could ever take away the hope that Marcus would make it until he actually died.

As soon as I stopped fighting back at what I could not change and decided to focus on helping Marcus, I let go of so much negative energy and heavy feelings. Anger and disappointment are not part of healing. Acceptance is. The holding was taxing on the body and mind. I think that letting go of despair and fear is the key to acceptance. Once I accepted that Marcus was brain damaged and I had a different Marcus to take care of, I embraced it and continued on with those new terms. The acceptance allowed my mind to think and plan constructively in collaboration with Marcus's medical teams. The acceptance empowered me and made me stronger. Negative thoughts made me weak, vulnerable, and unstable.

I believe that trust is imperative for any healthy relationship between human beings. I especially had a hard time trusting the doctors at TCH after what happened to Marcus during the Nelarabine incident. I had trusted the TCH doctors and unintentionally, they harmed Marcus. In the greater perspective, Marcus's brain damage was still a product of their medical judgments. Thus, I struggled for a long time coming to terms with that. Life is not black and white, and the medical world is certainly not black and white. Treatment comes with great risks, but life, too, comes with great risks as illustrated in the saying, "Life is dangerous—you risk dying."

Luckily, I was able to rebuild my trust in the medical system. I witnessed firsthand the help and support that was extended to us from our community. I felt privileged to have experienced such willingness to help us. It's a beautiful feeling worth treasuring. I felt grateful for what MD Anderson had done for Marcus by taking on his relapsed leukemia case when TCH failed to do so. I felt grateful for HealthBridge, the Epic home nurses, TIRR, and the hospice team who stepped up to help during Marcus's last months in our home.

I felt thankful for all the support, love, and care from family members and friends who, in any capacity, showed up on our doorstep and helped us throughout this journey. We were indebted to everybody who took care of Marcus so diligently and loved him. Seeing other people care and love Marcus the way I experienced it was a tremendous gift that melted my heart deeply. Many professional caregivers often told me that Marcus was so lovable, and they were right. You could not help adoring and admiring him. The support we experienced helped heal us both during Marcus's disease process and after. Even help we had not asked to receive.

After Marcus died, my life changed, my husband's life changed, and Lucas's life changed. Many aspects of our lives changed. My husband and I had lost a child; Lucas had lost his brother at age seven. From now on, things were not only different, but we had also started to think differently about things.

On my end, I learned to deeply appreciate even the smallest details in life and enjoy living more in the moment. This encouraging quote by Marcia Smith sums up the essence of this philosophy in a graceful manner: "Cancer is not a death sentence, but rather it is a life sentence; it pushes one to live."

I started to distinguish between what was fixable or not. If a problem was fixable, I would not bother too much about it. After having spent two years fighting and hoping for Marcus to get out on the other side of illness, nothing can ever compare to that hardship I had been through. I was convinced that I could manage anything from now on. No task or challenge was big enough. It was all a matter of how I decided to approach the challenge. If I were to encounter hardship, I knew I would find a way to deal with it. Small or big problem, it didn't matter because I had so much self-confidence and felt incredibly strong after having been by Marcus's side through his leukemia journey.

My father used to say that nothing is difficult if you know how to do it. This is true for me. Now I know how to do this. I possess the recipe. I'm ready to move on in life with all this knowledge of beautiful achievements.

Like in the poem above, my husband, Lucas, and I were set free too when Marcus died. Marcus set us free. He is safe now, and so are we. His physical presence is gone, but altogether he is not gone at all. Personally, I have given Marcus a new space in my life. His spirit is still here with me. He is in my heart, and I think about him and honor him every day.

It was a gradual process for me to come to this understanding. Looking back, I changed over time as I went through different phases and experienced different feelings. When Marcus got sick and brain damaged, I was overwhelmed with tremendous blame and grief because of the amplifications and loss of the old Marcus. Then I made some choices and moved into an acceptance mode. All along, I allowed laughter to be part of the journey, as humor was one of my best survival tools—in fact, the best coping medicine I could think of. It was a mixed-up process, of course, and some feelings repeated itself again when Marcus died.

Indeed, Marcus's inevitable death was a relief for him and us because it could not be any other way. However, losing Marcus was unimaginable, the pain so deep and enormous even words could not describe. Marcus did not complete his life just like the green painting he started painting but never finished when he was home during the first month of his treatment.

Just recently, looking at Marcus's unfinished painting, Lucas asked me why Marcus didn't complete his painting. I replied to Lucas that this was a good question but one I didn't know the answer to. I told him we couldn't always expect to find answers to all our questions in life, but we had to come to terms with that.

After this two-year experience, I believe that deep down I have a good grasp of life now. Marcus is still with me cheering for me as he cheered for his father when he ran his first Houston Marathon. Nobody can take Marcus away from me. There is always going to be this invisible string connecting us. Our relationship and love are eternal, and as mentioned in the poem above, I will never forget Marcus's eight healthy years before he fell ill. Marcus's story was just a small part of his amazing life.

Death ends a life, not a relationship.

—*Mitch Albom*

APPENDICES

Templates for Organizing Medical Information

You will need one binder and one set of dividers for preparing your medical information file. Here's how I recommend organizing it:

1. treatment plans
2. medication/medical care checklist (see template below)
3. lab results
4. other test results
5. insurance
6. business card protectors to keep business cards from medical contacts
7. documents regarding patient rights and responsibilities
8. miscellaneous and protective sheets for pamphlets

Template of Medication/Medical Care Checklist

Medication/ Medical Care	Date	AM	Noon	PM
(Name of medicine) XX mg for (reason for taking it)	(Write date)	(Check ✓ and add time for administration of the medicine)	(Check ✓ and add time for administration of the medicine)	(Check ✓ and add time for administration of the medicine)
PICC line care				(Check ✓ and add time for PICC line care and who did it, and where: home or at hospital)

Notes

- Here you can add comments about side effects such as pain, nausea, fever, trouble sleeping, or anything you want to discuss with your doctor next time you have an appointment.

- If you called the hospital that day for advice, write down who you talked to and the advice given.

- Note any physical activity you did that day: walk, yoga, etc. Any effect?

- Note any wellness treatments you got: foot massage, healing, etc. Any effect?

- Print out the list, complete, and put in the binder you bring to the hospital for appointments.

Template for an Online Diary in Google Drive

For Caretakers or Caregivers

You can share your diary with family members or close friends. The advantage is that what you write can be read in real time as you write it down. That way, you don't have to make endless phone calls. This will allow you to focus on the treatment instead. You can write it yourself or as a parent, a spouse, or any other caregiver.

If you do not want to share the diary, keep it a personal word document.

Date

- Write about hospital visits, appointments with doctors, milestones reached, and treatment plans.

- Write down the names of your doctors and medical personnel who follow your treatment. Create your own Dream Team of favorite doctors and other medical personnel. Ask for their business cards. Ask for recommendations.

- Write about personal achievements and observations.

- Write about exciting news and statements from the doctors and other medical personnel.

- Write about what you need help with and if you believe your care can be improved. Discuss it with your medical team next time you have an appointment. Write about your feelings, thoughts, and frustrations.

- Share any concerns with your medical team. Remember, they are there for you. Ask them for advice about what you can do to feel better in terms of improving your diet and physical, emotional, and spiritual practice.

Templates for Organizing Medical Information

Date

Date

Date

Date

Date

Acknowledgments

Thank you to the following people:

Book coach and mentor Ginger Moran: For believing in this project and teaching me how to write a memoir. With this, you have been an enormous support and inspiration.

Dr. Kevin Madden: For writing the beautiful foreword in which you show your deep understanding for Marcus and our family in such a kind-hearted way.

Website designer Chuck Moran: For creating my author website and coaching me patiently through this process.

Book cover designer Lilly Hallquist: For designing the incredible book front cover using all your creativity while letting Marcus's spirit shine through your work.

Copyeditor and proofreader Shaya Raquel: For masterfully editing the manuscript and making sure I express all my messages clearly.

Interior book designer Melinda Martin: For your amazing technical work in making this book accessible to readers.

ABOUT THE AUTHOR

Benedicte T. Nielsen

Danish author Benedicte T. Nielsen is a lawyer and paralegal who studied in France and lived in India. A Texas resident, she has experienced the worst a parent can—the loss of a child—and found a depth of knowledge and resources she is committed to sharing with other families and medical personnel. Through her story, she builds bridges for parents and caregivers where there were so few on her own journey. She is the author of *Marcus's Story*.

Connect with the Author

benedictenielsen.com

www.ingramcontent.com/pod-product-compliance
Lightning Source LLC
Chambersburg PA
CBHW030308080526
44584CB00012B/492